Indian Gaming: Who Wins?

Indian Gaming: Who Wins?

Edited by
Angela Mullis and David Kamper

UCLA American Indian Studies Center
3220 Campbell Hall, Box 951548
Los Angeles, California 90095-1548

CONTEMPORARY AMERICAN INDIAN ISSUES SERIES NO. 9

Cover artwork by Jacob Goff

Publisher: Duane Champagne
Publications Manager: Pamela Grieman
Assistant Editor: Amy M. Ware
Cover design and layout: Lisa Winger

Printed by Sheridan Books
Library of Congress Catalog Number 00-103282
ISBN 0-935626-53-0 (paperback)

Contents

THE GAMBLER'S STYLE

TRIBAL PERSPECTIVES

Introduction:
The Mimicry of Indian Gaming

David Kamper

In an acerbic yet incisive twist on the Manifest Destiny adage, "The only good Indian is a dead Indian," Jack Campisi has remarked that "the only thing more despicable than a poor Indian is a rich Indian."[1] His comment reflects the frustrations of many American Indian communities currently defending their right to run gaming operations on Native land. Considering the fervor expressed by many state and federal politicians who want to limit or abolish gambling in Indian Country, many Native people have come to view the gaming debate as a battle for sovereignty. On the other hand, state politicians profess their right to regulate all activities within their state's borders and federal government representatives have legitimized this claim through the implementation of the Indian Gaming Regulatory Act of 1988 (IGRA).

Such debates and legislative actions place much more than the theoretical politics of governance at stake. The restriction of Indian gaming hinders tribal economies. Such regulatory actions as IGRA have dual consequences: they not only limit a tribe's power to govern, but also attack a community's economic self-sufficiency. In fact, Indian casinos make up approximately 11 percent of the $44 billion legal gaming industry in the United States.[2] Gaming provides many Indian communities with the tremendous resources required to improve their standards of living and maintain their traditional cultures.

The current status of Indian gaming, with its external interventions and threats of prohibition, leaves Native communities facing a unique paradox. In its most recent form, this paradox arises from the sovereignty debate surrounding Native gaming ventures. While many Indian communities appreciate and utilize the legal protection of their sovereignty, there remains a more fundamental and organic source of self-governance. This kind of self-governance derives from a traditional understanding of community and the deep historic sense of autonomy that can be traced to long before European contact. As it applies to the right to operate reservation gaming, this traditional notion of sovereignty often contradicts legal conceptions of self-government. Many Indians believe that they possess the inherent right to govern their communities. Due to external forces, however, they must abide by a more limited model of sovereignty, one engendered by and based on United States law. Herein lies the paradox: federal- and state-sanctioned Indian gaming creates situations in which Indian communities must compromise some of their legal sovereignty in order to maintain economic independence.

The power conundrum that binds many Indian communities is indicative of the unique colonial/post-colonial space Indian communities occupy. As a result of common colonial histories, many Indian communities have had to move away from traditional economic subsistence, leaving them to rely on a combination of government subsidies and capitalist enterprises. Through a number of military campaigns, government policies, and missionary efforts, Euro-Americans have historically encouraged and compelled Native Americans to participate in a consumer economy. Concurrently many tribes, since earliest contact, have also recognized the benefit of economic interaction with Euro-Americans—even if it means engaging in a foreign economic system. Many communities have exploited livestock markets, commercial fishing, construction and resource extraction industries, arts and crafts, or the tourist trade.

Gaming is the most recent and perhaps the most strategic of such economic choices. Its advantages lie in the low strain on natural resources and the high profit margin. The adverse responses to Indian gaming can be best understood by the menace that Indian high-stakes gaming poses to state governments. Through the employment of a successful Euro-American-style economic venture, Indian communities around the country threaten to disorder the political, economic, and social power dynamics that maintain Euro-American hegemony.

State and federal governments' motives for intervening in Indian gaming are based on self-interest and illustrate the colonial situation Homi Bhabha has described as mimicry, which arises from the ambivalence of colonial discourse, defined by Bhabha as "the desire for a reformed, recognizable Other, *as a subject of a difference that is almost the same, but not quite.*"[3] The colonizer wants the colonized to assume the civilized tropes of the colonial power, while at the same time maintaining enough difference to justify and preserve the hierarchy of colonial discourse.

The ambivalence of colonial discourse is betrayed in the United States as Euro-Americans perennially preach the virtues of economic and cultural assimilation. At the same time these ideas are being discussed, Euro-Americans keep Indians' progress in check through allotment policies, boarding schools, and coerced urban migration, among other efforts. And while not all federal policy works toward the assimilation of American Indians, some policies intending to preserve autonomy produce a "'not quite/not white'" mimicry effect.[4] The clichéd idea of "pulling yourself up by your bootstraps" informed the concept behind self-determination. Indian gaming is a direct product of this policy.

It is important to note the subtle distinction between self-determination and sovereignty. Both words describe a concept of independence; however, each has a different emphasis. Frequently the federal government uses the term *self-determination* because it emphasizes the formulation of economically substantial institutions, and thus not only increased participation in the large American consumer economy, but also decreased the federal government's financial burden of supporting Indian communities. Native communities tend to use the word *sovereignty* to express independence because it demarcates a space of power and privilege compatible with the nation-state status they generally believe themselves to possess. Self-determination is about making virtuous, productive, and independent American citizens; sovereignty is a project that promotes vital, soluble, and distinct communities whose members desire exclusive self-governing rights. The distinction between these two concepts of independence betrays the danger of mimicry and provides an explanation for external resistance to Indian gaming.

Self-determination seeks to make American Indian communities like other American communities inasmuch as they economically support themselves with their own resources and are not dependent on federal subsidies. However, self-determination does not promote these communities to US government-like status: Indian communities are still considered domestic dependent nations. This fixes what Bhabha calls the "'partial' presence" of colonial subjects.[5] Giving complete sovereignty to Indian communities weakens the power of federal and state governments by disrupting the tenuous hierarchical control these authorities possess in American democracy. Thus, rather than give full power to Indian communities in the form of sovereignty, policies lean towards the partial empowerment of self-determination. As Bhabha suggests, the power of a colonial situation

> is dependent ... upon some strategic limitation or prohibition *within* the authoritative discourse itself. The success of colonial appropriation depends on a proliferation of inappropriate objects that ensure its strategic failure, so that mimicry is at once resemblance and menace.[6]

Indian gaming represents this kind of mimicry. It is the very act of limiting what Indian communities can do that continually (re)defines them as wards of the state. And in the most practical terms, an Indian community that makes money is one that no longer needs the subsidies that represent the clearest demarcation of its subordinate position to the federal government.

Without an "almost, but not quite" attitude, non-Indian communities cannot preserve the difference between themselves and Indian communities. Difference is necessary for non-Indian communities to be able to define Indians. Standard Euro-American history provides Euro-Americans with a narrative that clearly delineates who Indians are and how they act. Control over the definition of American Indians translates to control over individuals and their community's behavior. Thus, this "knowledge" of Indian essence seemingly justifies the paternalistic attitude that traditionally and still frequently informs the interaction between non-Indians and Indians. This desire to preserve Indians as knowable Others motivates policy directed at Indian gaming.

As Bhabha suggests, mimicry arises with the desire to reform. But civilizing has it limits because full reformation extinguishes the need for colonial authority and its paternalistic policies. This problem approaches the supreme danger of mimicry: its movement beyond colonial control. Mimicry is an act of camouflage and can threaten colonial authority when the colonized close the gap between colonizer and colonized. The more Indians outwardly act and succeed in the way non-Indians do, the more threatening they become. Indian gaming is exactly such an action. Native communities that participate in gaming disguise their identity to the external world. Indian gaming confuses an essential understanding of Indian communities because they are participating in an action they have never before performed and are practicing a custom that is not seen as "traditional" and that generates unprecedented financial success. The benefits of Indian gaming put Indians more in control of their future than they have been since European contact.

Through Indian gaming, Native communities have negotiated the restrained independence of self-determination policies and have boldly asserted the self-governance of sovereignty. In doing so, they are moving from a partial presence forced upon them by a colonial authority to taking control of that partial presence, turning the gaze back on the authority, and baffling that authority. Complaints from state governments and the resulting IGRA should be read as an attempt to recuperate power and surveillance over Indian communities. Its regulatory authority restores limited independence and forces Indian communities to fully reveal themselves to state government through the compact process. IGRA allows the federal and state governments to define Indian gaming and restores Indian communities as a knowable entity. US governments' attempts to delineate a space for Indian gaming unveil the camouflage of its mimicry and stabilize the power dynamic by defining its difference as subordinate—not ambiguously independent and successful. It restores the institutionalized failure that Bhabha theorizes as a limitation of the possibility for reform of the colonized.

What has been so significant about the development of Indian gaming is that, while external forces have worked to attack the independence of Indian gaming, many Indian communities have vocally and boldly asserted their sovereignty. They have done so in way that blur difference and repeatedly unsettle the definition of how an Indian community acts and what an Indian community has the right to do. Indians have pushed the envelope on Indian gaming with such contemporary tactics as television and radio ad campaigns, political lobbying, a ballot referendum, and ingenious legal maneuvers.

Indian Gaming: Who Wins? reveals the strategies and attiudes that many Indian communities have toward gaming, and seeks to engage the various perspectives that make up the Indian gaming debate. The book was inspired by a conference of the same name, held in the spring of 1997 at the University of California, Los Angeles (UCLA) and hosted by the university's American Indian Studies Center and School of Law. The conference addressed concerns in the legislative, scholarly, and tribal arenas and featured talks by several well-known speakers and activists on both sides of the gaming divide. Several chapters in this book are based on these presentations, while others have been added to expand the analysis of gaming's effects, to contextualize the debates, and to detail recent developments.

Contributors include tribal leaders, lawyers, policymakers, consultants, and academics who are on the front lines of Indian gaming. In *Indian Gaming: Who Wins?*, the strategies, tactics, and attitudes that many Native communities have toward gaming are revealed. These essays illustrate the success and potential of mimicking Euro-American techniques. Indian communities lie on the cutting edge of political and economic strategies that obfuscate their foes' understanding of what constitutes an Indian community.

The book is divided into four sections. The opening section—"Legislative Bets"—starts with Chad M. Gordon's "From Hope to Realization of Dreams: Proposition 5 and California Indian Gaming," which brings the reader up to date on some of the more recent debates surrounding Indian gaming. These issues focus on the hotly contested Indian gaming campaign that has raged over the last few years in California. The high profile of California's Proposition 5, the Indian Gaming and Self-Reliance Act, has already shaped Indian gaming across the country and undoubtedly will continue to do so. The November 1998 passage of the proposition created a template gaming compact for California Indian tribes that wished to conduct casino gambling. Gordon looks at the reasons why Proposition 5 came about, the legal maneuvers managed both by the proposition's drafters and the California Supreme Court, and the prospects for future California Indian gaming ventures and referendums. The second article, Sioux Harvey's "Winning the Sovereignty Jackpot: The Indian Gaming Regulatory Act and the Struggle for Sovereignty," presents a thorough explication of the recent legal and political history of Indian gaming in the United States. This detailed piece lays the historical context for a discussion of the social, political, and economic effects and repercussions of tribal gaming.

The following two articles in the "Legislative Bets" section deal specifically with legal challenges to a tribe's right to conduct Indian gaming. Both Joseph G. Nelson's and Carole E. Goldberg and Indian Law Professors' contributions examine a gaming compact from California. While Proposition 5 passed with notable voter support—63 percent—its powerful opponents sought to challenge the law's constitutionality. What ensued was a court battle in which the California State Supreme Court struck down Proposition 5 on the grounds that it violated federal law by permitting a type of gambling prohibited in the rest of the state. Nelson's "California High Court Strikes Down Indian Gaming in *Hotel Employees and Restaurant Employees International Union* v. *Davis*" details the events and arguments leading up to and contained in the state supreme court's decision that declared Proposition 5 unconstitutional. By analyzing the history of gaming legislation in California, Nelson cogently argues that the court's decision was faulty and incorrect. He demonstrates that the provisions in California law that the court used to knock down Proposition 5 were actually intended to foster—not limit—gambling. Much of the court's argument, and consequently Nelson's focus as well, revolves around definitions and notions of what gambling is and what its different classifications are. Nelson shows that despite the California State Supreme Court's arguments to the contrary, the kind of gambling established by Proposition 5 and practiced in many California tribal casinos is not prohibited by state law, and therefore is not unconstitutional.

Goldberg and her colleagues have provided a brief that they submitted to the state supreme court in reaction to the court's decision regarding

Proposition 5. This persuasive brief emphasizes the necessity to maintain coherence in Indian law at both the state and federal levels. Like Nelson's article, this brief addresses actions and rulings of the California Supreme Court; however, Goldberg focuses on the faulty legal logic of the petitioners trying to strike down Proposition 5 and not the decision made by the court, per se. This brief's in-depth discussion of what type or class of gambling a tribal-state gaming compact can legally permit or prohibit enacts the strategies used by lawyers who are on the front lines of defending Indian gaming rights.

Alexander Tallchief Skibine's contribution is based on his presentation at UCLA's Indian gaming conference. His article not only adds to the gaming debate between tribal and state governments, but also discusses the role of the federal government in Indian gaming. Skibine's article closely analyzes the legal technical maneuvers made by the US Supreme Court justices. His discussion skillfully speaks to both legal professionals and laypersons. Skibine's most interesting conclusion is his suggestion that due to the anti-Indian sentiments expressed in many recent Supreme Court rulings, legislative efforts may not be the best solution to ensure and defend Indian gaming. Instead, he proposes that tribes consider appealing to the executive branch of the federal government to request that the secretary of the Interior intervene on behalf of tribes that are having difficulty negotiating tribal compacts—agreements, required by federal law, to be made between tribal governments and state governments in order to determine the structure and nature of Indian gaming in any given state—with states.

Concluding the first section of the book, Thomas Gede's "Indian Gaming: The State's View" elaborates the state of California's objection to tribal casinos. Much like the other authors in this section, Gede constructs his commentary on legal interpretations. In this case, Gede looks at the state's legal grounds for challenging the kinds of gaming compacts desired by California Indian tribes. This insightful and sincere piece not only poses questions that California Indian tribes must confront as they seek to establish compacts and expand tribal casinos, but also posits important inquiries that any proponent or opponent of Indian gaming must consider.

In the second section of this book, "Community Prospects," Katherine A. Spilde examines the communal effects of Indian gaming. Utilizing a non-Native community—that which surrounds the White Earth Reservation in Minnesota—as her subject, Spilde attempts to clear up misconceptions about the way Indian gaming affects tribal casinos' neighboring communities. Spilde's work emphasizes the tensions between a reservation supporting gaming and its non-Indian neighbors. She looks at the perceptions held by these concerned US citizens as they are expressed through local media, interviews, and anecdotes. Perhaps most importantly, Spilde's article provides an excellent practical model for allaying local non-Indians' anxieties about the consequences of tribal casinos on the surrounding community.

Joseph G. Jorgensen outlines the actual monetary and social costs and benefits of various Indian gaming ventures. His article applies both historical and economic approaches to in-depth analyses of Indian gaming. Jorgensen places the weight of failures in reservation economic development squarely on the shoulders of the US political and economic superstructure by detailing the policies of active repression and passive hindrance of economic development on reservations. Jorgensen advocates economic models that represent Indian communities as active agents in determining their economic futures, arguing that casino gaming provides an excellent example of Indian communities asserting their agency. What increases the richness and dynamism of this examination is the analysis of tribal community debates over the merits of casino gaming and its viablity as an economic venture. As Jorgensen illustrates, it is just as critical to pay attention to tribal members' opposition to Indian gaming as it is to study gaming's merits.

Finally, James V. Fenelon's "Traditional and Modern Perspectives on Indian Gaming: The Struggle for Sovereignty" examines the effects on and reactions of traditional Natives living in reservation communities that own casinos. Fenelon seeks to challenge the conventional ways in which social scientists perceive Indian gaming and its effect on reservation life. He reframes the gaming debate and considers gaming in relation to both the inevitable modernization on reservations and the effects on Native traditional lifeways.

Spilde's use of Laurence Shames' novel, *Tropical Depression*, as a metaphor to frame her argument creates a smooth segue into the next scholarly section, "The Gambler's Style." In this pair of articles, contributors Paul Pasquaretta and Karen L. Wallace analyze gaming as a pivotal theme in many American Indian narratives and literary ventures. Both essays delineate the ways in which traditional and modern Indian gaming plays into literature and, hence, into the Native community. Pasquaretta takes a historical view of gambling's literary life as it is developed in works by various Native authors, including John Rollins Ridge, Mourning Dove, Leslie Marmon Silko, Gerald Vizenor, and Louise Erdrich. Wallace, on the other hand, confines her analysis to a close reading of Erdrich's *The Bingo Palace*. Both authors suggest that gambling, as a literary device, acts as a powerful metaphor in describing the precarious economic condition in which many contemporary tribes find themselves. They demonstrate how Native authors frame casinos and economic development in general in terms of traditional and modern gambling. In the literary world, the gamble places more than just an individual's money at stake—an entire community's livelihood and culture is on the table. Both Pasquaretta and Wallace seek to explore the complexities of American Indian communities as much as of American Indian novels.

The last section of this monograph, "Tribal Perspectives," gives voice to those most affected by Indian gaming: tribal community members. This section consists of a collection of speeches given by tribal leaders at the 1997 gaming conference. Highlighted leaders include Ron Andrade, Mary Ann Andreas, Pricilla Hunter, Ernie L. Stevens, Jr., and Erma J. Vizenor. Here the trials, triumphs, and tribulations of Indian gaming are laid bare by those who should have the loudest voice on the form and status of Indian gaming. As the rest of the monograph shows, the decision to engage in casino-style gaming is not determined by tribal members alone. For this reason, a tribe's decision-making powers should not be taken for granted. As the community leaders in this section explain, the decision to pursue gaming is neither simple nor singular. The complex dialogue and planning required by Indian gaming must take many voices into account. It is easy to lose track of this complexity as the media simplifies the public debate over gambling and as gaming opponents depict tribal casinos as voracious capitalist ventures. The voice of these tribal leaders illustrate that tribal casinos are something much more than the average Euro-American capitalist venture.

As these leaders enumerate the benefits and social services achieved through gaming, it is clear that this type of venture does not seek to turn profits for an elite core of managers and executive officials, but intends to enrich an entire community. The authors in this final and definitive section elaborate the unique historic, economic, political, and social situation of American Indian communities and the ways in which gaming can act as an important mover to correct the marginalized position in which many Indian communities find themselves. Gaming, many of these contributors point out, empowers tribes, providing them with a forum to activate their political skills and ingenuity and their desire to preserve their communities in ways that give them unprecedented access to the reins of power in American society.

NOTES

1. Quoted in Paul Pasquaretta, "On the 'Indianness' of Bingo: Gambling and the Native American Community," *Critical Inquiry* 20:4 (Summer 1994): 694–714, 712.

2. N. Bruce Duthu, "*Crow Dog* and *Oliphant* Fistfight at the Tribal Casino: Political Power, Storytelling, and Games of Chance," *Arizona State Law Journal* 29:1 (Spring 1997): 171–250.

3. Homi K. Bhabha, *The Location of Culture* (London: Routledge, 1994), 86.

4. Ibid., 92.

5. Ibid., 86.

6. Ibid.

Legislative Bets

From Hope to Realization of Dreams: Proposition 5 and California Indian Gaming

Chad M. Gordon

From the earliest days of the United States, Indian tribes have been recognized as "distinct, independent political communities."[1] As such, they are qualified to exercise powers of self-government not by virtue of any delegation of powers from the federal government, but because of their original tribal sovereignty. The United States has long recognized tribes as separate governments through US Supreme Court decisions, congressional acts, and presidential executive orders declaring a government-to-government relationship. Although the United States has not always recognized or respected the full range of Indian nations' sovereign powers, it has never denied their existence.

While many Americans today are quick to categorize American Indians within racial and ethnic groups, the unique governmental status of Indian nations grants them a distinct legal position. As sovereign nations, tribes are generally free from state regulation of internal affairs unless Congress has legislated otherwise. For example, states generally may not regulate the conduct of Indians living within reservation boundaries because such regulation would interfere with a tribe's power to govern itself and its territory.

The formal US recognition of tribal governmental powers has coexisted with federal policies and administration designed to control and assimilate Indian people. Generally, these nationwide efforts have resulted in the marginalization of reservation economies and the impoverishment of individual Indians. Moreover, a long history of discriminatory federal and state policies has ranked California Indians in the lowest income, education, housing quality, and health brackets of any population group in the state.[2] Gaming has become one of the few means of remedying this situation. Alternative methods of economic development have included environmentally hazardous activities such as uranium mining and toxic-waste dumping. While Native people have learned that the gaming industry is by nature risky, they also know that it is no less treacherous than existing by subsidy and governmental fiat.

The 1987 Supreme Court decision *California* v. *Cabazon Band of Mission Indians*[3] affirmed the principle that the laws of states generally applied to activities in Indian Country to the extent that the law was *prohibitory* and involved criminal sanctions; other *regulatory* activities, however, did not generally fall under a state's legal code. Pursuant to this logic, the Supreme Court denied the state of California the right to impose its laws upon Indian tribes relating to the operation of bingo games, given that the state permitted a substantial amount of gambling activity and actually promoted gambling through its own lottery. In essence, *Cabazon* was the first Supreme Court decision to uphold sovereign Indian nations' right to engage in gaming.

In the wake of *Cabazon*, Congress enacted the Indian Gaming Regulatory Act (IGRA)[4] in 1988 with a declared purpose to "provide a statutory basis for the operation of gaming by Indian tribes as a means of promoting tribal economic development, self-sufficiency, and strong tribal governments."[5] IGRA divided Indian gaming into three classes, labeling them classes I,[6] II,[7] and III.[8] Class III, allowing what are traditionally the most lucrative forms of gaming, is subject to an additional clause that states in part that a class III enterprise must be "conducted in conformance with a tribal-state compact entered into by the Indian tribe and the state."[9] This need for a tribal-state compact in order to enter into class III gaming would be a point of contention between the California tribes and the state for years to come.

Given their expanding gaming operations and the increased tension with the state government, many tribes began to legitimately fear that it was only a matter of time until their operations were deemed class III, thus necessitating a compact.[10] Concerned for their businesses and livelihoods, several tribes in December of 1991 commenced joint negotiations with former Governor Pete Wilson in an effort to gain compacts. The meetings were short-lived however. In April 1992 Wilson refused to bargain with the tribes any further on what he considered a non-negotiable subject—the lucrative video-gaming machines that many Indian casinos employed. Wilson insisted that since slot machines were categorically banned by the California Penal Code,[11] he did not have to come to the bargaining table with any tribe that utilized the common video-gaming machines. In Wilson's opinion, tribal video machines were indistinguishable from what he considered an illegal slot machine. While Wilson's definition of a *slot* appeared to be quite broad, many of California's own video terminals, utilized for the state lottery keno game at that time, were virtually indistinguishable from what he considered an "illegal slot."[12] Wilson's definition was inconsistent—it was exceedingly broad when tribal interests were at stake and extraordinarily narrow when the state's own lottery was in question—leaving many tribes rightfully frustrated and angered at the governor's myopic attitude and lack of respect. In addition, the law at that time was unclear regarding the scope of the state's obligation to negotiate gaming compacts with some courts, upholding the view that if a state allowed *any* form of class III gaming, it was required to negotiate regarding *all* forms of class III gaming, including slot machines.[13]

At an impasse, the tribes and the state sought a judicial termination decision in a federal court in *Rumsey Indian Rancheria of Wintun Indians* v. *Wilson*,[14] as to the question of whether the state was obligated to enter into negotiations with regard to electronic devices and house-banked card games. While the district court sided with the tribes in *Rumsey* and agreed that the state was indeed obligated to negotiate over the games and devices in question, the ninth circuit reversed the district court's opinion, holding that IGRA did not require the state to negotiate a compact allowing those activities to be conducted in tribal gaming facilities. With the favorable court of appeals ruling in hand, Wilson ceased all compact negotiations with the tribes.

With Wilson gone from the bargaining table, the tribes could either continue their un-compacted gaming and risk shutdown or discontinue their profitable enterprises and go back to poverty until Wilson decided to bargain in good faith. Not surprisingly, many tribes chose the former. However, a source of indirect help was not far away. In 1996, the California Supreme Court, in *Western Telcon Inc.* v. *California State Lottery*,[15] addressed the legality of the California State Lottery's electronic keno game. While the decision was unfavorable to gaming interests in general, principles espoused by the court and subsequent actions by the state indirectly buttressed the Indian nations' position. The court held that the defining element of the game was its prize system and *not* the hardware on which it was played. The justices emphasized that since the California State Lottery's keno game did not maintain a dedicated "prize pool" to be distributed to winning players, it was illegal as a house-banked game under California's constitution.[16] Unwilling to abandon its highly profitable keno game, the state continued the game on the same machines and merely revised its prize system by establishing a dedicated player prize pool, or a sum of money fixed in advance, in which the state had no direct interest. While the state was able to preserve its keno game with its revised prize system, it inadvertently buttressed the tribes' position by resuming its keno game on hardware similar to the machines that the governor insisted were slot machines when in tribal hands. This duplicity on the part of the state would become both a rallying point and a source of power for the tribes in subsequent compact negotiations.

With the *Western Telcon* decision in hand, along with their growing power and influence on both state and national levels, the tribes regrouped and once again approached Wilson with the prospect of entering serious compact negotiations. Taking stock of the tribes' newfound position of power, Wilson reluctantly agreed. However, while Wilson agreed in principle to enter into fair and serious compact negotiations, the tribes soon found themselves mired in an all-too-familiar rut of political doublespeak and treachery. In October 1996 the gaming tribes persuaded Wilson to negotiate a compact with a single, non-gaming tribe—the Pala Band of Mission Indians of San Diego County—in an effort to produce a single compact that would be used as a model for all future negotiations with other California tribes. Central to the agreement for employing the Pala compact as a model for future compacts was the state's promise to allow the negotiations to act as an open forum for all tribes to voice their concerns and desires.

However, only a few months passed before Wilson and the Pala Band joined together in excluding other tribes from the bargaining process, a move in violation of their prior agreement. A non-gaming tribe at the time, the Pala Band was interested in opening a casino. Wilson, ever the political opportunist, was willing to cater to their desires on his own terms. While the gaming tribes looked on, Wilson and the Pala Band negotiated a compact in the absence of other tribes' input. Without the collective strength of the tribes in the negotiating process, the "negotiations" for the Pala compact quickly degenerated into what many commentators have called the "Wilson compact." The one-sided compact arbitrarily restricted tribes to using a single electronic gaming system and put a cap on the number of gaming machines each tribe could possess. In addition to the gaming restrictions, and perhaps most troubling to the tribes, the Pala compact sought to regulate areas that seriously impinged on tribal authority over matters close to the heart of tribal sovereignty: the environment, employment, and the size of the casino. Thus many tribes saw the Pala compact's provisions as deeply offensive, both as to the practicalities of serving the gaming market and in the larger and more fundamental sense of its alteration of the relationship between the sovereign tribes and the state in ways that many tribes felt could foreshadow the end of tribal sovereignty.[17]

For Wilson, the Pala compact was an important personal and political move, intended to counter his critics' claims that he was not coming to the bargaining table in good faith as mandated by IGRA. To some lay observers, "good faith" under Wilson's regime could only mean fair dealing by going through the motions, solemn governmental obligations twisted and turned to such a degree that only the most foolhardy or partial viewer could ascertain any semblance of obligation in an otherwise splintered carcass of justice—a prospect all too familiar to sovereign Indian nations.

Proudly hailing the Pala compact as an illustration of his willingness to bargain with the tribes in compliance with IGRA, Wilson touted the agreement as a model compact for all California tribes. In a bold and calculated final step, Wilson showed the rest of his cards to the tribes, a hand that he had been hiding for quite some time. The tribes soon learned the real reason behind his insistence on negotiating solely with the Pala Band. The former governor announced that any tribe seeking to enter into future compact negotiations would have to agree *in advance* to the provisions contained in the Pala compact or face immediate closure—hardly a negotiation by any standard. By insisting on applying a prepackaged and one-sided compact across the board for all tribes, Wilson again exposed his denial of the fundamental maxim of tribes as separate and sovereign governments.

Since many tribes refused to sign the prepackaged and inherently unfair Pala compact, the United States immediately responded with forfeiture actions against many tribal casinos under IGRA and the Johnson Act.[18] Tribes' arguments that they lacked compacts solely because of the bad faith conduct of Wilson were to no avail.

With their pleas falling on deaf ears in both state and national governments, the tribes regrouped and planned to take the issue directly to the California voters. They united to draft a 1998 ballot initiative, Proposition 5, in an effort to protect their sovereign rights and safeguard their businesses and livelihoods. In essence, Proposition 5, as drafted, guaranteed any federally recognized California tribe that had land eligible under IGRA the right to operate limited forms of class III gaming under a compact with specific terms. The proposition allowed tribes to: (1) use properly configured video terminal and card games, while continuing to restrict Indian casinos to federally designated tribal land; (2) create new revenue-sharing programs that dedicated part of the revenues from Indian gaming to help non-gaming tribes; (3) support local programs in communities near Indian casinos;

(4) reimburse the state for all regulatory costs; and (5) establish emergency medical services throughout California. Widely understood as an effective and fair compromise, the proposition properly affirmed tribal autonomy and acknowledged state concerns about proper controls.

Unlike the Pala compact, Proposition 5 was not mandatory for a valid gaming agreement in California; it just guaranteed a minimum set of terms. As such, Proposition 5 respected tribal sovereignty and the notions of government-to-government relationships between individual tribes and the state. By allowing the tribes the freedom to ignore the statutory compact and seek their own agreement with the state through individual negotiations, the drafters gave tribes a model compact that was less partisan than the Wilson-sponsored compact and provided a mechanism that respected the autonomy of separate sovereign Indian nations by allowing for separate negotiations.

Drafting the proposition was one feat, passing it with the voters of California was yet another. From the beginning, the "Yes on 5" campaign knew that any proposed initiative to protect Indian gaming would face well-funded opposition, including a broad range of unusual allies—the Republican administration of Governor Pete Wilson, Nevada gaming interests, organized labor, California's horse-racing industry and card clubs, the Religious Right, and anti-gaming groups. With less than a month until the petition-filing deadline, the campaign began an intensive signature drive that ultimately gathered more than one million signatures, far surpassing expectations.[19]

The campaign's official name, "Californians for Indian Self-Reliance," reflected its central strategy: focusing on the inherent right of tribal nations to determine their own destinies and collective well-being. The notion that voters should help Indians maintain their self-reliance resonated well with liberals, who believe that governments should assist the disadvantaged, and with conservatives, who believe firmly in independence and self-determination. Since the campaign focused on tribes' rights to self-reliance, it was important to garner the support of non-gaming tribes as well. By doing so, the campaign was able to underscore the central theme of self-reliance and dispel criticism that the measure was merely about high-stakes gambling. Ultimately, the campaign's efforts were successful as eighty-eight gaming and non-gaming tribes linked arms in support of the proposition.

The early stages of the campaign were largely focused on exposing the big Nevada gaming interests as the primary opponents, and inoculating the public against their deceptive and self-serving messages. Countering ads that attempted to persuade the public that tribal casinos were polluting the environment and not affording basic worker protections, the campaign employed television ads that utilized tribal spokespersons and Indian scholars with empirical evidence that the opposition's commercials were misleading and inflammatory. In addition to countering the opposition's claims, the ads also recounted the tumultuous history of California Indians and the positive effects gaming has brought many reservations. Many of the ads were presented from the perspective of tribal members affected by the proposition.

While some ads focused on the benefits that gaming revenues provided, such as the introduction of running water and electricity in some disadvantaged reservation communities, other commercials highlighted improvements in medical care as well as the creation of scholarships enabling tribal members to further their education. By showcasing Indian people as positive and contributing members of both reservation life and larger society, the commercials provided a sorely needed contemporary view of Indian people in the wake of years of media-induced cultural stereotypes.

One of the more familiar faces throughout the campaign was that of Mark Macarro, chairman of the Pechanga Band of Luiseño Mission Indians, and official campaign spokesperson. A charismatic speaker, Macarro voiced trust in the ability of the voters to see through the Nevada gaming industry's rhetoric, and to recognize the validity and soundness of the tribes' position. His faith would be confirmed in the November election.

After the most expensive initiative campaign in US history,[20] the tribes' efforts proved fruitful as 5 million Californians voted Proposition 5 into state law on 3 November 1998. In the nation's most populous state, 63 percent of the voters upheld tribal sovereignty and affirmed the right of tribal governments to maintain limited forms of gaming, providing jobs to thousands of California workers and economic benefits to surrounding business. The passage rate of 63 percent speaks volumes as to the effectiveness of the campaign, given that early opinion polls showed the public support in the low fifty-percentile range.

Even though California voters overwhelmingly supported Indian gaming in the November election, the proposition's constitutionality was soon tested in the California State Supreme Court by the Hotel Employees and Restaurant Workers Union (HERE).[21] In a controversial decision in August of 1999, the court invalidated the proposition by focusing in large part on an obscure provision within section 19(e) of the 1984 State Lottery Initiative that amended the state constitution to provide that "The Legislature has no power to authorize, and shall prohibit casinos of the type currently operating in Nevada and New Jersey." In defining the type of casino "currently operating in Nevada and New Jersey," the court stated that such a casino "may be understood, with reasonable specificity, as one or more buildings, rooms, or facilities, whether separate or connected, that offer gambling activities including those statutorily prohibited in California, especially banked table games and slot machines."[22] Equating California Indian casinos with the type "currently found in Nevada and New Jersey," the court invalidated the will of the voters and stated: "In a conflict between statutory and constitutional law, the Constitution must prevail."[23]

The tribes had made two basic arguments: (1) that the video gaming terminals located in many of the tribal casinos were not illegal slot machines and (2) that a holistic assessment must be employed when defining a casino "of the type found in Nevada or New Jersey." The tribes argued that just because a tribal casino may possess one forbidden characteristic of a Nevada casino, the state should not categorically make such an establishment unconstitutional. For example, dissimilarities from the impermissible "Nevada-type casinos," such as the absence of free alcohol to patrons or the utilization of craps or roulette should be some of the many factors considered when making the final assessment as to whether a tribal casino is of the proscribed Nevada type. Unfortunately for the tribes, the court did not agree.

In lone dissent, Justice Joyce Kennard stressed that voters should be allowed final say in the matter: "One of the fundamental powers reserved to people of this state is the power to enact legislation by initiative.... Indeed, it is our solemn duty to jealously guard the precious initiative power, and to resolve any reasonable doubts in favor of its exercise."[24] Relying on an interpretation of IGRA, Justice Kennard found that Congress, not the state legislature, had authorized tribal gaming. Hence, there could be no violation of the California Constitution.

While the tribes were disheartened by the California Supreme Court's ruling, they were optimistic that a new governor might deal with them in a respectful and dignified way—a decorum that the tribes felt they had been without for so long and so richly deserved. The November election giving tribes victory in Proposition 5 also elected Gray Davis, the state's first Democratic governor in sixteen years. Frustrated by the disrespect and treachery characterized by the previous administration, the tribes had contributed heavily to Davis' campaign coffers. Thus, even though the proposition had been defeated in the California Supreme Court, the tribes were optimistic that they still might be able to reach a compact with the new governor.

Upon taking office, Davis knew that the days of wholesale denial of tribes' sovereign rights was a thing of the past. The tribes were now a powerful political force to be reckoned with and had the backing of the California voters. Davis proceeded to appoint former ninth circuit Judge William Norris as his representative in compact negotiations with the tribes. While Davis wanted to reflect the will of the people in their support of Indian gaming, Davis received pressure from organized labor lobbying for collective bargaining rights within the casinos as well as from traditional conservative groups advocating only a modest expansion of tribal gaming.

During a period of less than two weeks, Davis and his representatives crafted a model compact for the tribes that would serve as a starting point for all future negotiations. The model compact was for a term of twenty years with a three-year option to reopen negotiations on the number of devices and revenue sharing, and it limited each reservation to a maximum of two gaming facilities. Important to the tribes was a provision that gave tribes the ability to utilize any kind of slot machine and offer all house-banked card games. The compact sought to establish a cap on the total number of slot machines statewide, but controversy has arisen over the exact number specified in the agreement. Under the compact, tribes were also able to keep all of their existing slot machines, with annual increases of up to 7 percent.

Silencing critics who protested that gaming tribes would receive a windfall due to the exclusion of the state government and neighboring non-gaming tribes, the compact included revenue-sharing programs for both.[25] Revenues shared with the state are planned to assist programs for gambling addiction, the support of state and local government agencies impacted by tribal gaming, and compensation for regulatory costs incurred by the state. Should a tribal government decide not to engage in gaming, it is estimated that the revenue-sharing program with non-gaming tribes could net such tribes approximately $1 million a year.

Of great concern to many tribes during the compact negotiations with

Davis was the governor's insistence upon collective bargaining rights for organized labor. Central to the tribes' concern was that in no other state had a tribe been forced to recognize outside labor unions. While organized labor tried to color the issue as a concern for workers' rights, the larger and more appropriate question concerned the propriety of a foreign entity being thrust upon a separate and sovereign nation.[26] In stark opposition to many of their opponents' criticisms, California Indian casinos consistently evidence a firm commitment to the well-being of their employees. A brief survey of many of the current employees of California Indian casinos evidences a large number of workers who relocated to California from traditional gambling meccas such as Las Vegas and Reno to take advantage of the superior compensation, hours, and benefits that many tribal casinos provide.[27]

Facing Davis' unwavering position on organized labor, the tribes reluctantly agreed to incorporate their own tribal labor relations ordinances guaranteeing workers at tribal casinos the right to organize in exchange for the compacts that had eluded them for many years. While the compacts were heralded as a major breakthrough for California Indian nations, the inclusion of a mandatory labor agreement is a serious compromise of tribal sovereignty that may have far-reaching consequences in the future. When a sovereign nation gives up a portion of its ability to dictate the terms and conditions of its governmental structure or rules of conduct, the gradual erosion and eventual destruction of that revered and self-defining attribute is not far behind.

While many tribes object in principle to the forced collective bargaining agreements, the tribes have ample reason to protest the language contained within the proposed Tribal Labor Relations Ordinance as well. Largely fashioned after the National Labor Relations Act (NLRA),[28] which regulates the relationship between unions and employers in the United States, the Tribal Labor Relations Ordinance similarly defines the collective bargaining rights of the tribal casino employee and the responsibilities of the tribal employer. However, while the Tribal Labor Relations Ordinance mirrors the NLRA in many of the collective rights afforded to tribal employees, conspicuously absent from the tribal ordinance are some of the same substantial safeguards afforded to employers within the NLRA.

Unlike their non-tribal counterparts, tribal casino employees under the ordinance have the right to enter onto casino property at any time to talk to employees and post propaganda in order to facilitate the organization of employees. Under the NLRA, employees are subject to strict standards regulating when, where, and in what fashion they may engage in those types of activities.[29] In addition, the ordinance allows unions to engage in secondary boycotts[30] after an impasse has been reached in negotiations without suffering any penalty proscribed by the NLRA.[31]

While fifty-nine tribes signed compacts with Davis, the validity of the compacts is contingent upon a separate ballot measure to go before the California voters in March 2000. Proposition 1A, a proposed constitutional amendment, would overcome the obstacle Proposition 5 encountered by specifically exempting Indian tribes from section 19(e) of the state constitution. If passed, it would give tribes the exclusive right to offer Nevada-style machines and house-banked card games. Without passage of this constitutional amendment, the compacts signed between Davis and the tribes will be void. At the time this article is being written, many tribes are optimistic about the proposition's chance for success, given that early reports indicate that many of the Las Vegas gaming interests that contributed so heavily to anti-Proposition 5 efforts in the November 1998 election are not interested in a repeat of an expensive battle to try to change the public policy in another state. In addition to the retreat of the Las Vegas interests, the tribes have attracted the support of their other Proposition 5 adversary: organized labor. With signed compacts giving organized labor bargaining rights at the tribal casinos and the promise of lucrative member fees, organized labor has a vested interest in the proposition's passage.

While the California voters have yet to vote on Proposition 1A, and with the legality of the compacts signed by Governor Davis and tribal nations in September 1999 hinging upon their decision, the overwhelming support of California voters for tribal gaming, as evidenced in Proposition 5, lends optimism that voters will similarly voice their support in March 2000. If indeed tribes are victorious with Proposition 1A, it will be the result not only of the hard work of the Proposition 1A campaign, but also of the foundation laid nearly a year earlier in Proposition 5.[32] This proposition was successful in appealing to the California voters not because it was a vote on gaming, but because it was an affirmation of the most basic tenet of self-government: that people have the inherent right to govern themselves and to make basic decisions affecting their collective well-being. As Mark Macarro, chairman of the Pechanga Band of Luiseño Mission Indians, has said regarding Proposition 5: "For the first time in history, tribes have established what the public policy of a state is, and succeeded in putting a debate forward and having the public side with the tribes in that debate. It seems that tribes no longer have to be relegated to being history's doormats, but can actually engage in public debate and set policy in terms favorable to tribes."[33] Indeed, throughout history, the state and federal governments have used their power to take away the land, resources, and even the lives of California Indians. Although numerous Native people lost much that was sacred, dignity and pride as a people have never been sacrificed. Any negotiations between sovereign Indian nations and the state and federal governments should include mutuality and respect for different cultural values. Perhaps the best solution may be found in the wisdom of the Iroquois wampum belt presented to Europeans during the Encounter era:

> The two rows will symbolize two vessels, traveling down the same river together. One, a birch bark canoe, will be for the Indian people and their laws, their customs, and their ways. The other, a ship, will be for the white people and their laws, their customs and their ways. We shall each travel the river together, side by side, but in our own boat. Neither of us will try to steer the other's vessel.[34]

In an effort to reverse the effects of years of discriminatory federal and state policies, Indian people are now taking control of their own destinies, deciding what is best for their people and communities. Eighty-eight tribes, representing 96 percent of California Indians, supported Proposition 5, with 63 percent of the California voters passing it in November of 1998—an indelible fact that is testimony to the determination and collective strength of Indian people. Indeed, as the new millennium dawns, California Indian gaming nations, through their hard work and unwavering commitment, have crossed the bridge that leads from hope to realization of dreams.

NOTES

1. *Worcester* v *Georgia*, 31 US (6 Pet.) 515 (1832).
2. Carole Goldberg-Ambrose and Duane Champagne, et al., *A Second Century of Dishonor: Federal Inequities and California Tribes*, report prepared by the UCLA American Indian Studies Center for the Advisory Council on California Indian Policy (27 March 1996).
3. 480 US 202.
4. 25 USC §2701.
5. Id., §2702 (1).
6. Class I gaming is defined as "social games solely for prizes of minimal value or traditional forms of Indian gaming engaged in by individuals as a part of, or in connection with, tribal ceremonies or celebrations" (25 USC §2703[6]).
7. Class II gaming is defined to include: "(1) the game of chance commonly known as bingo" and "(2) card games that are explicitly authorized by the laws of the State" or "are not explicitly prohibited by the laws of the State and are played at any location in the State, but only if such card games are played in conformity with those laws and regulations (if any) of the State regarding hours or periods of operation of such cards games or limitations on wagers or pot sizes in such card games" (25 USC §2703[7][A]). The act excluded from its definition of class II gaming: "(1) any banking card games, including baccarat, chemin de fer, or blackjack" and "(2) electronic or electromechanical facsimiles of any game of chance or slot machines of any kind" (Id., §2703[7][B]).
8. Class III gaming is defined as "all forms of gaming that are not class I or class II" (Id., §2703[8]).
9. Id., §2710(d)(1).
10. Tribes may engage in class III gaming so long as: (1) the tribe adopts an ordinance authorizing such gaming; (2) the tribe is located in a state that "permits such gaming for any purpose by any person, organization or entity"; and (3) the gaming is conducted in accordance with a tribal-state gaming compact (25 USC §2710).
11. Cal. Pen. Code §330(a).
12. Jerome Levine, "California's Legal Quagmire," *International Gaming and Business Wagering* (February 1999): 26.
13. *Mashantucket Pequot Tribe* v *Connecticut*, 913 F.2d 1024.
14. (9th Cir. 1994) 64 F.3d 1250.
15. 13 Cal. 4th 475.
16. Cal. Pen. Code §330.
17. Levine, "California's Legal Quagmire," 27.
18. The Johnson Act (15 USC §1175) prohibits the possession of gambling devices on Indian lands. IGRA waives this prohibition when the gaming is conducted by a tribe under a valid tribal-state compact.

19. Under the impression that they would be unable to acquire the necessary signatures for a constitutional amendment, the campaign decided to present their plan in the form of a statutory initiative.

20. Total campaign expenditures surpassed $92 million. The tribes spent a total of $63 million while the opposition spent more than $29 million.

21. *Hotel Employees and Restaurant Employees International Union* v *Davis*, 21 Cal. 4th 585.

22. Id., 602.

23. Id.

24. Id.

25. *Tribal Government and Economic Self-Sufficiency Act*, §5.

26. Among the many critics of the mandatory agreements with organized labor within the compacts was Republican Congressman J. D. Hayworth of Arizona. On 30 September 1999 Congressman Hayworth introduced legislative bill HR 2992 into the United States Congress. The bill would protect the sovereignty of Indian tribes by prohibiting collective bargaining requirements from being part of future tribal-state gaming compacts and revoking the compacts recently negotiated in California. As of this writing, the bill is scheduled for debate in the House of Representatives.

27. Field notes at Pechanga, Morongo, and Viejas casinos, 23 May 1998 to 23 June 1998 in possession of the author.

28. 29 USC §151 et seq.

29. Id., §157.

30. A secondary boycott is defined as union pressure in the form of strikes, picketing, threats, or other coercion aimed at an employer or other person with whom the union has no labor dispute, with the object of persuading or coercing that neutral party to stop dealing with a primary party with whom the union has a dispute, and thus ultimately persuading the primary party to meet union demands.

31. Id. at §158(c).

32. [In March 2000, Proposition 1A passed in California.]

33. Mark Macarro, chairman of the Pechanga Band of Luiseño Mission Indians, interview by Chad M. Gordon, November 1999.

34. Robert A. Williams, Jr., "The Algebra of Federal Indian Law: The Hard Trial of Decolonizing and Americanizing the White Man's Indian Jurisprudence," *Wisconsin Law Review* (1986): 223.

♠

Winning the Sovereignty Jackpot: The Indian Gaming Regulatory Act and the Struggle for Sovereignty

Sioux Harvey

What Congress did when it passed the IGRA in 1988 would change the political landscape of tribal-state relations in ways no one could have possibly anticipated when the first small Indian bingo parlours were opened.[1]

Since World War II American Indians have built sovereignty through political, economic, and cultural incorporation. I define *incorporation* as the process by which a group and its members are drawn into the institutional practices of larger and more powerful political economies and their attendant cultural formations. *Incorporation* is a term drawn from world-systems theory and has mainly been deployed to argue or imply that groups undergoing incorporation lose power and become dependent or assimilated into the core. According to my definition, the term *core* is the mainstream economic, political, and cultural streams of American life. This chapter argues that tribal incorporation of the United States' political culture has provided tribes with greater sovereignty and independence. Since they became involved in policy implementation and moved into the entertainment business via gambling, tribes have exercised greater control over their lives. Scholars and others have often looked for Indian sovereignty in the wrong place. By focusing on the process in which we might least expect to find it—incorporation into the dominant political economy—I hope to show that Indian sovereignty is much more viable than has been thought. I will also shed light on the process, in this case gaming legislation, through which a once dependent people can achieve self-determination.

The idea of self-determination and its economic engine, gaming legislation, has evolved over time in both ideological and political ways. Once the ball started rolling toward self-determination in the early 1970s, the intention of the federal government shifted away from Termination policies. Nevertheless, Indians continued the fight to gain control of their land, economies, health care systems, educational methods, and religions. The battle for change in Indian Country was slow but steady and ultimately brought increased tribal sovereignty, a consequence that neither Indians nor the United States government accurately predicted.

Sovereignty is defined by *Webster's Dictionary* as "supreme power over a body politic; freedom from external control; autonomy; controlling influence."[2] In this article *sovereignty* will be used to define the point at which tribes can call their own shots, in the sense that they are financially independent from the United States government and are politically and culturally able to direct their lives on the reservations according to the tribes' desires. This idea of sovereignty includes freedom from federal and state interference in economic, political, religious, cultural, legal, and educational decisions.

As mentioned above, a big part of this increase in tribal sovereign power is economic independence from the federal government. This chapter will provide an overview of the historical events that occurred to bring about the passage of the Indian Gaming Regulatory Act (IGRA) in 1988. This act may be seen as a continuation of the American Indian self-determination policies that began under Richard Nixon. One of the problems with this policy's implementation and success, however, was the lack of adequate funding required to get Indian people on their feet economically. Gaming has provided some tribes with the cash flow necessary to gain financial independence from the federal government and to experience true sovereignty.

The passage of IGRA helped bring about an explosion in Indian-run casinos. While the many tribes that opened casinos in the early 1980s added to the need for the hearings and passage of this act, many other tribes were waiting for the act's passage before they opened their own casinos. Therefore, the act caused a gaming boom in many Indian nations. Amounts earned by Indian nations in Class III gross revenues were about $1 billion in 1990. This grew to $5.4 billion in 1995; $6.2 billion in 1996; $7.4 billion in 1997; and $8.1 billion in 1998.[3] Twenty-three states now have Indian casinos.[4]

This steep increase in cash flow has changed the face of Indian participation in politics—tribes are now in the business of political giving. According to *Mother Jones* magazine, the Mashantucket Pequot have given both political parties more than $1 million in federal soft money since 1993. In California, the California Indian Nations Political Action Committee has spent more than $870,000 on contributions to lobbyists.[5]

Gambling is the fastest growing business in America and Indians are taking advantage of the trend. How did the tides turn? This chapter will trace the history of these changes and will provide an overview of: (1) the economic trends on Indian reservations; (2) how the United States government has sought ways to assist Indian nations in becoming self-determined since the 1970s, including the passage of IGRA; and (3) the current gaming battles between the three sovereign powers in America: the federal government, the states, and the Indian nations.

A HISTORY OF COURT CASES: DEFINING THE LEGALITY OF BINGO ON INDIAN RESERVATIONS

Large-scale gaming on Indian lands started in the early 1980s. Tribes noticed the success of state lotteries and the bingo being used as fundraisers by churches and other charities. Indians in Florida and California began to raise revenue by offering bingo with larger prizes than were allowed under state law. The states threatened to sue if the tribes did not stop their gaming. The tribes, in turn, sued in federal court.[6] This series of court cases in the early 1980s declared that Indian tribes could legally host games on their reservations. The first case, *Oneida Tribe of Indians* v. *State of Wisconsin*, was decided on 27 July 1981. There were three primary decisions made: "1) In absence of consent of tribes or express authorization of Congress, state law does not govern on-reservation conduct involving only tribal members; 2) In some cases, tribal laws may control activities of non-Indians on the reservations; and 3) Wisconsin's bingo laws were civil/regulatory, and thus, not enforceable by the state in Indian country [because of Public Law 280]." In this case, the Oneidas argued that they did not have to comply with Wisconsin law because they had treaty-based immunity to state-to-state laws and because they had the right to self-govern. The tribe argued that because bingo laws were "civil/regulatory" as opposed to criminal in nature, they did not fall under Wisconsin's Public Law 280 (PL 280) requirements.[7]

In the court's opinion, Indians hold broad authority to govern themselves as established by *Worcester* v. *State of Georgia* in 1832, which decided that the state could not enforce its laws on the Cherokee Reservation. The Court also emphasized that the question was, absent acts of Congress, can states infringe on reservations' right to make their own laws and rule by them? It was then stated that the nature of tribal and state authority on the reservation has become less clear, but that state law cannot govern on-reservation acts regarding tribal members without express authorization from Congress. In conclusion, the Court opined that "Congress did not intend to allow states to use licensing requirements in an attempt to create jurisdiction to enforce otherwise civil regulation on Indian reservations." In addition, the Court stated that Wisconsin's state laws could not be enforced on the Oneida Reservation under PL 280 because it conflicted with current federal policy encouraging tribal self-governance.[8]

The second case defining PL 280 was *Seminole Tribe of Florida* v. *Butterworth*, decided on 5 October 1981. The Seminole sued the sheriff of Broward County, who sought an injunction against the tribe because they refused to let the state regulate the Seminole's bingo hall. This case reaffirmed reservations' self-governing power, deciding that states lack jurisdiction over Indian reservation activity until granted such authority by the federal government. In addition, *Seminole* v. *Butterworth* declared false the state's contention that only Indians could play bingo on the reservation. The opinion stated that reservations are not required to differentiate between Indians and non-Indians. The appeal again questioned PL 280. Florida argued that PL 280 gave the state the right to exercise criminal and limited civil jurisdiction over the tribe.[9] However, the court cited that this portion of PL 280 was repealed by PL 284, Title IV s 403, 82 Stat. 79, which required the consent of the tribes themselves before any further assumption of jurisdiction. In addition, the decision stated that "if Congress in enacting PL 280 had intended to confer upon the States general civil regulatory powers, including taxation over reservation Indians, it would have said so."[10] Therefore the Supreme Court concluded that "states do not have general regulatory power over Indian tribes."[11]

After this and other similar rulings in other circuits, more than eighty tribes started their own bingo parlors. In hearings held in Washington in 1985, Seminole

Tribal Chairman James E. Billie testified that due to the infusion of capital from their bingo operations the tribe had been able to make positive steps forward in funding projects supporting the health, education, and welfare of his people. The money was also used to support other tribal businesses and to loan tribal members cash to start their own businesses. Billie added that now the tribe had a new source of education not available in schools—the value of trial and error.[12]

After the addition of bingo, the Seminole tribes' unemployment went from 60 percent to the teens; more kids graduated from high school in the 1980s than in the entire history of the tribe; all the tribal houses were upgraded with plumbing; and they earned renewed pride in their cultural and political heritage—something of greater value than any of the other effects of gaming. These are the gains that self-determination can bring when a tribe struggles for financial independence.

In another case, held in the ninth circuit, *United States* v. *Farris*, supra 624 F. 2nd 890, the court found that the Puyallup tribe could open a casino in spite of the state of Washington's objections, because the state had not assumed jurisdiction over gambling offenses. Washington argued that under the Organized Crime Control Act of 1970 the state could prohibit reservation gambling laws that violated the surrounding state's laws. The federal courts concluded that gambling activities, which are regulated rather than prohibited by state law, are not against the public policy of the state and therefore not in violation of the Organized Crime Control Act.[13]

Another big case in California (a PL 280 state), *Barona Group of the Capitan Grande Band of Mission Indians, San Diego County, California* v. *Duffy*, once again reaffirmed what the previous cases had. The case confirmed that whether state and county laws were applicable to Indian tribes' bingo enterprises on the reservation depended on whether state laws were classified as civil/regulatory or criminal/prohibitory according to California state law. Once again, the court stated that the states' enforcement of bingo on Indian reservations went against the grain of current federal Indian policy that was supportive of self-determination.[14]

After the California and Florida cases, bingo began to appear on Indian reservations across the United States. This started a heated debate as tribes began to expand their gaming activities and states tried to block their efforts. A compromise was needed, and so Congress held hearings on the proposed regulation of Indian gaming. The major architects of the Indian Gaming Regulatory Act were senators Daniel K. Inouye (D. Hawaii) and Daniel J. Evans (R. Washington). IGRA was passed in hopes of ending the conflict, but I. Nelson Rose cites that the passage of the act has only shifted the conflict from Congress to the states, federal courts, and the National Indian Gaming Commission.[15]

In 1986, the Supreme Court began to hear *California* v. *Cabazon Band of Mission Indians*, which helped formulate some of the background for the passage of IGRA. This case was decided in favor of the Indians in 1987. Nancy McKay in the *Gonzaga Law Review* stated that "the primary issue in *Cabezon* was whether the State of California had authority to enforce its gambling laws within the reservation occupied by the Cabezon Indians."[16] This case confirmed what tribes had been arguing: that if a state legalized some form of gambling, as the state of California did when it allowed charities to hold bingo events with large jackpots, then Indian tribes could do the same, without state injunction. I. Nelson Rose stated that the Supreme Court held in this decision that federal policy actively supports Indian gaming.[17]

A HISTORY OF THE CONGRESSIONAL HEARINGS PRECEDING THE PASSAGE OF THE INDIAN GAMING REGULATORY ACT

The House and Senate conducted hearings on Indian Country gambling in 1985. It was hoped that regulations would ease the tensions resulting from the explosion of Indian gaming throughout the country. The Department of the Interior estimated that nearly eighty tribes were conducting gaming, chiefly bingo, and that twenty to twenty-five of these were high-stakes operations, some grossing up to $1 million monthly. Some of these operations were tribally owned and operated, while others involved outside management companies or were independently owned and operated by individual Indian residents.[18]

The government's basis of concern was the connection between lucrative gambling operations and organized crime. They believed large amounts of cash acted as a magnet to such organizations and could be a source of potential corruption. History had demonstrated that large amounts of cash are very seductive to these elements and if regulations could be legislated then it was hoped that background checks would stop these people from operating within the Indian gaming sphere. Some senators, however, such as Arizona Republican John McCain, believed that states' gaming interests went beyond such stated interests—they were really concerned with protecting their own games from competition.[19]

Tribes were concerned with protecting their rights through the legislation of regulations. States such as California refused to accept the previous six court decisions that made gaming legal on Indian lands and ignored the ninth circuit court's decision regarding the Barona tribe. California was forcing other tribes, such as the Morongo Band of Mission Indians, to relitigate the Barona case. In the hearings, attorney Barbara Karshmer, representing the Morongo Indians, explained that this was part of a pattern in California that contested tribes' right to self-government and self-determination on the reservations.[20]

Indians have stated that sovereignty—their government-to-government relationship with the federal government—is guaranteed by the United States Constitution. They argue that this historic relationship should insure their independence from state laws. It is this author's opinion, however, that most states do not appreciate the historic relationship between tribes and the federal government. They look at Indian nations within their borders as they would any other constituency. When state laws are broken on reservation lands, local governments want to assume control over the reservation, forgetting that only the federal government has jurisdiction over tribes. With gaming, states such as California perceive tribes as renegades who are breaking state laws by hosting "illegal" casinos.

For example, until 1997 California refused to negotiate a compact with gaming tribes. California stalemated negotiations, arguing that because the gaming tribes were operating illegal casinos, they were not required to negotiate with them until the tribes shut down their operations. The state had formerly asserted that it was illegal for tribes to host bingo when it actually was not. Since tribes believed that the federal government supported them, the Indians opened bingo halls in reaction to California's statement. When Class III gaming appeared in Indian casinos outside California and the state still persisted in its resistance to negotiation with tribes that wanted to expand, tribes installed Class III machines. California continued to maintain that these casinos were illegal but refused to confer to make them legal. Governor Pete Wilson took this hard line and stood firm until he began to negotiate with the Pala Band of Mission Indians, a non-gaming tribe.

The first hearings in the House began in November of 1985.[21] Marion Black Horn, the principal deputy solicitor of the Department of the Interior (DOI), testified that tribes' unregulated gambling held an unfair competitive advantage over the states' regulated gambling. She continued, stating that there were no state imposed limits on the size of jackpots, no limits on the hours of operation, no licensing fees, and no state-imposed taxes.[22]

This speech by Horn demonstrates that she and most other federal employees of the Department of the Interior and the Bureau of Indian Affairs (BIA) were either unaware or dismissive of the trend towards self-determination for Indian peoples. In her conclusion, she asserted that the DOI's approach is a step toward tribal sovereignty. Her attempts to gain approval for state control over Indian gaming activities invalidates this point—control by the state or federal governments over Indian activities on the reservation is not what self-determination policy intended. Horn testified without speaking to any Indians about her proposals for new legislation. In addition, no one from the DOI attended the hearings at which Indians testified as to their desired legislation. Once again the federal mandate was ignored.[23]

The National Tribal Chairman's Association (NTCA) testified that:

> We are resolved to control our future and we, therefore, declare that our control must become part of the fabric of the U.S. government documents. Our people must give expression to our collective existence through Indian governments. It is kind of sad to see that the Department of the Interior's representative and the Justice representative are not here to hear some of the comments by these Indians gathered at this podium to give our point of view.[24]

NTCA furnished the House Committee on Indian Affairs with a letter containing three major points of the benefits gaming provided for Native peoples. These were:

I.   Gaming provides an essential and vital source of revenue to the tribes.
    A. Reduces the tribes' dependency on public support.
    B. Provides local establishments with spill over benefits in the form of increased money.
    C. In some instances it gives local governments an addition to their tax base (Seneca, Fox, and Sac).
    D. On the reservation it provides additional jobs.

     E. The source of money flows mainly from off-reservation to
        on-reservation.
  II. Gaming provides a socio-economic function-generator. There are
     few other activities on the reservation that provide the opportuni-
     ty for Indians and non-Indians to interact.
     A. Gaming brings new technology to the reservation (electronic
        funds transfer, telex, Visa and Mastercharge).
     B. Gives the Indians incentive to organize in a business-like
        manner.
     C. Teaches the tribe management skills.
     D. Encourages entrepreneurial instinct.
  III. Provides an important opportunity for Indians to participate in
     current economic trends.
     A. Attracts off-reservation monies that would otherwise be spent
        elsewhere.
     B. A growing number of states are already resorting to lotteries
        for raising revenue.
     C. One of the few ways that reservation tribes are able to raise
        capital.
     D. Without such a source of revenue Indians cannot participate in
        the general economy as equals, but will forever be wards of the
        state.[25]

Indians themselves also furnished information to the House committee about the possibility of organized crime coming to the reservation once gaming expanded. In light of this, the National Gaming Task Force was created to examine the concerns of the Justice Department. Sixty tribes were represented and this task began its work two years before the 1983 hearings. The chairman, Mark Powless, was an elected official of the Oneida Tribe of Wisconsin. He stated for the record that tribes were also concerned about the possibility of organized crime and therefore supported the group.[26] The task force acknowledged that the Department of Justice did have good reason for concern. There were some instances in which there appeared to be involvement by organized crime members. However, they could not find the criminal elements within the tribe. It always came from an outside management or consulting firm. The task force found no evidence of criminal involvement on any Indian reservation.

    The task force also highlighted the need for DOI and BIA assistance. Without any policies, regulations, or guidelines from the governmental organizations, tribes would have no aid in the development and management of their gaming operations. Confusion would be the result. They asked that legislation be provided so that tribes could receive technical and financial assistance for gaming proposals on the basis of their economic merit. Finally, they asked that gaming be regulated by tribal-state compacts.[27]

    In 1986, the hearings continued, except that they now were focused on the establishment of federal standards and regulations for gaming, as opposed to the previous hearings' focus on background information.[28] The report submitted by the Select Committee on Indian Affairs was to recommend that HR 1920, once amended, be passed by the House. This would establish federal standards and regulations for gaming. HR 1920 was introduced by Democratic Representative Mark Udall from Colorado on 2 April 1985.[29]

The regulations were amended to ensure that tribal governments take a stronger role in gaming than the previous legislation proposed. The committee also reported that it found no evidence of criminal involvement on Indian reservations and that a heavyhanded approach by the federal government was inappropriate. The committee did recommend a strong federal presence, however, arguing that it would help insure gaming's integrity, although only the tribes were to reap the benefits of running a casino.

The regulations set up by this bill were similar to the ones included in the bill that passed two years hence. For example, it stated that tribes could conduct Class II gaming if such games were permitted in the state. In addition, the bill stated that if a tribal-state compact gave them permission, a tribe could conduct Class III gaming.

By mid-1986, 108 tribes had gaming facilities and 104 of these conducted bingo. The combined receipts for these gaming activities were estimated to be $100 million annually. Forty-five states permitted some form of bingo, while only five states prohibited the game completely. The committee saw gaming as "a welcome source of funds to replace dwindling Federal dollars." Since Ronald Reagan's administration affirmed sovereign tribal rights, the committee believed that this legislation would mirror his directive.[30] In his Indian policy statement Reagan said,

> It is the policy of this Administration to encourage private involvement, both Indian and non-Indian, in tribal economic development. In some cases, tribes and the private sector have already taken innovative approaches which have overcome the legislative and regulatory impediments to economic progress.
>
> Since tribal governments have the primary responsibilities for meeting the basic needs of Indian communities, they must be allowed the chance to succeed.[31]

Congress believed that Indian gaming was a promising source of revenue that would assist Indian people in gaining their economic independence. The legislators also saw that the passage of this bill would demonstrate support for the trend toward Indian self-determination, an idea articulated in all three branches of government.

In 1987, hearings were again held to establish federal standards and regulations for Indian gaming. There were two reasons why Congress had to act. First, since gaming on reservations was uncontrolled, Congress needed to organize the situation. Second, since the Supreme Court had reaffirmed tribal jurisdiction over gambling on reservations, Congress needed to act to formulate the best possible federal policy.[32] Concerns with the legislation were varied, the most commonly cited being the reconfirmation of formerly approved management contracts between tribes and private companies. Investors who were helping tribes gather seed money would examine these contracts with great interest before investing. If Congress validated previously approved contracts, it would send a strong message to companies considering such investments. Another area of importance was law enforcement. There was concern over the criminal elements and the legality of Class III gaming on reservations. Congress needed to balance tribal and outside interests without changing the historic federal-tribal relationship.[33]

Current legal cases such as *California v. Cabazon Band of Mission Indians* were interpreted differently by Congress and Indian tribes. This case found that activity not criminally prohibited by the state may be regulated by tribes under their own laws, just as bingo had been. Tribes saw the decision as a complete affirmation of their sovereignty. State representatives who testified at these hearings were concerned largely because the proposed legislation contained no strict regulations on Indian gaming. The states sought to control what would happen inside their borders. For example, Nevada sought legislation that would license people or entities only after extensive background checks into the person's or people's character(s), associations, financing, and business acumen. The state also wanted to require investigations of management, vendors, lenders, and financial and legal advisors.[34]

Some senators, such as McCain, also sought regulation, licensing, and oversight activities by the federal government. In doing so, he acknowledged that the real issue was Indian sovereignty. McCain expressed concern over Congress giving states jurisdiction over Indian gaming. He argued that this move would go against the current policy of self-determination and self-government. The responsibility over Indian people, McCain said, belonged to the federal government—not to the states. He said that the historical record was clear: tribal sovereignty was protected through treaties. The government-to-government relationship, McCain claimed, began with the inception of the United States. He advocated a partnership, not a paternalistic approach.[35]

Another factor important to this story is the outgrowth of the National Indian Gaming Association (NIGA). NIGA was formed by the BIA and the Ninety-eighth Congress. Before NIGA, tribes and the BIA had set up the Indian Gaming Task Force. However, tribes found that they were at odds with the BIA and set up their own organization for two main reasons: (1) to formally answer this proposed legislation and (2) to serve the interests of gaming and non-gaming tribes. The membership of NIGA originally included twenty tribes that operated either bingo or other card game operations.[36]

NIGA supported the current legislative approach to Indian gaming, although it did not agree that Indian gaming was currently unregulated, citing *Cabazon* to contend that states had no power to regulate affairs on Indian land. NIGA saw that the responsibility of the federal government was to protect Indians from state interference and to protect the economic interests that states represent—not a very easy task.[37]

Even in PL 280 states, tribes could not legislate against gaming because it was considered a civil (versus criminal) activity. So once again, the battle was over sovereignty or as NIGA stated, "a balancing test" between "[t]raditional notions of Indian sovereignty and the Congressional goal of Indian self-government, including its 'overriding goal' of encouraging tribal self-sufficiency and economic development."[38]

The final area of contention was the regulation of Class III gaming. NIGA stated its position by declaring that the Supreme Court, in *Cabazon*, rejected Congressional action for Class III games. There were two major reasons for this: (1) NIGA felt that Congress had no business either insulating non-Indian gaming interests from those with whom they had no "fiduciary relationship," or protecting tribal interests due to some moral constitutional and congressional responsibility; and (2) In the ten-year period since the Seminole tribe had revitalized itself through bingo, tribes have had a fantastic gaming record. NIGA pointed out that states argued the old racist belief that Indians are an inferior race incapable of regulating such a complex enterprise as the complicated Class III gaming activities. Tribes, in NIGA's assertion, were perfectly capable of complex activity—they had proven themselves with their bingo track record and other gaming developments.

THE INDIAN GAMING REGULATORY ACT PASSES IN 1988—AND THE CONGRESSIONAL HEARINGS CONTINUE

The Indian Gaming Regulatory Act, Public Law 100–497, passed on 17 October 1988.[39] This is one of the most important Indian legislation acts passed by Congress since the Indian Reorganization Act of 1933. IGRA divides all gambling into three classes: Class I encompasses social and traditional games; Class II is limited to bingo, including pull-tabs, electronic aids, and non-banking card games like poker; Class III includes primarily slot machines, casino banking and percentage games, off-track betting, and lotteries. Class III is viewed as the most dangerous. The basic structure (although there are exceptions) is that a federally recognized tribe may operate a Class I game without restriction, a Class II game with oversight by the new National Indian Gaming Commission, and a Class III game only if it reaches a compact with the state in which it resides. Class II or III gaming is allowed only in states that have not completely prohibited that particular game.[40]

In 1992, after IGRA had been in operation for four years, hearings were held on the implementation of the act. The problems sounded familiar. Senator Inouye said in his opening statement that four years after passage, the Department of the Interior had not presented its management plan to the secretary. The Department of Justice was awaiting finalization of regulations on the definitions of Classes II and III before it pursued violations of the act. Because the National Indian Gaming Commission was still in the process of developing regulations, there was much to be done. Inouye stated that he and the others who worked on the "long and tortuous route" to this act's passage had attempted to strike a balance and recognize state and tribal sovereignty.[41]

There were those who opposed the act's passage. The state of Nevada, whose gaming interests spent millions (tribes say $100 million a year) to stop Indian gaming in California, was the first to testify that there was an uncontrolled spread of Indian gaming, legal and illegal. The state also asserted that organized crime was trying to infiltrate these gaming establishments. Another major opponent was Slade Gorton, a senator from Washington state, who was elected in the furor that occurred after the 1975 Boldt decision gave half of the annual salmon catch to Indian tribes in the state. Gorton has repeatedly held that Class III gaming was an "unmitigated disaster" for the people who have it forced on them because of federal acts.[42]

Gorton's statements were countered by senators John McCain, Henry Reid, and Thomas Daschle. McCain affirmed the fact that the Supreme Court decision left Congress little choice but to enact enabling legislation. The Supreme Court stated that Indians should be allowed to engage in the same type of activities that are allowed in non-Indian Country. Daschle, from South Dakota, said he agreed with Gorton but took exception to some of the things he said. Daschle found it difficult to describe what had happened in his state as an "unmitigated disaster." He said that some reservations had 80 percent unemployment before IGRA, but many reservations now not only had full employment, but also benefited the surrounding communities. He said, "So to the skeptics who, with amazing consistency, said, 'It's impossible for an Indian reservation to get its act together to develop economic activity to the point where they themselves can deal with the problems economically,' we've got exhibit A."[43]

Congress found it difficult to agree that gaming was harmful and should not be allowed. On the contrary, it saw a possible rebirth for many Indian people. And because gaming was providing Indian people with a means to self-determination, the stated federal policy, Congress decided to move ahead with gaming legislation. As Eddie Brown, assistant secretary for Indian Affairs, stated, "The department has had responsibilities in Indian Gaming since at least 1984. We recognize that a proper balance has to be struck between the concerns of law enforcement in asserting some measure of control over high-stakes gaming as a revenue source."[44] Brown continued, stating that Indian gaming regulations were difficult to nail down because of the complexities of the situation. And due to these challenges, he said, some tribes were operating with unapproved management contracts; some were conducting Class III without tribal-state compacts (such as California); and some tribes were distributing income without having their plans approved by the law.

Indian gaming grew so fast that the federal agencies were initially unable to keep up with its expansion. The Department of the Interior was unable to properly monitor gaming activities on Indian reservations because the BIA was understaffed. There were three underlying reasons for this: first, tribal gaming exploded beyond anyone's predictions; second, new technology (such as video gaming machines) came out after the law was passed in 1988 and before there were any agreements about which games were legal and which were illegal; and third, the DOI and the BIA both thought that the National Indian Gaming Commission would be taking over regulatory responsibility once it was established. This did not occur, however.

In 1992 the hearings continued. The first hearing, which took place in February, was focused on the way federal agencies implemented the act. The second, in March, examined the tribal-state compacting process. This hearing was to direct attention to the actions that tribal governments have taken to implement the act in terms of law enforcement and regulation.[45]

Senator Inouye, in his opening statement, gave an overview of the regulations' standing. Since gaming law began its development in 1987, much had happened. The Supreme Court ruled on the *Cabazon* case and still there were no regulations in place to control gaming activities. Due to the unique federal-tribal trust relationship, Congress decided to maintain the exclusion of states having jurisdiction over this federal activity. The Senate select committee first considered a federal commission that would be responsible for Indian gaming regulation as well as the associated law enforcement responsibilities, planned to be shared by tribal governments.

Inouye reported that most Indian leaders were favorable to this proposition because it continued the traditional relationship between tribes and the federal government. However, once the states got wind of this agreement they became concerned. States argued that because these activities occurred within their borders, they too deserved a role in deciding what gaming activities would be conducted on reservation lands. The states wanted tribal-state compacts. They wanted to negotiate with the tribes on a government-to-government basis, so that, in their eyes, the playing field would be leveled.

Inouye explained that he, as chairman of the committee, had to urge Indian governments to accept this new idea of negotiating with states instead of the federal government. He felt this was the only agreement that would allow for passage. A deal was made wherein Indians set aside some of their sovereignty in return for what Congress and the tribes thought would be a "rational scheme of management of gaming activities on Indian lands."[46] In this way Indians ended up with tribal-state compacts instead of federal-tribal compacts.

In exchange for tribes giving up some sovereignty, Congress waived the Johnson Act whenever a tribal-state compact was in place. Congress also provided that if a state allowed Class III gaming for charitable purposes, then Class III could be negotiated and compacted between tribes and states.[47] One problem Inouye noted was that at this point in time states were avoiding compacting with tribes by asserting Eleventh Amendment immunity—they used the amendment to argue that the federal government cannot tell states what to do. Inouye said this practice was happening more and more frequently.[48]

Inouye was the primary sponsor of IGRA and the chair of the select committee on Indian affairs. He conveyed that he was constantly approached by states who wanted to amend the act and wanted to ask his fellow senators what they wanted to do. He was in a conundrum: the states did not want tribal-state compacts; they did not want the secretary of the Interior to prescribe contracts; and they did not want the secretary of the Interior to proscribe procedures for the conduct of Class III gaming.[49] He further commented that without regulations, the allowance of the *Cabazon* decision to control the activity would only result in chaos. If he allowed Indian gaming to linger at this impasse, he was not leading as he thought he should and was acting unfairly to the Indian nations.[50]

Senator Inouye chose as his star witness George Mickelson, senator from South Dakota, who had successfully negotiated five compacts with nine tribes residing in his state. According to Inouye, he did not use the Eleventh Amendment to evade his responsibilities. Mickelson testified that what he thought the states wanted was to fix ambiguities in the law that impeded the progress of negotiations. He did not see this as a large problem—the clarification that was needed, he said, could easily be accomplished. One of the ambiguities he cited was that tribes ran Class III gaming when it was illegal in the state in which the tribes reside.[51]

Until the recent passage of Proposition 1A, this argument raged in

California. Tribes in the state argued that video lottery terminals (VLTs) are the same machines that the state uses in its lottery games. California argued that VLTs are slot machines and are illegal in the state. This disagreement was one reason why the state refused to negotiate with any tribes that had casinos with VLTs—at the time, this was all but one gaming tribe in California. And the one tribe that did not have VLTs was unable to get the governor to negotiate with them either.

Mickelson expressed concern for another area of confusion: tribal authority over non-Indians on reservation lands. Some tribes in the United States sought to open casinos on lands outside their trust lands. If this is part of the negotiation process, Mickelson believed IGRA should be amended to state such options. He wanted the rules to be clear. South Dakota had developed a unique partnership with local tribes, allowing them to participate as individual operators in the state's lottery. While Mickelson knew that this was a special arrangement, he thought it would be helpful to clarify the gaming act's amendments.[52] As the hearings continued, state representatives asked that a more complete explanation be inserted into the gaming regulations. The tribes also supported clarification of the act, since misunderstandings hindered their progress.

Hearings in the House in 1992 brought up the same concerns. Assistant Secretary Eddie Brown commented that background checks needed to be more thorough in protecting the industry from organized crime. The Federal Bureau of Investigation was responsible for conducting the checks; however, there was no specified completion date. Brown argued that a deadline was imperative to the act's success.[53]

There were a few other areas of import highlighted during the hearings. Representative Thomas Glidden, for example, asked the Department of Justice to look into the embargo placed on states' and tribes' options to sue each other and to provide a legal opinion on the matter. Another area in need of clarification concerned the Santee Sioux in Nebraska, a state in which gaming is illegal. The Santee Sioux purchased land in Iowa, where gaming is legal, and petitioned the secretary of the Interior to add this new land to their trust lands so that they might open a casino in Iowa. The fact that this request crossed state lines made it a federal matter. There was no precedence, however, for making a decision on the issue. Within IGRA, the issue of taking land into trust for gaming purposes is addressed, but not when the purchase of land crosses state lines—so the secretary declined the tribe's request.[54]

Tony Hope, the chairman of the National Indian Gaming Commission (NIGC), testified that there were four major contributors to the slow pace at which the regulations had been formulated. To begin with, the challenge of regulating a new industry, one that had grown astronomically even as the regulations were being considered, was very difficult. The complexity of the issues also made it difficult to get the regulations formulated. This was especially true because NIGC had to balance interests among three sovereigns: the states, the federal government, and the Indian tribes.[55] Second, Hope explained that the regulations had to follow the Administrative Procedure Act, the Privacy Act, the Paperwork Reduction Act, the Freedom of Information Act, the National Environmental Policy Act, the Regulatory Flexibility Act, and Executive Order

12291. Conforming to each of these required a great deal of time. The third problem was the difficulty of working through the fact that Indians used the NIGC as they did the BIA's office of trust, economic development, or tribal government services. Indians demanded that the NIGC abandon its regulatory stance because they misread the purpose of the organization. The tribes apparently misunderstood the commission's responsibility as stated in the act and continued to argue for the removal of any NIGC oversight.[56] Fourth, Hope explained that the most recent proposed regulations defining the differences between classes II and III had caused tremendous disagreement among tribes. Many of the tribes, as well as their supporters, felt that electronic technology and electronic facsimiles were Class II games—not Class III as the NIGC had defined them. This definition was detrimental to tribes, since video gaming counts for about 70 percent of casino revenue and most states did not allow Class III gaming.[57]

The purpose of the 1992 hearings was to gather information on gaming's progression. In 1994, Congress conducted hearings on amendments to IGRA. In April and July of 1994, the Senate held hearings in Washington, DC. To begin, they heard testimony on regulatory systems that several states had established to govern Indian gaming. These regulations were compared to those that the executive branch had both implemented and proposed.[58]

Senator Reid of Nevada testified that no federal agency had the mechanism or the expertise to regulate Class III gaming. Even though the FBI had only found one tribe in California who did hire, by mistake, a management company with Mafia ties, Reid assured the Senate that the only reason it did not find more connections was because it was not conducting the right investigations. Reid suggested that wiretaps were the best way to discover organized crime. He conjectured, however, that Indian tribes would most likely not agree to FBI wiretaps. Senator Reid also declared that the management companies currently working with Indian tribes must be siphoning off large amounts of cash from tribal casinos. He provided no evidence for his accusations.[59]

Tony Hope, who two years previous was just beginning to organize the NIGC, had since been able to better comprehend the scope of Indian gaming. Since tribes were free to conduct Class II gaming without the commission's approval, he focused instead on Class III. The commission discovered that the agreement worked well for those states with a strong regulatory system in place for Class III. Problems were found in states with a weak regulatory system or one in which the system was strong but poorly enforced.[60] Hope stated that in the past fifteen months the commission had brought eighty-seven tribal ordinances into compliance with IGRA, and that it was currently processing another sixty. It had forty management contracts awaiting approval, had closed three illegal casinos, and had stopped illegal activity at a fourth. Workshops were conducted to assist Indians with compliance. Field representatives had visited all the Class II and most of the Class III operations to explore how their regulations worked.[61] In his concluding remarks, Hope pointed out that it took many years for Nevada and New Jersey to come up with strict regulations that worked well. Gaming regulation was a trial and error system, just as it is for Indian gaming. Chairman Inouye reported that the state of New Jersey spends $55 million a year on regulation and asked the NIGC to come up with an appropriate budget.[62]

The fifteenth congressional hearing on Indian gaming legislation in four years convened in July 1995.[63] Since the last hearing, several months before, there had been much discussion about section 12 of the proposed bill, which dealt with the secretary of the Interior acting as a mediator between states and tribes in the development of a Class III compact. States were hostile toward the idea of federally enforced gaming negotiations between them and tribes. The other two areas emphasized by Chairman McCain were: (1) the enactment of legislation that would provide minimum federal standards applicable to all Class II and Class III gaming on Indian reservations and give life to an independent federal agency with a strong authority to "vigorously enforce these standards";[64] and (2) the stoppage of the enactment of any legislation that would turn back or overturn the Supreme Court's decision in *Cabazon*. His reason for this was that in 1988, when IGRA was passed, tribes had to give up some of their sovereignty to states because they wanted regulations to help ease the pressure and confusion that occurred without them. *Cabazon* provided a good backup for this because it essentially stated that Indian tribes could conduct gaming on reservations lands without state involvement. He said that the halls of Congress were ringing with cries from states for more rights, but that these cries could not drown out the "solemn trust obligations to American Indians and the government-to-government relationship with Indian tribes."[65]

The National Governors Association was the leading dissenter in these hearings. Raymond C. Scheppach, the organization's executive director, expressed two major concerns. First was the scope of gaming. Scheppach reiterated what many states argued: the states did not want to be forced to negotiate gaming compacts with tribes. In addition, the association felt uneasy regarding trust lands acquired by tribes. Governors felt that they—not the federal government—could best determine what was best for their citizens. Chairman McCain asked Scheppach a series of questions about which rules he was willing to follow. He agreed that he would follow the Supreme Court's decisions.[66]

Some Indians also testified at this hearing, describing how gaming had changed their lives for the better. Melanie Benjamin, a member of the Mille Lacs Band of Chippewa, said:

> I'm here today because Washington needs to understand what's really at stake. You've heard from the Donald Trump allies. You've heard from those [who] for their own profit or political purpose want America to turn it's [sic] back on the First Americans, to break another promise. The promise is called the Indian Gaming Regulatory Act. It has helped give Indian people, our mothers and our fathers, our sons and daughters, our grandmothers and grandfathers, the first taste of self-determination that leads to what some call the American dream.
>
> I'm talking about real people with real American dreams. People like Molly Big Bear, once a welfare mother, and now a coordinator of guest services at our Band's Grand Casinos. Molly has just proudly and successfully completed a prestigious statewide leadership program. People like Monica Kegg, who recently graduated from our Band's modern new high school. Monica is an Academic Olympic Team Member who admits she would have dropped out of high school long ago if she had

to face the prejudice in the public school system.

People like Robert Mitchell, a talented and hardworking man other employers passed over and over again until he came to work for the Grand Casinos. Today, Robert has fulfilled his promise to his wife that some day they would own a home where they could raise their children. Imagine his pride, and the pride of his wife and those children. Think about the powerful example he has set.

And people like Richard Johnson, an ordinary Minnesotan who lost his job after a serious car accident. Richard applied for nearly 130 jobs, but the only place that would give this non-Indian the chance to work again was our Band. Richard is getting much more than a paycheck from Grand casinos. He says he has regained the pride and confidence that he had lost in his accident.

These people, Monica, Robert, Molly, and Richard and thousands more like them are what this hearing is all about, Senators. Not amendments, not legal maneuvering, not fatter, more outrageous profits for multimillionaires who take so much for granted.

Now, in my written testimony, I've described in detail the over $21 million the Mille Lacs Band had given back to Indian families and Indian children.[67]

This is an emotional testimony that has been echoed around the country—gaming has brought a flourishing economy and a new sense of security to some Indians who were once dependent on the federal government. Senator Inouye stated that, historically, of 800 treaties entered into by both parties, 430 were simply rejected out of hand or disregarded by previous senators; of the 370 that were ratified, the United States violated every one of them.[68] Some people argue that we let this history stand and stop treating Indians differently from other Americans. Those in government who have studied these issues, however, believe that the solemn trust between the federal government and American Indian tribes needs to be respected—this relationship means that Indians must be given the opportunity to act as self-determined peoples.

CONCLUSION

The two primary purposes of the Indian Gaming Regulatory Act of 1988 were: (1) to help protect Indian gaming from organized crime and (2) to establish a federal regulatory authority for gaming. Indian gaming has exploded across the United States since this legislation passed. Presently, more than 250 of the 552 federally recognized tribes have some form of gaming on their reservations. By early 1994, there were 225 casinos and high-stakes bingo halls on Indian reservations. In 1993, for the first time in the history of our nation, more Americans visited some type of casino (Indian or not) than attended a major league ball park—over 92 million trips.[69] Of the $550 billion spent in legal wagering in 1996, about $49 billion was spent in Indian casinos.[70]

Indian gaming continued its explosive growth through the mid-1990s. Twenty-three states had Indian casinos in 1996.[71] By 1998, gaming had spread even further. *Indian Gaming* reported in April of that year that there were

188 gaming tribes operating 285 gaming operations in 28 states. Of the 188 gaming tribes, 24 are operating gambling facilities which offer Class II games only. The remaining 164 tribes are offering either a combined Class II/III gaming facility, or a facility that offers Class III gambling only. As of November 19, 1997, the Secretary of the Interior has approved 158 compacts with 147 tribes in 24 states. The states with the greatest number of compacts include Arizona (16), New Mexico (16), and Washington (17).[72]

There is an erroneous belief among many people that all Indian tribes are becoming "filthy rich" off their casinos. A report in December 1996 by the General Accounting Office explained that ten tribes took in more than 50 percent of the $1.6 billion received by Indian reservations from tribal gaming. In addition, it stated that one-third of all federally recognized tribes have gaming on their reservation.[73] Even with the limited success of many casinos, Indian tribes still have the highest poverty rate of any minority—a staggering 31 percent. Indian unemployment is still six times as high as the national average. The statistics on Indian education and welfare are still very low. Of the tribes that conduct gaming, only 2 to 3 percent are highly successful. For the most part, the money generated is just beginning to ease the troubles of unemployment and poverty.

Tribes are required by federal law to use casino revenue to fund essential tribal services such as education, law enforcement, tribal courts, economic development, and improvements in infrastructure. In addition, they use this money to fund social service programs, scholarships, health care clinics, new roads, new sewer and water systems, adequate housing, and substance abuse programs. Casino revenue is making it possible for some tribes to pull themselves out of economic destitution.

Indian gaming has provided many tribes with the experience and money to help them strengthen their own sovereignty. For decades, Indian people have suffered from poverty. Past experience demonstrated that the federal government was impotent in its attempt to build reservation economies; the Indians needed to do this themselves. Gaming has provided some tribes an opportunity to learn entrepreneurial skills and to use the economic windfall to rebuild their tribal infrastructure. As Joseph P. Kalt and Jonathan B. Taylor wrote in their response to Senator Slade Gorton's means testing proposal, which attacks the government-to-government relationship between tribes and the federal government:

> Over the last two decades, Indians on reservations have fought to reestablish long-lost powers of self-rule. Governed by institutions, tribes now have powers akin to those of the U.S. states, including powers to make rules and regulations, to wield law enforcement and judicial authority, to tax, and ... like states ... run gaming operations. Self-rule is the indispensable first ingredient needed to turn reservation economies around.[74]

and

> The common thread in economic growth for Indian tribes is their successful assertion of their rights to govern themselves. Money from gam-

ing can be earmarked for education, health and welfare, economic development, charities, and funding tribal government operations or programs.[75]

This chapter is intended to show the ways in which tribes have incorporated into US political culture. Through this consolidation they have gained greater sovereignty and independence. Gaming has strengthened sovereignty because "sovereignty is power and it increases with knowledge." The knowledge and experience from working with both the state and federal governments in creating Indian gaming policy, conceiving, building, running a business, and dealing with the range of business problems, has been a catalyst for greater tribal power. It also has increased tribes' financial strength and their opportunities to build a more secure future. As tribal experiences expand, so do the opportunities for human growth.[76]

NOTES

1. Robert Goodman, *The Luck Business: The Devastating Consequences and Broken Promises of America's Gambling Explosion* (New York: Martin Kessler Books, 1995), 113.

2. *Webster's Ninth New Collegiate Dictionary* (Springfield, MA: Merriam-Webster, Inc., 1991), 1129.

3. Dan Means, "The Casino Question," *The Blood Horse* (3 December 1994): 5970–5976; also "Assessing Indian Gaming," *The Blood Horse* (1 April 1995): 1564; Eugene M. Christiansen, "Industry Rebounds With 8.4% Handle Gain," *International Gaming and Wagering Business* 14:7 (15 July–14 August 1995): 12–35; phone interview with Kyle Nayback at National Indian Gaming Association, November 1999.

4. "Heavy Betting: How the Gambling Industry has Spread Its Wings—and Its Political Clout," *Mother Jones* (August 1997): 40–41. The states that have casinos are: Arizona, California, Colorado, Connecticut, Florida, Idaho, Iowa, Kansas, Louisiana, Michigan, Minnesota, Mississippi, Montana, Nebraska, Nevada, New Mexico, New York, North Carolina, North Dakota, Oregon, South Dakota, Washington, and Wisconsin.

5. Ibid.

6. "The History of Tribal Gaming," *Indian Gaming Magazine* (June 1998): 16.

7. Ibid. Public Law 280 was an act passed by Congress in 1953 that transferred criminal and civil jurisdiction in Indian Country from the federal government to the states of California, Minnesota, Nebraska, Oregon, and Wisconsin (after 1959 to Alaska). Other states were given the option to assume jurisdiction by legislation. In 1968, PL 280 was amended to require tribal consent to the transfer of jurisdiction (Duane Champagne, ed., *The Native North American Almanac* [Washington, DC: Gale Research Inc., 1994]).

8. Ibid., 718–720.

9. *658 Federal Reporter, 2nd Series, Seminole Tribe of Florida v Butterworth*, 658 F, 2nd. 310 (1981): 310–317.

10. Ibid., 313.

11. Ibid.

12. US Senate Select Committee on Indian Affairs, *To Establish Federal Standards And Regulations For The Conduct Of Gaming Activities Within Indian Country, And For Other Purposes*, 99th Congress, 1st sess., 26 June 1985 (Washington, DC: Government Printing Office, 1985), 597.

13. *Seminole Tribe of Florida* v *Butterworth*, 315.

14. *658 Federal Reporter, 2nd Series, Barona Group of Capitan Grande Band, etc.* v *Duffy* , 694 F. 2nd 1185 (1982): 1185–1190.

15. I. Nelson Rose, "The Future of Indian Gaming," *Journal of Gambling Studies* 8:4 (Winter 1992): 383–399.

16. Nancy McKay, "The Meaning of Good Faith in the Indian Gaming Regulatory Act" *Gonzaga Law Review* 27:3 (1991–1992): 471–486.

17. Rose, "The Future of Indian Gaming," 383–399.

18. US Senate Select Committee on Indian Affairs, *To Establish Federal Standards and Regulations*, 99th Congress, 1st sess., 139.

19. Ibid., 33.

20. Ibid. *Barona Group of the Capitan Band of Mission Indians San Diego County* v *Duffy*, 692 F. 2nd 1185 (1982): 1185-1190.

21. US House of Representatives Committee on Interior and Insular Affairs, *Indian Gambling Control Act*, 99th Congress, 1st sess., 14 November 1985 (Washington, DC: Government Printing Office, 1987), 37.

22. Ibid.

23. Ibid.

24. Ibid., 66–67.

25. Ibid.

26. Ibid.

27. Ibid., 82–83.

28. Senate Report 99-493, *To Establish Federal Standards and Regulations for the Conduct of Gaming Activities on Indian Reservations and Lands, and for other Purposes*, 99th Congress, 2nd sess. (24 September 1986), 2–4.

29. Ibid.

30. Ibid.

31. Ibid., 4.

32. US House of Representatives Committee on Interior and Insular Affairs, 100th Congress, 1st sess., 25 June 1987 (Washington, DC: Government Printing Office, 1989).

33. Ibid.

34. Testimony of Richard H. Bryan, Governor of Nevada, US House of Representatives Committee on Interior and Insular Affairs, 100th Congress, 1st sess., 25 June 1987, 2–3.

35. Testimony of Senator John McCain of Arizona, US House of Representatives Committee on Interior and Insular Affairs, 100th Congress, 1st sess., 25 June 1987, 159–161.

36. Testimony of William J. Houle, chairman of the National Indian Gaming Association, US House of Representatives Committee on Interior and Insular Affairs, 100th Congress, 1st sess., 25 June 1987, 236–245.

37. Ibid.

38. Ibid.

39. Duane Champagne, ed., *The Native North American Almanac: A Reference*

Work on Native North Americans in the United States and Canada (Detroit: Gale Research, Inc., 1994), 95.

40. 25 USC 2703 (definition of Class II gaming), 2710 (Class II and III permitted), 1992.

41. Testimony of Senator Daniel K. Inouye, US Senate Select Committee on Indian Affairs, *Oversight Hearing on Status of the Activities Undertaken to Implement the Gaming Regulatory Act*, 102nd Cong., 2nd sess., 5 February 1992 (Washington, DC: Government Printing Office, 1992), 11.

42. Ibid. 5–6

43. Ibid.

44. Testimony of Eddie Brown, assistant secretary of Indian Affairs, US Senate Select Committee on Indian Affairs, *Oversight Hearing*, 102nd Congress, second sess., 11.

45. US Senate Select Committee on Indian Affairs, *Implementation of the Indian Gaming Regulatory Act*, 102nd Cong., 2nd sess., 6 May 1992 (Washington, DC: Government Printing Office, 1992): 1–3.

46. Testimony of Senator Inouye, US Senate Select Committee on Indian Affairs, *Implementation of the Indian Gaming Regulatory Act*, 102nd Cong., 2nd sess., 1–3.

47. The Johnson Act, passed in 1951 and subsequently amended, prohibited the sale, transportation, or possession of gambling devices on federal lands, including Indian lands, or in states that have not acted to exempt themselves from the application of the Johnson Act. The Indian Gaming Regulatory Act provides for a waiver of the Johnson Act when the secretary of the Interior approves a tribal-state compact to govern the conduct of Class III gaming activities on Indian lands. However, in the world of Indian gaming, the federal regulatory presence is limited primarily to Class II gaming.

48. Testimony of Senator Inouye, US Senate Select Committee on Indian Affairs, *Implementation of the Indian Gaming Regulatory Act*, 102nd Cong., 2nd sess., 1–3.

49. Ibid.

50. Ibid.

51. Ibid.

52. Testimony of Senator Mickelson from South Dakota, US Senate Select Committee on Indian Affairs, *Implementation of the Indian Gaming Regulatory Act*, 102nd Cong., 2nd sess., 6–15.

53. Testimony of Eddie Brown, 11.

54. Testimony of Timothy W. Glidden, counselor to the secretary and chairman, US House of Representatives Committee of Interior and Insular Affairs, *Implementation and Enforcement of the Indian Gaming Regulatory Act, Public Law 100-497*, 102nd Cong., 2nd sess., 9 January 1992 and 4 February 1992 (Washington, DC, Government Printing Office, 1992), 1–12.

55. Testimony of Anthony J. Hope, US House of Representatives Committee of Interior and Insular Affairs, *Implementation and Enforcement* , 102nd Congress, 2nd session, 10–18.

56. Ibid.

57. Ibid.

58. US Senate Committee on Indian Affairs, *Oversight Hearing on the Need For Amendments to the Indian Gaming Regulatory Act*, 103rd Cong., 2nd sess., 20 April 1994, Part I (Washington, DC: Government Printing Office, 1994).

59. Testimony of Senator Henry Reid, US Senate Committee on Indian Affairs, *Oversight Hearing on the Need For Amendments*, 103rd Cong., 2nd sess., 4–7.

Information regarding Mafia tie-in is included in these hearings.

60. Testimony of Anthony J. Hope, US Senate Committee on Indian Affairs, *Oversight Hearing on the Need For Amendments*, 103rd Cong., 2nd sess., 7–8.

61. Ibid., 8.

62. Testimony of Senator Inouye, US Senate Committee on Indian Affairs, *Oversight Hearing on the Need For Amendments* , 103rd Cong., 2nd sess., 14.

63. Testimony of Senator John McCain, chairman for the committee on Indian affairs, US Senate Committee on Indian Affairs, *To Amend the Indian Gaming Regulatory Act*, 104th Cong., 1st sess., 25 July 1995 (Washington, DC: Government Printing Office 1996), 1.

64. Ibid., 2.

65. Ibid.

66. Testimony of Raymond C. Scheppach, executive director of the National Governors Association, US Senate Committee on Indian Affairs, *To Amend the Indian Gaming Regulatory Act*, 104th Cong., 1st sess., 99–105.

67. Testimony of Melanie Benjamin, senior vice president of Administration and Finance, Mille Lacs Band of Ojibwe Indians, US Senate Committee on Indian Affairs, *To Amend the Indian Gaming Regulatory Act*, 104th Cong., 1st sess., 108.

68. Testimony of Senator Inouye, US Senate Committee on Indian Affairs, *To Amend the Indian Gaming Regulatory Act*, 104th Cong., 1st sess., 108–110.

69. "America's Gambling Craze: The Casino Boom is Growing Daily. But It Might Not Last Forever, and Its Ill Effects Are Potent," *US News and World Report* (14 March 1994): 42–46.

70. W. Ron Allen, "Feds Load the Dice Against Indian Gaming" *Native Americas* XIV:1 (Spring 1997): 6.

71. Ibid.

72. "What Are the Three Classes of Gaming?" *Indian Gaming* (April/May 1998): 21.

73. Timothy Eagen, "Senate Measures Would Deal Blow To Indian Rights: Operating Money at Risk: A Pair of Riders Causes Furor Among Nation's 554 Tribes—Sovereignty Is Issue," *The New York Times*, 27 August 1997, A1.

74. Stacey Kiehn, "Tribal Gaming and Sovereignty," *Indian Gaming* 8:4 (June 1998): 32–33.

75. Ibid.

76. The Urantia Foundation, *The Urantia Book* (Chicago: The Urantia Foundation, 1955), 1488.

♠

California High Court Strikes Down Indian Gaming in *Hotel Employees and Restaurant Employees International Union* v. *Davis*

Joseph G. Nelson

INTRODUCTION

Supporting Indian self-reliance, Californians overwhelmingly approved Proposition 5 on 3 November 1998.[1] Proposition 5 intended to resolve the impasse resulting from the failed gaming compact negotiations between former governor Pete Wilson and California's gaming tribes.[2] Soon after the initiative was approved, a Nevada labor union[3] and individuals[4] backed by the Nevada gaming industry appealed to the California court to block the measure.[5] The California Supreme Court accepted the case without first allowing review by the lower courts because they concluded that the case raised questions of "great public importance" that needed to be "resolved promptly."[6] The court properly recognized the importance of the issue in the case. As this article will argue, however, the holding of the case is wrong.

On 23 August 1999, the California Supreme Court invalidated Proposition 5[7] because it determined that the initiative violated Article IV, section 19(e) of the California Constitution, which provides that "the Legislature has no power to authorize, and shall prohibit casinos of the type currently operating in Nevada and New Jersey."[8] The primary question in the case was whether the tribal gaming devices and the card games authorized in Proposition 5's model compact operated as lotteries, which are legal under the Constitution,[9] or as house-banked games, which are prohibited by California statutes.[10]

Because of the ambiguity in section 19(e), the court, with much effort, was able to invalidate the measure. The initiative, for the most part, was primarily opposed by Nevada gaming interests.[11] The question of whether the gaming facilities provided for in Proposition 5 were of "the type currently operating in Nevada and New Jersey" could easily have been answered negatively.[12] In light of federal Indian law, the popular support for the initiative, and the differences between Nevada-type casinos and Indian gaming operations, the decision was misplaced.[13]

This chapter will argue that *Hotel Employees and Restaurant Employees International Union* v. *Davis*[14] was inappropriate in light of federal Indian law and the California initiative process. Included in this case note is: (1) a history of Indian gaming in California and a discussion of the federal Indian Gaming Regulatory Act of 1988 (IGRA); (2) a description of the act and a synopsis of the decision; (3) an analysis and critique of *Hotel Employees*; and (4) a conclusion contending that although the California Supreme Court improperly sided with Nevada gaming interests when it struck down Proposition 5, Californians and California gaming tribes surpassed the decision by amending the Constitution in March 2000.

CONTEXT AND BACKGROUND

Casino gambling on Indian reservations has breathed life into tribal governments throughout California. With gaming revenue, tribal governments have been able to provide basic governmental services as well as employment and educational opportunities to their members.[15] Both the tribes and the federal government have strong interests in the success of Indian gaming operations. As tribal government balance sheets flow, their reliance on federal funds ebbs. Casino gaming, however, has not been universally accepted as a means of revenue generation.[16] States may have competing interests in the growth of casino gaming and possible secondary effects,[17] as well as an interest in the financial success of numerous tribal members who are also potential voters and lobbyists.[18]

The type of gaming permitted by Proposition 5 invites regulatory participation from many sovereigns—the tribes, the federal government, and the states.[19] The following background material will show how this current dispute spawned out of a long and complex relationship between these governments.

The California Indians

Not long ago, California Indians were numerous, independent, and self-governing.[20] Although this is not the proper forum in which to analyze California Indian history, a restatement of a few generally accepted facts will provide the historical backdrop necessary to understand why Indian gaming is so important for both California Indians and non-Indian residents.

Most of California's tribes practice some form of gambling in their traditional cultures.[21] A complex trade network for exchange of material goods and social ideas existed in Native California long before the United States was established.[22] While gaming was not central to the Indian economy, gambling and complex economic enterprises were not foreign to their cultures.[23] The aftermath of the California Gold Rush along with the federal government's neglect[24] of Native peoples left California Indians struggling to survive on small remote reservations.[25]

In the early 1980s, tribal governments throughout the United States began turning to gaming as a source of revenue.[26] By the mid-1980s, more than one hundred tribes in the country had opened gaming facilities.[27] Most of these tribes ran high-stakes bingo parlors, but many also operated both house-banked and player-banked games such as slot machines and blackjack.[28]

Through gaming, California Indians found a way to again become self-reliant. Revenue from these operations was not lining the pockets of individual entrepreneurs—it was allowing tribal governments to function and provide community services. Many of these gaming tribes were once fully dependent on the federal government. Prior to opening their gaming facilities, tribes' investment opportunities were very limited for a few simple reasons, including lack of capital, lack of natural resources, and physical isolation. By bringing in outside money, gaming generated revenue for tribal governments, allowing them to shed the need for federal subsidies.

Presently, there are 107 Indian reservations[29] and more than one hundred federally recognized tribes[30] in California.[31] Forty-one of these tribes sponsor some form of gaming.[32] Revenue from these operations support governmental programs including but not limited to health, education, welfare, and police and fire department services.[33] Gaming has helped revive Indian communities, creating a higher quality of life on and near these reservations.

For many tribes, a gaming operation is not an end in itself. Income from gaming not only contributes to the health and welfare of these communities, but also gives tribes a chance to seize investment opportunities.[34] Each tribal government has its own reasons for making economic decisions, but it seems that many would rather diversify their portfolio than reinvest all their profits in casino expansion projects.[35]

History of Gaming Laws in California

The only reference to gambling in California's first constitution was a prohibition against state-sponsored lotteries.[36] When the 1849 constitution was adopted, California was in the midst of the Gold Rush and private gambling was not regulated. However, the California legislature soon thereafter prohibited lotteries and banking games.[37] The original 1872 penal code also defined and prohibited lotteries and banking or percentage games.[38] Bookmaking was prohibited in 1909,[39] and slot machines were added to the list in 1911.[40] For the most part, the statutory gaming prohibitions have remained unchanged since the enactment of the original penal code.

Every law passed by the people since 1849 has increased the scope of gambling. In 1933, an exception to pari-mutuel betting on horse races was created.[41] In 1976, charitable bingo was authorized,[42] and in 1984 the California Constitution was amended to authorize the state lottery.[43]

Overview of Federal Indian Law and the Indian Gaming Regulatory Act

American Indians, as the original inhabitants of North America, developed a unique relationship with the federal government based on the sovereign status of both parties. The treaties between tribes and early European emigrants acknowledged this relationship[44] and helped solidify it.[45] This government to government relationship has traditionally been maintained between individual tribes and the federal government.[46] The Commerce Clause of the United States Constitution left Indian affairs in the hands of Congress.[47]

History between Indian tribes and the federal government is categorized by periods, such as assimilation, relocation, termination, and self-determination, as defined by the prevailing policy of the time.[48] In 1953, during the termination era, Congress delegated some of its power over Indian affairs to a few states.[49] Public Law 280, as this decision is coined, extended state criminal laws to Indian Country and granted jurisdiction over Indian lands to six states, including California.[50]

This federal grant of authority to the states was not absolute, especially with respect to Indian gaming. The Supreme Court made this very clear when it handed down the landmark decision *California* v. *Cabazon Band of Mission Indians*.[51] In that case, California applied its penal code regulations to the Cabazon and Morongo bands of Indians that were operating federally authorized bingo games on their reservations.[52] State law did not entirely prohibit bingo operations, but limited the games to charitable organizations that limited prizes to $250 per game.[53]

The Court held that state "civil/regulatory" laws did not apply to Indian Country, while "criminal/prohibitory" laws did.[54] It further concluded that California regulates rather than prohibits gambling in general because the state allowed bingo and operated its own state lottery.[55]

Soon after the Supreme Court decided *Cabazon*, Congress passed the Indian Gaming and Regulatory Act (IGRA) in 1988.[56] Congress' response to *Cabazon* supported the holding. The act set out to reconcile the tribes' interest in self-sufficiency and the states' interest in regulating gaming to avoid crime and other harmful effects. While Congress had the well-being of tribal governments in mind when it passed IGRA, it also had to take into consideration the states' interest in regulating such activities within their borders. In doing so, IGRA divided gaming into three categories, Class I, Class II, and Class III: Class I games include tribal ceremonial games and social games for prizes of minimal value.[57] Class I games are regulated exclusively by the tribes.[58] Class II games consist of bingo and non-banked card games that are authorized by the state.[59] These are regulated jointly by the tribes and the National Indian Gaming Commission, which operates under the Department of Interior.[60] Class III includes all games that are not Class I or Class II games.[61] Class III gaming is lawful if (1) the tribe adopts an ordinance authorizing such gaming; (2) the tribe is located in a state that "permits such gaming for any purpose by any person, organization, or entity"; and (3) the gaming is conducted in accordance with a tribal-state compact.[62]

Under IGRA, tribes can contact a state and request to enter into negotiations. If an agreement is not reached within 180 days following the request, a tribe may submit its case to a federal court to determine whether or not the state negotiated in good faith. If the court finds that the state did not negotiate in good faith, a mediator is appointed to submit a last offer, which the state can either accept or reject. [63] If the state rejects the last offer, the secretary of the Interior will determine and impose the terms of the compact after consultation with the Indian tribe alone.[64]

In the event that a tribe opens a gaming operation in violation of IGRA, the state has no power to prosecute the offending tribe.[65] Under IGRA, only the federal government may enforce gaming laws on Indian reservations.[66]

Failed Negotiations with Pete Wilson

California tribes entered into negotiations with the state soon after IGRA passed.[67] In April 1992 the negotiations broke down because former Governor Pete Wilson refused to negotiate over electronic and video gaming.[68] IGRA requires states to negotiate in "good faith,"[69] so Wilson and the tribes agreed to have a federal court determine the scope of the state's negotiatory obligation.[70] Eventually the ninth circuit court of appeals held that the state was not required to negotiate for the games in dispute, with the exception of slot machines in the form of video lottery terminals.[71] In February 1994, Governor Wilson repudiated the agreement and broke off all negotiations.[72] In fact, Wilson wanted to prosecute tribes that were operating what he called illegal slot machines.

Negotiations resumed in October 1996 between the state and a non-gaming tribe—the Pala Band of Mission Indians.[73] This compact was to serve as a model for other tribes.[74] However, Wilson and the Pala Band excluded the other tribes from the negotiations entirely.[75] The state refused to conduct any negotiations with tribes that were operating any Class III gaming and offered the Pala compact on a take-it-or-leave-it basis to non-gaming tribes.[76] The other tribes did not find the Pala compact acceptable.[77] The secretary of the interior concluded that the State was acting in bad faith and could not require tribes to accept the Pala compact.[78]

PROPOSITION 5 AND HOTEL EMPLOYEES

Refusing to concede their gaming hopes to one man, California tribes took their case to the people with Proposition 5.[79] The initiative set out to establish a model compact allowing gaming tribes to keep their casinos open and allow non-gaming tribes to open their own gaming facilities in accordance with IGRA.[80]

The Act

Proposition 5 was drafted on the premise that tribal gaming was a means for California Indian tribes to strengthen "self-sufficiency through the creation of jobs and tribal economic development."[81] It also established that the tribal gaming facilities permitted by the act were materially different from "casinos of the type currently operating in Nevada and New Jersey," because such casinos, unlike tribal facilities, commonly offered a broad spectrum of house-banked games and were privately owned.[82]

Pursuant to these goals, the act provided a model statutory tribal-state compact that was available to any tribe willing to be bound by its terms.[83] The model compact and the act itself provided for four limited types of gaming on tribal land: (1) tribal gaming terminals that do not have handles and do not dispense currency, and that pay prizes "solely in accordance with a players' pool prize system"; (2) card games actually operated in a tribal gaming facility on 1 January 1998, also so long as prizes are paid according to the players' pool prize system; (3) other lottery games; and (4) off-track betting on horse races.[84] The "players' pool prize system" is defined in the Statutory Compact as "one or more segregated pools of funds that have been collected from player wagers, that are irrevocably dedicated to the prospective award of prizes in authorized gaming activities, and in which the house neither has nor can acquire any interest.[85] Under the act, tribes are required "to submit to substantial State regulation in exchange for the right to conduct limited gaming."[86] The state has a right to participate in its own background checks and licensing through its own set of requirements.[87] The state can object to the selection of potential employees, other than members of a recognized tribe.[88] Licenses for tribal members are reviewed by the National Indian Gaming Commission.[89] Disputes in the background and licensing process are resolved by binding arbitration.[90]

The tribal building and safety codes, under the model compact, are required to be at least as stringent as local building and safety codes or the uniform building and safety codes.[91] Other than through the statutory compact, tribes are not bound by non-tribal building codes.[92] The compact also requires tribes to follow federal health and safety codes, make reasonable provisions for emergency services,[93] provide workers' compensation,[94] and submit to various audit and inspection procedures.[95] Under these procedures, the state is permitted to conduct on-site inspections of gaming facility books and records without prior notice.[96]

If a tribe decides that it wants to open a gaming facility and agrees to accept the model compact, the governor is then compelled to sign the compact within thirty days.[97] The governor can offer and negotiate other terms and conditions with the tribe.[98] If the governor fails to sign the compact within the thirty days, the compact is automatically approved, as if he did sign it, after the secretary of Interior approves it.[99]

Court Invalidates the Initiative

Although nearly 63 percent of California voters favored the initiative, it only took four California Supreme Court justices to deliver a fatal blow. In the end, six justices struck the law down, leaving only a single Proposition 5 supporter on the bench.

In *Hotel Employees* the California Supreme Court found that Proposition 5 violated section 19(e) of the state constitution by allowing "Nevada-type and New Jersey-type casinos."[100] Because the constitution does not define "Nevada-type" casinos, the court turned to California statutes to interpret the clause. In deciding the case, the court raised a statutory prohibition[101] to a constitutional[102] level and then concluded that the "players' prize pool" permitted in Proposition 5 was a house bank and therefore illegal under California penal code, thereby violating the state's constitution.

Analysis

The California Supreme Court in *Hotel Employees* invalidated a popular initiative by finding that it violated the California Constitution. While the court recognized the power of the people as expressed through the initiative,[103] it continued to defy the will of the people with their decision. Although it only took six justices to strike down a law approved by a majority of the state's citizens, the question was constitutional and the state supreme court's interpretation is final regarding such questions. The will of the people is one of the influences from which the court is supposed to be shielded. Although the process was not flawed in its logistics, the court's reasoning and ultimate conclusion was.

The following analysis will critique the court's reasoning in finding a constitutional violation. This section will also consider the federal preemption issues that were raised peripheral to the holding. Finally, the analysis will critique a portion of the dissenting opinion regarding California's ability to "authorize" Indian gaming.

The Constitutional Bar to Proposition 5

The following analysis will attempt to prove that the holding in *Hotel Employees* was wrong. The reasoning of the majority was flawed because (1) the purpose of the 1984 initiative, which adopted the prohibition of Nevada-type casinos, was to increase the scope of gambling in California rather than prohibit the type of gaming permitted by Proposition 5; (2) the statutory prohibition of banked games was not a constitutional barrier to Proposition 5; and (3) the tribal gaming facilities permitted by Proposition 5 were not Nevada- or New Jersey-type casinos. The majority of the court determined that the constitutional prohibition against "Nevada and New Jersey-type casinos" meant that slot machines and house-banked games were illegal, and since Proposition 5 authorized such games; the initiative was therefore unconstitutional.

The purpose of the 1984 initiative was to legalize more gambling in California rather than prohibit the type of gaming authorized by Proposition 5. The Lottery Act of 1984 (Proposition 37) amended the California Constitution to allow a state-sponsored lottery and prohibit "Nevada-type and New Jersey-type casinos." However, prohibiting casino gaming was not the primary purpose of Proposition 37. Instead, its purpose was to expand the scope of gaming in California. Specifically, Proposition 37 was enacted to establish a state lottery that would generate money for education.[104] Section 19(e), the Nevada-type casino provision, was mentioned only fleetingly in the ballot materials.[105] "There is no reason to believe that the People conditioned their vote for the lottery on the addition of that proscription."[106]

Interestingly, the Proposition 37 campaign also involved funding from out-of-state gaming interests. Scientific Games, Incorporated, a subsidiary of Bally Manufacturing Corporation, which owned a hotel and casino in Atlantic City and later acquired MGM Hotel and Casinos in Las Vegas and Reno, funded the Proposition 37 campaign.[107] At the time, Scientific Games, Inc. was a manufacturer of lottery tickets and paraphernalia.[108] If the people were concerned about limiting specific types of gaming in California, they easily could have included more precise language. Instead, the language in Section 19(e) is specifically worded to protect out-of-state gaming interests from competition.

The court introduced its opinion in *Hotel Employees* with the following:

> In 1984, the people of California amended our Constitution to state a
> fundamental public policy against the legalization in California of casi-
> no gambling of the sort then associated with Las Vegas and Atlantic

City: "The Legislature has no power to authorize, and shall prohibit casinos of the type currently operating in Nevada and New Jersey."[109]

The court's statement is only a partial truth. A more precise statement might read: the people of California, by passing Proposition 37 in 1984, amended the constitution to create the California State Lottery. Assuming that Section 19(e) was not merely inserted to protect out-of-state gaming interests, it is reasonable to conclude that the electorate intended to limit the legislature's ability to expand gaming. If the new state-operated lottery successfully generated income for public education, the electorate may have adopted section 19(e) to preclude any temptation to increase state-operated gaming to generate income for government spending in other areas.[110] In any event, the primary purpose of Proposition 37 was to increase—rather than limit or prohibit—gaming in California. In its effort to give meaning to "Nevada-type and New Jersey-type casinos," the court ignored the circumstances under which the amendment was adopted and may have misinterpreted the legislative intent that drove section 19(e).

The statutory prohibition against banked games is not a constitutional barrier. The California Constitution, on its face, does not prohibit the type of gaming authorized by Proposition 5. The vagueness of "Nevada-type and New Jersey-type casinos" allowed the court to create an obstacle to the initiative in the absence of a clear constitutional violation. The question turned on whether the "players' prize pool" authorized in the initiative operated like a lottery or a house-banked game. If the players' prize pool operates like a lottery, it does not violate state law since the state allows such gaming activities.[111] On the other hand, if players' prize pool is really just a house bank, as the court found in this decision, it is prohibited by state law.[112]

In *Western Telcon* v. *California State Lottery*,[113] the court discussed lotteries and banked games at length. Initially the court found these two categories of gambling to be mutually exclusive,[114] distinguished "not by the manner of play, but by the nature of the betting itself."[115] In a lottery, the operator offers a prize and does not bet against any of the participants.[116] The operator does not place any wagers. In other words, the lottery operator has no interest in the game's outcome.[117] In contrast, the operator in a banking game is "the one against the many."[118] The operator does compete with the other participants and therefore has a direct interest in the outcome of the game.[119]

The court identified consideration, chance, and prize as defining elements of a lottery.[120] "'Consideration' is the fee that a participant pays the operator for entrance."[121] "'Chance' means that winning and losing depend on luck and fortune rather than, or at least more than, judgment and skill."[122] "'Prize' encompasses property that the operator offers to distribute to one or more winning participants and not to keep for himself."[123] The prize may arise from participant fees, like in a pari-mutuel system,[124] or it may exist separately.[125]

The gaming permitted by Proposition 5 is operated under the players' pool prize system. This system is defined as "one or more segregated pools of funds that have been collected from player wagers, that are irrevocably dedicated to the prospective award of prizes in authorized gaming activities, and in which the house neither has nor can acquire any interest."[126] By definition, the operator in a players' pool prize system does not retain an interest in the game's outcome. The operator collects fees from the players and does not rely on the outcome of the game.[127] Justice Joyce Kennard (dissenting) properly recognizes that the players' pool prize system operates like a lottery and is not a bank.[128] Games operating according to the players' pool system are lotteries because participants pay a fee—or offer consideration—to play for a share of the pool, or prize.

The majority, however, came to a different conclusion, determining that the players' pool permitted by Proposition 5 was actually a bank in nature[129] because the house retained an interest in the outcome of play.[130] According to the majority, the tribal gaming operator retains an interest because

> the more the players' pool collects from losers and the less it pays to winners, the lower the tribal operator's costs—the less likely it will be compelled to lend seed money to the players' pool in the future, the more likely it will be able to obtain repayment of seed money lent to the pool in the past.[131]

Moreover, the court suggests that the operator has an interest in maintaining ample funds in the pool because a depleted pool will decrease players' odds on bets, which will in turn decrease the amount of betting and the amount of fees collected.[132]

The court's reasoning is not compelling because its description of the tribal gaming operator's interest cannot be distinguished from lotteries. In the players' pool, the operator's income, in any given round of play, is fixed and does not change as a result of the outcome of play. Therefore, the operator does not have an interest in the outcome of the game. The fact that a high pay-out has delayed or prevented the repayment of past loans to the prize pool does not give the operator an interest in the outcome of play. The amount collected by the operator does not change with the outcome of the game; rather, much like a lottery, it is the number of participants that determines how much revenue is generated. According to the majority, lotteries become banks merely because their revenue does not exceed the cost of the prize offered. The operator's interest in the players' pool, if it can be described as such, cannot be distinguished from the interest that the operator of the California State Lottery has in that pool.[133] Although it is suspiciously creative, the players' pool does distinguish the Proposition 5 gaming from house-banked games.

The tribal gaming facilities were not Nevada or New Jersey-type casinos. Proposition 5 supporters acknowledged the potential constitutional conflict and half-heartedly attempted to address the problem by finding that the gaming permitted by the act was materially different[134] from "casinos of the type currently operating in Nevada and New Jersey."[135] It goes unquestioned that Indian gaming operations are significantly different from the casino operations in Las Vegas and Atlantic City. The court, however, did not squarely address this issue. Instead, it read an expanding meaning into what the prohibition against Nevada-type casinos attempted to forbid by looking to the California penal code.

The Supreme Court is the final arbiter of the California Constitution, so this decision and methodology is within its prerogative. By raising statutory prohibitions to a constitutional level, however, the court substantially manipulated the question of whether the tribal gaming facilities permitted under Proposition 5 were in fact Nevada-type casinos.

Respondents argued that the tribal gaming facilities permitted by Proposition 5 were materially different from Nevada and New Jersey casinos in a number of ways. First, Nevada and New Jersey casinos operate cash-dispensing slot machines and other house-banked games. Tribal video terminals, on the other hand, cannot have handles or dispense cash and they operate under the players' pool prize system.[136] Second, Nevada and New Jersey casinos' revenue comes from players losing their bets; tribal gaming revenue is derived from fees charged on a per play, per hour, or percentage basis.[137] Third, Nevada and New Jersey casinos are clustered together in dense areas and tribal facilities are dispersed on isolated tribal reservations.[138] Fourth, casinos in Nevada and New Jersey are privately owned, whereas tribal facilities must be owned by the tribe and revenues must be used solely for governmental purposes.[139] Fifth, Nevada and New Jersey casinos routinely serve free alcohol, while tribal facilities are prohibited from serving complimentary cocktails.[140] Finally, tribal facilities are prohibited from offering house-banked games including roulette, craps, and wheel of fortune.[141]

In addition to these distinguishing characteristics, respondents note that the gaming facilities permitted under Proposition 5, as a matter of law, could not be licensed in either Nevada or New Jersey because both states prohibit the operation of lotteries in casinos.[142] Respondents also introduced survey evidence indicating that people believed tribal gaming facilities to be significantly different from casinos in Nevada and New Jersey.[143] Interestingly, the surveys indicated that, "were location not a factor, [survey respondents] would choose a Nevada casino over a tribal facility."[144] Thus, given these distinctions it is clear that the tribal gaming facilities permitted by Proposition 5 are materially different from Nevada and New Jersey-type casinos.

Proposition 5 addresses the concerns held by the electorate when they amended the constitution in 1984. As discussed earlier, Proposition 37 was adopted in 1984 for the purpose of creating, in part, the California State Lottery by amending the constitution.[145] However, Proposition 37 also amended the constitution to prohibit Nevada and New Jersey-type casinos. The out-of-state gaming industry's motive for including this clause has already been suggested,[146] and the lack of legislative history supporting section 19(e) supports this conclusion. However, the electorate did adopt the amendment. If organized crime was their primary concern, Proposition 5 sufficiently addressed this issue. To put it succinctly, Proposition 5 is in accord with the goals of Proposition 37.

Tribal gaming facilities authorized under Proposition 5 are managed and operated by tribal governments.[147] As such, casino managers are accountable to the tribal government and their constituents—not to private companies. Proposition 5 also allows substantial state regulation of tribal gaming facilities. The state may perform independent background checks of potential employees[148] and may also inspect the tribal facility and its books and records without prior notice or permission.[149]

With regard to the organized crime potential, the players' pool eliminates house temptation to cheat because the outcome of the game does not matter. Finally, through IGRA, the federal government adds another layer of regulation to tribal gaming facilities to which Nevada and New Jersey casinos are not subject. For example, IGRA requires a tribal-state compact[150] for Class III gaming and requires that gaming revenue be used for either tribal governmental purposes[151] or for the general welfare of the Indian tribe.[152]

The Court Avoids Federal Preemption Issues

Regulation of Indian affairs traditionally lies somewhere between individual tribes and the federal government. However, as noted in earlier sections, Congress has at times, passed some of its authority in Indian affairs onto the individual states.[153] Indian gaming, as authorized by IGRA, is regulated for the most part by the tribes and the federal government under the National Indian Gaming Committee. However, states are allowed to participate in Indian gaming regulation through the state-tribal compacting process.

Federal authority in Indian affairs and in gaming in particular is superior to state authority. Federal legislation enables tribes to operate gaming facilities on tribal trust land. The same legislation provides the regulatory guidelines, which happen to leave room for state participation. When state and federal laws conflict, the doctrine of preemption provides that federal law will prevail.

The parties in this case have submitted opposing federal preemption arguments that cannot coexist. First, petitioners argue that Proposition 5 violates IGRA and is therefore preempted by IGRA because it authorizes tribes to conduct gaming that is otherwise illegal in California. This argument fails because the games permitted by Proposition 5 are lotteries and the California Constitution authorized the state lottery.[154] Meanwhile, respondents argue that if IGRA is unclear, ambiguities should be construed in favor of the Indians.[155]

The majority decided *Hotel Employees* based on their interpretation of the California Constitution and did not address the federal questions, while dissenter Justice Kennard eagerly accepted federal dominance in the field of Indian gaming regulation. According to the dissent, federal preemption under IGRA is such that the state cannot authorize or prohibit gambling on Indian lands.[156] Through the tribal-state compact in Proposition 5, Kennard argued that the state was merely facilitating Indian gaming.[157] Since the adoption of Proposition 5 would merely have facilitated Indian gaming, there was no authorization of "casinos of the type currently operating in Nevada and New Jersey." Therefore, there can be no violation of article IV, section 19(e).

The dissent properly acknowledged that federal law is paramount in the regulation of Indian affairs, and federal canons of construction suggest that ambiguities be construed in favor of the Indians, while the majority ignored federal Indian legislative histories as well as the legislative intent behind certain state laws. However, by ignoring the fact that Congress granted much of its regulatory powers over Indian land to the state in 1953,[158] the dissent overstated the supremacy of the federal law.

CONCLUSION

In *Hotel Employees* the California Supreme Court reached deep into its hat of tricks to invalidate a popular Indian gaming initiative. The court looked to the penal code to clear up the ambiguous constitutional prohibition of "Nevada-type and New Jersey-type casinos" and concluded that the gaming in Proposition 5 was unconstitutional because it authorized banked games and slot machines.

In reaching this conclusion, the court ignored the context in which the constitutional amendment in question was adopted. The circumstances surrounding the 1984 amendment clearly indicates that the voters' primary concern was to create a state lottery to generate revenue for education—not to prohibit Indian gaming on tribal land.

The court also raised a statutory prohibition to a constitutional level without a solid justification. In 1984 the people voted in favor of public education and created a state lottery. If they intended to outlaw house-banked games and slot machines, they could have done so with clear and convincing language.

Even if the games permitted by Proposition 5 were slot machines and banked games, the tribal gaming facilities authorized by the act were materially different from Nevada and New Jersey-type casinos. Many things distinguish tribal gaming facilities from the type of casinos operating in these states, the most significant factor being that the tribal gaming facilities are operated by and for sovereign tribal governments on tribal land.

The dissent courageously concluded that federal law is supreme in the field of Indian gaming. Tribal gaming, however, is subject to various levels of regulation by the tribal, federal, and state governments. In the end, both the Proposition 5 campaign and the *Hotel Employees* decision proved that Indian gaming is not shielded from private out-of-state interest groups.

NOTES

1. Proposition 5, also known as the Tribal Government and Economic Self-Sufficiency Act of 1998, passed with 62.4 percent of the vote in the November general election.

2. *Hotel Employees and Restaurant Employees International Union v Davis*, No. S074850, S074851, XX Cal. XX, XX P.2d XX, 1999 Cal. LEXIS 5529 (1999) (6 to 1 decision with Justice Joyce Kennard dissenting), 25.

3. Brief for Respondent, 1 n.1 (on file with author). Hotel Employees and Restaurant Employees International Union represents Nevada Casino employees (id.).

4. Brief for Petitioner, 6 (on file with author). Petitioner Eric Cortez lives near the Bear River Band of Indians; petitioner P.A. LeDoux is the president of the Grassy Run Community Services District and the Grassy Run Homeowners' Association near the Shingle Springs Band of Miwok Indians; petitioner Cathy Nash is the president of the Indian Lakes Estates Property Owners' Association, located near the Chukchansi Band of Indians; petitioner West Bell Group is a California partnership with investments in three card clubs in Bell Gardens; and petitioner Frank Tyson owns a business near the

Agua Caliente Band of Cahuilla Indians. All petitioners claim to be harmed by Indian gaming operations authorized by Proposition 5. See id.

5. *Hotel Employees, supra* 7 n.2.

6. *County of Sacramento* v *Hickman*, 66 Cal.2d 841, 845, 59 Cal Rptr. 609, 428 P.2d 593 (1967).

7. *Hotel Employees, supra* n.2.

8. Cal. Const., art. IV, §19, subd. (e), added by initiative, gen. elec. (6 November 1984).

9. Cal. Const., art. IV, §19, subd. (d), authorizes the California State Lottery.

10. Cal. Penal Code §330 (Deering, 1994).

11. Christopher E. Skinnell, "The Opponents of Proposition 5: An Analysis of Campaign Expenditures in Opposition to Proposition 5," [http://www.pechanga.net], 19 November 1999. Copies of this document may also be obtained by calling the Rose Institute at (909) 621-8159. More than 77 percent of the funding for the No on Proposition 5 Campaign came from Nevada casinos.

12. Cal. Const., art. IV, §19, subd. (e).

13. The Indian Gaming Regulatory Act of 1988 (25 USC §§2701-2721) requires tribes and states to enter compact agreements before certain types of gaming are allowed to take place on Indian lands. Following the California Supreme Court's invalidation of Proposition 5, Governor Gray Davis and the tribes reached an agreement and signed state-tribal compacts. The state legislature will put a measure on the March 2000 ballot to create a specific constitutional exception for Indian gaming on tribal land. See Dan Morain, "Davis, Tribes OK Accords to Allow More Gambling," *Los Angeles Times*, 11 September 1999, A1.

14. No. S074850, S074851, 1999 Cal. LEXIS 5529 (Cal. 23 Aug. 1999).

15. Tom Gorman, "Indian Casinos Fund Diverse Portfolios," *Los Angeles Times*, 23 Aug. 1999, A1. Casino revenues allow tribes to provide housing, health care, and scholarships (see ibid.).

16. Ibid. Some tribes have not opened casinos because their reservations are too remote or because agreements have not been reached with the state.

17. Eric Lichtblau, "California Shortened on Tribal Police Funding," *Los Angeles Times*, 28 October 1999, A3. Authorities warn that crime will increase as Indian gaming operations expand because of the increase in traffic, cash, and alcohol on reservations that already suffer from crime and a lack of law enforcement.

18. "Proposition 5's Legacy," *California Journal* (1 October 1999). Tribes donated more than $1 million in combined tribal donations to Governor Gray Davis, nearly $500,000 to Assemblyman Tony Cardenas, and sizeable contributions to Attorney General Bill Lockyer.

19. IGRA requires state-tribal compacts for the regulation of Class III gaming on tribal land.

20. Dolan H. Eargle, Jr., *The Earth Is Our Mother: A Guide to the Indians of California, Their Locales and Historic Sites* (San Francisco: Trees Company Press,1986).

21. Mary B. Davis, ed., *Native America in the Twentieth Century* (New York: Garland Publishing, Inc., 1994), 205.

22. Dolan Eargle, Jr., *California Indian Country: The Land and the People* (San Francisco: Trees Company Press, 1992), 21. Obsidian, shells, feathers, minerals, salt, fish and other foods, pelts, furs and hides, and bone and antler goods traded for hundreds of

miles. Religious leaders also established trade networks.

23.   Davis, *Native America*, 205 n.19.

24.   Eric Lichtblau, "California Shortened on Tribal Police Funding," *Los Angeles Times*, 28 October 1999, A3: "'underfunding of California-based tribes reflects a history of federal inattention to the state's Native American population'" (quoting Carole Goldberg). In 1953, with Public Law 280, Congress granted civil and criminal jurisdiction over tribal lands to a few states, including California. See also Carole Goldberg-Ambrose, *Planting Tail Feathers: Tribal Survival and Public Law 280* (Los Angeles: UCLA American Indian Studies Center, 1997).

25.   See Albert L. Hurtado, *Indian Survival on the California Frontier* (New Haven: Yale University Press, 1988).

26.   Davis, *Native America*, 205 n.19.

27.   Ibid. Approximately 180 tribes were conducting bingo in 1983.

28.   Ibid. By 1993 more than sixty-three tribes were in casino agreements with states.

29.   Ibid.

30.   Often referred to as *bands* in California.

31.   Fifty-three California tribes are currently seeking federal recognition. See Bureau of Indian Affairs, "Branch of Acknowledgement and Research, Summary Status of Acknowledgement Cases as of October 29, 1999," [http://www.doi.gov/bia/bar/indexq.htm], 2 November 1999.

32.   Maura Dolan and Tom Gorman, "State High Court Overturns Indian Gaming Initiative," *Los Angeles Times*, 24 Aug. 1999, A1.

33.   Davis, *Native America*, 205 n.19.

34.   Gorman, "Indian Casinos Fund Diverse Portfolios," A1.

35.   Many tribes have chosen not to enter into the gaming industry. See New York ex rel. *Abrams* v *Anderson*, 137 A.D.2d 259, 529 (1988). The court decided that intertribal disputes regarding gambling should be decided in tribal court.

36.   Cal. Const. art. IV, §27 provided: "No lottery shall be authorized by this State, nor shall the sale of lottery tickets be allowed."

37.   Stats 1851 ch. 28 p.211; Stats 1855, ch. 103 §1, p.124; Stats 1857, ch. 230 §1, p.267.

38.   Cal. Penal Code §319 and §330.

39.   Stats 1909, ch. 28, §1, p.21; Cal. Penal Code §337a.

40.   Stats 1911, ch. 483, §1, p.951; Cal. Penal Code §330a.

41.   Cal. Const. of 1933, art. IV, §25a; See also Stats. 1933, ch. 101, p.3160.

42.   Cal. Const. of 1976, art. IV, §19(c); See also Stats. 1975, ch. 869, §1, p.1942; Cal. Penal Code 326.5.

43.   Cal. Const. of 1984, art. IV, §§19(d),(e); Gov. Code, §§8880–8880.72 (1984).

44.   *United States* v *Winans*, 198 US 371 (1905) held that Indian treaties are not a grant of rights to the Indians, but a grant of rights from them. Any rights not granted to the United States by the Indians were retained.

45.   Many of these early treaties are still being enforced today. See *United States* v *Washington*, 520 F.2d 676 (9th Cir. 1974), cert. denied, 423 US 1086 (1976), which held that Washington state tribes retain rights to 50 percent of salmon harvest as guaranteed by an 1855 treaty. Compare Hurtado, *Indian Survival*, *supra* 140 n.25 (treaties negotiated with California tribes never became effective because the California legislature refused to ratify them).

46.   See *Worcester* v *Georgia*, 31 US (6 Peters) 525 (1832), holding that Georgia could

not extend its laws to Cherokee territory without their consent.

47.   US Const. art. I, §8(3): "Congress shall have Power ... to regulate Commerce with foreign Nations, and among the several States, and with the Indian Tribes."

48.   David Getches, et al., *Federal Indian Law: Cases and Materials* (St. Paul: West Publishing, 1993), 723.

49.   Goldberg-Ambrose, *Planting Tail Feathers*, 280.

50.   Pub. L. No. 280 (1953), 67 Stat. 588. The other five states are Alaska, Minnesota, Nebraska, Oregon, and Wisconsin. See id.

51.   480 US 202 (1987).

52.   Ibid., 205.

53.   Ibid.

54.   Ibid., 211.

55.   Ibid. In *Cabazon* the Court relied on its earlier interpretation of Public Law 280 in *Bryan* v *Itasca County,* 426 US 373 (1976). In that case, the Court decided that section 2 of the law granted California broad criminal jurisdiction, while section 4 granted the state only a limited jurisdiction over civil matters. In other words, it must be determined whether the law is criminal or civil in nature.

Two federal courts of appeals subsequently used the civil/criminal distinction in *Bryan* in favor of Indian gaming. In *Barona Group of Capitan Grande Band of Mission Indians* v *Duffy*, 694 F.2d 1185, 1187 (9th Cir. 1982) the ninth circuit held that California penal code §326.5 was regulatory rather than prohibitory. Therefore Public Law 280 did not authorize the state to enforce that law on an Indian reservation. The court of appeals for the fifth circuit used the same analysis to reach a similar result in *Seminole Tribe of Florida* v *Butterworth*, 658 F.2d 310,316 (5th Cir. 1981).

56.   Pub. L. No. 100-497, §23, 102 Stat. 2487, 25 USCA §§2701–2721 (1988). §2701 stated the findings:

> The Congress finds that—
> (1) numerous Indian tribes have become engaged in or have licensed gaming activities on Indian lands as a means of generating tribal government revenue;
> (2) Federal courts have held that section 2103 of the Revised Statutes (25 USC 81) requires Secretarial review of management contracts dealing with Indian gaming, but does not provide standards for approval of such contracts;
> (3) Existing Federal law does not provide clear standards or regulations for the conduct of gaming on Indian lands;
> (4) a principle goal of Federal Indian policy is to promote tribal economic development, tribal self-sufficiency, and strong tribal government; and
> (5) Indian tribes have the exclusive right to regulate gaming activity on Indian lands if the gaming activity is not specifically prohibited by Federal law and is conducted within a State which does not, as a matter of criminal law and public policy, prohibit such gaming activity.

57.   25 USC §2703(6).

58.   25 USC §2710(a)(1).

59.   25 USC §2703(7)(A). Blackjack (21), baccarat, and *chemin de fer* are excluded from Class II.

60.   25 USC §2710(b).

61. 25 USC §2703(8).

62. 25 USC §2710(d)(1)(A)-(C).

63. Getches, et al., *Federal Indian Law*, 723.

64. Ibid.

65. 25 USC §2701 (d)(7)(A)(i–iii), which provides that United States district courts have jurisdiction over causes of action arising out of the tribal-state compacts.

66. Ibid.

67. Brief for Respondent, *supra* 10 n.3.

68. Ibid.

69. IGRA 25 USC §2710 (d)(3)(A).

70. *Rumsey Indian Rancheria of Wintun Indians* v *Wilson*, 1993 WL 360652, (E.D. Cal. 1993).

71. *Rumsey Indian Rancheria of Wintun Indians* v *Wilson*, 64 F.3d 1250 (9th Cir. 1994).

72. Brief for Respondent, *supra* 10 n.3.

73. Ibid., 11.

74. Ibid.

75. Ibid.

76. Ibid.

77. Ibid.

78. Brief for Respondent, *supra* 11 n.3.

79. Ibid. Both a constitutional amendment and a statute require a majority vote by referendum. See George Skelton, "In This Poker Game, the Indians Hold the Best Hand," *Los Angeles Times*, 30 August 1999, A3. To qualify for the ballot, however, a statute initiative required 419,260 signatures, while an initiative for a constitutional amendment required 693,230 signatures. The Proposition 5 campaign collected 1.2 million signatures in three weeks. See id.

80. Gov. Code, §98001(a); see also Brief for Respondent, 12.

81. Gov. Code, §98001(a); see also Brief for Respondent, 12.

82. Gov. Code, §98001(c); see also Brief for Respondent, 12.

83. Gov. Code §98002; see also Brief for Respondent, 12.

84. Brief for Respondent, *supra* 12 n.3; see also Gov. Code 98006; and Compact §4.1.

85. Brief for Respondent, *supra* 12 n.3; see also Gov. Code 98006 (a),(b); and Compact §2.17.

86. Brief for Respondent, *supra* 13 n.3.

87. Ibid.

88. Compact §6.5.6; see also Brief for Respondent, *supra* 13 n.3.

89. Ibid., n.11.

90. Compact §9; see also Brief for Respondent, *supra* 13 n.3.

91. Compact §6.4.2(b); see also Brief for Respondent, *supra* 13 n.3.

92. Ibid., 14 n.12.

93. Compact §10.1(d), 10.2; see also Brief for Respondent, *supra* note 3, at 14.

94. See Compact §10.1(e); see also Brief for Respondent, *supra* note 3, at 14.

95. Compact §§7.4.1–7.4.3; see also Brief for Respondent, *supra* 14 n.3.

96. The model compact also requires the tribes to create three trust funds. "Two percent of the net revenues from Tribal gaming terminals go to benefit non-gaming Tribes in California" (Compact, §5.2). "Another three percent of net revenues from Tribal gaming terminals is paid to the State to supplement emergency medical care resources, with

one-half of one percent of these revenues dedicated to programs for compulsive and addictive gambling" (Compact, §5.3). "Finally, one percent of net revenues goes to cities and counties near Tribal lands to meet local community needs, including the mitigation of any off-reservation impacts of Tribal gaming projects" (Compact, §5.4).

97. Brief for Respondent, *supra* 13 n.3; see also Gov. Code §98005; 25 USC §2710(d)(1)(A).

98. Gov. Code 98010; The negotiated compact can be approved by the governor alone if it does not "expand the scope of gaming beyond that permitted in the Statutory Compact, create or confer additional power on a State agency, or infringe upon the Legislature's power to appropriate funds.... Otherwise, a compact other than the Statutory Compact requires additional approval by the Legislature." Ibid.

99. Gov. Code 98005; 25 USC §2710(d)(1)(A); see also Brief for Respondent, *supra* 13 n.3.

100. *Hotel Employees, supra* n.2.

101. Cal. Penal Code §330, prohibiting house-banked and percentage games.

102. Court concluded that by amending the constitution to prohibit "Nevada-type and New Jersey-type casinos," the people intended to declare slot machines and house-banked games illegal. See *Hotel Employees, supra* n.2.

103. *Legislature v Eu*, 54 Cal. 3d 492, 816 P.2d 1309 (1991). The initiative power is to be liberally construed; presumptions favor validity of initiative; and measures are to be upheld unless their unconstitutionality is clear and unmistakable.

104. Brief for Respondent, *supra* 7 n.3.

105. Ibid.

106. Ibid.

107. Brief for Respondent, *supra* 8 nn.3, 8.

108. Brief for Respondent, *supra* 6 n.3.

109. Hotel Employees, *supra* 4 n.2.

110. Respondent suggests that the petitioner's reading of section 19(e) does not make sense because the people would not intend to restrict their initiative powers in such manner. Rather, they amended the constitution to prevent the legislature from increasing gaming. In so doing, they intended to reserve control over gaming to themselves. See Brief for Respondent, *supra* 20 nn.3, 17.

111. IGRA 25 USC 2701 (d)(1)(B).

112. Cal Penal Code §330.

113. *Western Telcon v California State Lottery*, 13 Cal. 4th 475, 917 P.2d 651 (1996).

114. Ibid., 487.

115. Ibid. See for example In re *Lowrie*, 43 Cal. App. 564, 566-567, 185 P. 421 (1919).

116. *Western Telcon, supra* 488 n.113.

117. Ibid.

118. Ibid.; *People v Ambrose*, 122 Cal. App. 2.d Supp. 966, 970, 265 P.2d 191 (1953).

119. *Western Telcon, supra* 488 n.113.

120. Ibid.

121. *Hotel Employees, supra* 11 n.2.

122. Ibid.

123. Ibid.

124. *Western Telcon, supra* 486 n.113. In a pari-mutuel system bets are pooled and the prize is shared among all of the winning bettors after operator fees are deducted. See id.

125. *Hotel Employees, supra* 11 n.2.

126. Compact, §2.17; see also Gov. Code, §98006(a),(b); see also Brief for Respondent, *supra* 12 n.3.

127. Compact, §2.17; see also Gov. Code, §98006(a),(b); see also Brief for Respondent, *supra* 22 n.3.

128. See *Hotel Employees* (dissent), *supra* 92, 93 n.2. A players' pool prize system has none of the characteristics of a banked game. See id.

129. *Hotel Employees, supra* 46 n.2.

130. Ibid., 50.

131. Ibid., 49.

132. The flaw in the court's reasoning was concisely summarized in the following editorial:

> In striking down Proposition 5, the court majority decided that the video slot machines and card games authorized by the initiative are the kind of "Nevada and New Jersey" casino games outlawed by the state constitution.
>
> That conclusion, the logic of which the justices labor greatly to explain, simply doesn't jibe with what any gambler knows to be true.
>
> When you play against the house, the house has a direct stake in the outcome of the game. It gets to keep your wager if you lose but has to pay you if you win. In theory, it can be broken—every player at the table might bet big and win. Or it might reap a windfall—every player could bet big and lose.
>
> In the kind of games authorized by Proposition 5 (and the constitution), that crucial element is lacking. The tribes charge a fee for participation, but the players' wagers are pooled and divided among the winners. If everyone wins, each gets a smaller share of the pool; if no one wins, the unclaimed pool rolls over to the next game. Since the house gets no share of that pool, it has no stake in the game's outcome.
>
> If this sounds familiar, that's because it is precisely the method by which the California Lottery operates. And because the lottery is legal in California, the state has no authority under federal law to prohibit sovereign Indian tribes from doing the same thing (Staff editorial, "Court Blows Call in Gaming Case," *Ventura County Star*, 25 August 1999, B8).

133. Ibid.

134. Gov. Code, §98001(c); see also Brief for Respondent, *supra* 12 n.3.

135. Gov. Code § 98001(c); see also Brief for Respondent, *supra* 12 n.3.

136. Brief for Respondent, *supra* 30 n.3.

137. Ibid.

138. Ibid.

139. Ibid.

140. Ibid.

141. Ibid.

142. Ibid., 31. Respondents also state that the tribal facilities would fail to meet minimum bankroll requirements in Nevada and a requirement that casinos be attached to hotels in Atlantic City. See ibid.

143. Brief for Respondent, *supra* 32 n.3.

144. Ibid.

145. Cal. Const., art. IV, §19 (d),(e).

146. Ibid.

147. Brief for Respondent, *supra* 33 n.3. However, while tribes can initially employ outside organizations to manage the facilities, they must work toward the placement of tribal members and, ultimately, tribal management. Ibid. See also IGRA 25 USC §2710 (a)(2)(B) requiring revenues to be used for tribal government operation.

148. Brief for Respondent, *supra* 13 n.3; Compact §6.5.6.

149. Id.

150. 25 USC §2710 (d)(1)(C).

151. 25 USC §2710 (b)(2)(B)(i).

152. 25 USC §2710 (b)(2)(B)(ii).

153. See generally Goldberg-Ambrose, *Planting Tail Feathers*, *supra* n.24.

154. Cal. Const., art. IV, §19(d).

155. Any ambiguity in statutes designed for the benefit of Indians must be construed liberally in the Indians' favor. *County of Yakima* v *Confederated Tribes and Bands*, 502 US 251, 269 (1992); see also S. Rep. No.100-446, 15: "the committee trusts that courts will interpret any ambiguities [in IGRA] in a manner that will be most favorable to tribal interests."

156. *Hotel Employees*, *supra* 81 n.2.

157. Ibid.

158. See generally Pub. L. No. 280; 18 USC §1151.

♠

Amici Curiae Brief of Indian Law Professors in the Case of *Hotel Employees and Restaurant Employees International Union* v. *Wilson*

Carole E. Goldberg and Indian Law Professors

INTRODUCTION

On 23 August 1999, the California Supreme Court issued its opinion in *Hotel Employees and Restaurant Employees International Union* v. *Wilson*, 21 Cal.4th 585, 981 P.2d 990, 88 Cal. Rptr.2d 56 (1999), invalidating Proposition 5, the California tribal gaming initiative that had passed the previous November with 63 percent of the popular vote. Proposition 5 would have allowed California Indian nations to conduct prescribed forms of gaming on their lands in accordance with tribal-state compacts and the federal Indian Gaming Regulatory Act of 1988 (IGRA). It also established minimum terms for such compacts, subject to modification by agreement between the tribes and the state. The California Supreme Court found that Proposition 5 conflicted with Article IV, §19(e) of the California Constitution, which was added in 1984, when California authorized the state lottery. According to this provision, "The Legislature has no power to authorize, and shall prohibit, casinos of the type currently operating in Nevada and New Jersey."

Opponents of Proposition 5 had challenged the measure under federal law as well. They had argued that Proposition 5 was incompatible with the Indian Gaming Regulatory Act, because it allowed tribes to carry on forms of gaming that were outlawed elsewhere in the state. Indeed, they argued that if the Indian Gaming Regulatory Act were interpreted to permit state laws that allow only tribes to conduct specific types of gaming, then the federal gaming act violated the equal protection guarantees of the United States Constitution. These were serious attacks on Proposition 5; but the California Supreme Court declined to address them once it found that the proposition violated state law.

The amici curiae ("friends of the court") brief that appears below focuses on the federal law issues that the California Supreme Court chose not to address. It was filed on behalf of thirteen law professors who teach federal Indian law, including the coeditors of the 1982 treatise, *Felix S. Cohen's Handbook of Federal Indian Law*; authors of casebooks in the field; and faculty who teach the subject at California law schools. Included in this group are: Jo Carrillo, professor at Hastings College of Law; Reid Chambers, part-time faculty member at Yale Law School; Robert N. Clinton, professor at University of Iowa College of Law; Richard B. Collins, professor at University of Colorado School of Law; Arturo Gandara, professor at University of California, Davis School of Law; Gerald Gardner, part-time faculty member at University of California, Berkeley, Boalt Hall; David Getches, professor at University of Colorado School of Law; Raleigh Levine, part-time faculty member at Loyola, Los Angeles School of Law; Nell Newton, dean at University of

Denver School of Law; Monroe Price, professor at Cardozo Law School, Yeshiva University; Rennard Strickland, dean at University of Oregon School of Law; Charles Wilkinson, professor at University of Colorado School of Law; and myself, Carole E. Goldberg, professor at Univeristy of California, Los Angeles School of Law. Our interest in this case was in maintaining the coherence of Indian law and the integrity of long-tested principles in that field. Because initiatives similar to Proposition 5 may be presented to other states, the issues that this amici curiae brief tackles have continuing significance.

— Carole E. Goldberg

[Editor's Note: The brief that appears below is on file with the California Supreme Court and is reprinted in its original form with minor editorial changes.]

I. TRIBAL SELF-GOVERNMENT MAY BE ALTERED ONLY BY A CLEAR AND SPECIFIC STATEMENT OF CONGRESS

Tribal self-government is genuinely and profoundly at stake in this case. As Congress proclaimed in the Declaration of Policy in IGRA, the purpose of the act "is to provide a statutory basis for the operation of gaming by Indian tribes as a means of promoting tribal economic development, self-sufficiency, and strong tribal governments," 25 USC §2702[1]. The passage of Proposition 5 was necessary to enable tribes in California to exercise the governmental function of authorizing and regulating gaming as a form of economic development. A major national study of tribal gaming by the Economic Resources Group of Cambridge, Massachusetts has documented how this form of tribal economic development has benefited reservation communities through increased employment and generation of resources for the enhancement of governmental infrastructure, cultural revitalization, and augmented tribal social services to reservation citizens (Stephen Cornell, Joseph Kalt, Matthew Krepps, Jonathan Taylor, *American Indian Gaming Policy and Its Socio-Economic Effects: A Report to the National Gambling Impact Study Commission* [July 31, 1998]). Tribal self-government entails the capacity to make such choices about economic development and to provide for the economic welfare of tribal members.

One of the most fundamental principles of Indian law is that tribal powers of self-government may be extinguished only by a clear and specific expression of Congress. The 1982 edition of the *Cohen* treatise twice articulated this principle:

> Once powers of tribal self-government or other Indian rights are shown to exist, by treaty or otherwise, later federal action which might arguably abridge them is construed narrowly in favor of retaining Indian rights. The principle of a "clear and plain statement" before Indian treaty rights can be abrogated also applies in nontreaty contexts.... The canons are variously phrased in different contexts, but generally they provide for a broad construction when the issue is whether Indian rights are reserved or established, and for a narrow construction when Indian rights are to be abrogated or limited.... (Cohen, 224–25, footnotes omitted)

> Before holding that treaties or statutes limit tribal powers ... the courts have insisted upon a clear and specific expression of congressional intent to extinguish traditional prerogatives of sovereignty. (Cohen, 242, footnotes omitted)

This principle has been applied in cases construing Congressional delegation of jurisdiction over Indians to states, *Bryan* v. *Itasca County*, 426 US 373, 392 (1976): "[S]tatutes passed for the benefit of dependent Indian tribes ... are to be liberally construed, doubtful expressions being resolved in favor of the Indians" (quoting *Alaska Pacific Fisheries* v. *United States*, 248 US 78, 89 [1918]); in cases construing federal laws directly limiting exercises of tribal sovereignty, *Santa Clara Pueblo* v. *Martinez*, 436 US 49, 60 (1978): "Although Congress clearly has power to authorize civil actions against tribal officers,... a proper respect both for tribal sovereignty itself and for the plenary authority of Congress in this area cautions that we tread lightly in the absence of clear indications of legislative intent"; and in cases construing congressional acts that arguably contract the territorial basis for tribal sovereignty (i.e., Indian Country), *Solem* v. *Bartlett*, 465 US 463, 472 (1984): "When both an Act and its legislative history fail to provide substantial and compelling evidence of a congressional intention to diminish Indian lands, we are bound by our traditional solicitude for the Indian tribes to rule that diminishment did not take place and that the old reservation boundaries survived the opening." In each instance, the Court has required either an express statement in the statutory text or some unmistakable indication from the circumstances surrounding the enactment before it would allow tribal self-government to be diminished. When there was ambiguity or uncertainty regarding congressional intent, the principle dictated, and the Court insisted, that tribal self-government remain intact.

In applying the requirement of a clear and specific statement, it is not enough to identify the more persuasive rendering of Congress' intent between two competing versions. Under this incorrect approach, the principle of clear and plain expression would function only as a "tie-breaker" in the event the Court could not find one version more persuasive than the other. Rather, more like the burden of persuasion in criminal cases, the Court must determine whether there is any reasonable basis for doubting that Congress intended to extinguish tribal self-government. If any reasonable doubt exists, then the principle requires that tribal sovereignty be upheld. Thus, when this Court has been confronted with constructions of statutes and treaties that would effectively "reverse the general policy of the government towards the Indians," it has said that "[t]o justify such a departure ... requires a clear expression of the intention of Congress...." Ex parte *Crow Dog*, 109 US 556, 572 (1883).

The principle of clear and specific expression, and the cases that apply it, "reflect a pervasive influence of (a) the tradition of federal policy to encourage the development and exercise of tribal self-governing powers and (b) the assumed federal obligation to preserve and protect those powers" (*Cohen*, 242–43). Since publication of the 1982 edition of the *Cohen* treatise, this policy and the associated federal responsibility have been more widely and fully elaborated than at any time since the early treaty period of United States-tribal relations. See, e.g., Clean

Air Act, 42 USC §7601(d), 7602(r) (tribes treated as states); Tribal Self-Governance Act of 1994, 25 USC §§450n, 450aa note, 450aa–450gg (extending and making permanent systems for tribal control over federally funded services to tribes); Defense Appropriations Act for FY 91, Pub. L. No 101-938, §8077(b)-(d) (1990) amending 25 USC §1301(2) (affirming tribal criminal jurisdiction over non-member Indians); Office of the Administrator, United States Environmental Protection Agency, EPA Policy for the Administration of Environmental Programs on Indian Reservations (November 8, 1984) (recognizing tribes as governments responsible for making decisions and carrying out program responsibilities affecting reservations); Indian Tribal Justice Act, 25 USC §3601 et seq. (affirming that tribal justice systems are the appropriate forums for the adjudication of disputes affecting personal and property rights). Thus the historical and doctrinal foundations for the principle remain secure.

The normative basis for the principle of clear and specific expression is found in fundamental works of Anglo-American political theory and finds full expression in the United States Constitution. This theory makes political legitimacy turn on "the consent of the governed." See John H. Ely, *Democracy and Distrust* (1980); Richard Collins, "Indian Consent to American Government," 31 *Arizona Law Review* 365 (1989). Indians, unlike most other Americans, were of course not incorporated into the American body politic by virtue of voluntary immigration. Their consensual adherence to the American commonwealth must thus be predicated on the treaties and other agreements with tribes that established rules protecting tribes and their members on reservations in their exercise of self-government and freedom from state control. See generally Philip P. Frickey, "Marshalling Past and Present: Colonialism, Constitutionalism and Interpretation in Federal Indian Law," 107 *Harvard Law Review* 381, 413–19 (1993). Accordingly, when Congress exercises its broad constitutional power over Indian affairs,[1] particularly when it exceeds the powers acknowledged in treaties, the legitimacy of its action is questionable under any theory requiring "consent of the governed." See *Worcester* v. *Georgia*, 31 US (6 Pet.) 515, 542(1832) (Marshall, C.J.).[2] Under this circumstance, the principle of clear and specific expression operates to limit federal incursions into tribal sovereignty, while maintaining Congress's ultimately broad power.

In this case, the Court is asked to construe a federal statute, the Indian Gaming Regulatory Act of 1988 (IGRA), 25 USC §§2701 et seq. The principle of clear and specific expression provides a distinct framework for interpreting this statute as applied to Proposition 5.

II. THE INDIAN GAMING REGULATORY ACT OF 1988 DOES NOT PREEMPT PROPOSITION 5

Petitioners in this litigation have argued that Proposition 5 conflicts with §2710(d)(1) of IGRA because it authorizes tribes to engage in gaming that is otherwise impermissible within the state. The relevant language in the federal act allows Class III gaming activities[3] on Indian lands only if these activities are "(B) located in a State that permits such gaming for any purpose by any person, organization, or entity" and "(C) conducted in conformance with a Tribal-State

compact." Petitioners contend that Proposition 5 fails to satisfy this requirement because there is no state law other than the proposition that authorizes the
forms of gaming addressed in the proposition.

Even assuming *arguendo* that California law otherwise prohibits the forms
of gaming allowed in Proposition 5, there is no basis for finding a conflict
between the proposition and IGRA. Neither the language itself, nor the context
and legislative history surrounding its enactment, suggest that Congress intended
to prohibit a state from enacting laws that affirm compacts with tribes to carry
on games that are otherwise unlawful within the state. If this Court finds there
is any ambiguity about the application of this statutory language, the canons of
construction discussed above dictate an interpretation that would uphold the
proposition.

A. Proposition 5 Is Consistent with the Language of 2710(d)(1)

The language of §2710(d)(1)(B), read literally, allows gaming under Proposition
5 because the proposition itself is a state law that "permits such gaming for any
purpose by any entity," to wit, the tribes. The language of §2710(d)(1)(C),
which further requires any such gaming to be "conducted in conformance with
a Tribal-State compact," casts no doubt on this reading of the statute.

Petitioners argue that if the existence of a tribal-state compact were sufficient
by itself to satisfy the requirement that state law "permit" a given form of gaming, there would be no need for both subdivisions (B) and (C). Thus, they contend, Congress must have intended that state law "permit" the gaming by some
person or entity other than the tribes. Their argument is faulty for two reasons.

First, compacts, standing alone, do not always have the effect of law. In many
states compacts must be confirmed by the legislature before they can "permit"
conduct such as gaming.[4] Proposition 5 combines these two functions in one,
thereby satisfying both requirements; but subdivision (C) of §2710(d)(1) seems to
have anticipated the more frequent occurrence of a compact separate from state
"permission" in the form of legislative confirmation. Under this reading, the separate requirements that the state "permit" the gaming and "conformance with a
Tribal-State compact" make perfect sense, even if tribes are the only entities "permitted" to conduct that form of gaming under the state law in question.

Second, petitioners can achieve their reading of the statute only by miscon-
struing the requirement of subdivision (C) of §2710(d)(1). That subdivision
demands more than the mere *existence* of a tribal-state compact. It requires tribal
"conformance" with that compact. Tribal-state gaming compacts under IGRA,
such as Proposition 5, typically entail detailed regulations specifying the manner and circumstances of tribal gaming, and often impose obligations on tribes
to pay the cost of state services associated with gaming, 25 USC §2710(d)(3)(C);
Proposition 5, §16.2. Subdivision (C) of §2710(d)(1) insists that Class III gaming will satisfy IGRA only if the tribe *is conforming with* the terms of that compact. This requirement is separate from the subdivision (B) requirement that
state law "permit" the particular form of gaming for any entity. A compact/law
such as Proposition 5 could "permit" certain forms of tribal gaming, but the
tribes could nonetheless be failing to "conform" with the terms of that compact.

Under such hypothetical circumstances, subdivision (B) could be satisfied but not subdivision (C). Hence there is no reason to view the two subdivisions as redundant.

Petitioners also argue that Proposition 5 cannot be the law that "permits" Class III gaming for purposes of §2710(d)(1)(B) because as a matter of federal Indian law states lack regulatory authority over tribal activities on reservations, even in Public Law 280 states such as California. According to this argument, if states lack such regulatory authority, they must be incapable of "permitting" gaming on Indian lands. Thus, §2710(d)(1)(B) must be referring to state law that "permits" such gaming outside of reservations.

Even if petitioners are correct that states entirely lack regulatory authority over tribal gaming,[5] they fail to acknowledge that Congress can confer authority on states that states otherwise would lack. For example, Public Law 280 gives states certain civil and criminal jurisdiction over reservation Indians. See Carole Goldberg, "Public Law 280: The Limits of State Jurisdiction over Reservation Indians," 22 *UCLA Law Review* 535 (1975). IGRA is also such a statute. According to the Senate Report on IGRA, that law invokes Congress's power to alter jurisdictional arrangements within Indian Country. Senate Report 100-446 on S. 555, "Indian Gaming Regulatory Act," Select Committee on Indian Affairs at 3 (1988) [hereafter *Senate Report*]. IGRA prohibits all Class III tribal gaming unless it is conducted in accordance with the act, and confers upon states the power to "permit" such gaming. This scheme is fully consistent with Congress's acknowledged plenary power over tribes and with states' authority to exercise such power when it is delegated from Congress.

Petitioners have pointed to no previous court decisions construing the language of §2710(d)(1) as they propose. Both *Rumsey Indian Rancheria* v. *Wilson*, 64 F.3d 1250 (9th Cir. 1994), and *Cheyenne River Sioux Tribe* v. *South Dakota*, 3 F.3d 273 (8th Cir. 1993), construed §2710(d)(1) in a completely different context from the present litigation. These cases considered whether states were *required* to negotiate compacts over forms of Class III gaming prohibited throughout the state. For this purpose alone, the courts found that tribes had no "right" to conduct Class III gaming (that is, to insist on a compact) where such gaming was generally outlawed by the state. Neither of these cases presented a situation where the state had actually enacted a law such as Proposition 5 that "permits" Class III gaming on Indian land. Thus no language from these cases supports the assertion that gaming must be "generally permitted" on non-tribal land.

Petitioners' reliance on *Citizen Band of Potawatomi Indian Tribe of Oklahoma* v. *Green*, 995 F.2d 179 (10th Cir. 1993), is similarly misplaced. *Potawatomi* interpreted an entirely separate provision of IGRA, §2710(d)(6), not §2710(d)(1). But even if one is tempted to analogize from the interpretation of one subsection to another, *Potawatomi* should not help the petitioners' case. Section 2710(d)(6) sets forth requirements for waiver of the Johnson Act, a federal statute banning sale or possession of certain gambling devices. Under this provision of IGRA, the waiver operates as to any "gaming conducted under a Tribal-State compact that (A) is entered into ... by a State in which gambling devices are legal, and (B) is in effect." In *Potawatomi*, the tenth circuit rejected the tribe's argument that its tribal-state compact authorizing gambling devices was sufficient to render them "legal" in a state where they were otherwise prohibited. With very little supporting analysis, and no consideration of the obligatory canons of construction, the Court asserted that Congress must have intended that the gambling devices in question be legal outside of the tribal-state compact. This conclusion by the tenth circuit flouts congressional intent as reflected in the legislative history. During the Senate debate over IGRA, Senator Daniel Inouye, chair of the Senate Select Committee on Indian Affairs, stated specifically that IGRA "would not alter the effect of the Johnson Act except to provide for a waiver of its application in the case of gambling devices operated pursuant to a compact with the State in which the tribe is located," 134 Congressional Record S12650 (September 15, 1988).

But even if *Potawatomi* is treated as good law, it is distinguishable from the present case. In *Potawatomi*, there was no state legislation legalizing tribal gaming apart from the compact itself. By way of contrast, Proposition 5 constitutes state legislation as well as a compact, providing all necessary predicates for a Johnson Act waiver. Indeed, Proposition 5 contains a separate statutory authorization, independent of any compact, permitting the gaming at issue, Cal. Govt. Code §98006.

In contrast, there is one case that provides some support for the position that a state need not allow non-Indian gaming in order to enter into an IGRA compact. In *Forest County Potawatomi Community of Wisconsin* v. *Norquist*, 45 F.3d 1079 (7th Cir. 1995), the court rejected an argument that a tribe's Class III gaming compact was unlawful under IGRA § 2710(d)(1). The seventh circuit panel noted that even if it were to follow *Rumsey, supra,* and insist on a state law that otherwise "permits" the specific form of gaming addressed in the compact, it would be sufficient if another tribal compact allowed the form of gaming in question. In the court's words, "Assuming for argument that we agree with the Ninth Circuit's reading of the IGRA (on which we express no opinion), that case does not undermine the validity of the Potawatomis' Compact under the IGRA, because Wisconsin unlike California presently permits other Indian tribes within the state to carry on the exact gaming activities to be challenged here," 45 F.3d at 1083 n.1. Thus, under *Forest Potawatomi*, a compact alone suffices to demonstrate that the state "permits" Class III gaming.

B. Context and Legislative History Demonstrate That Proposition 5 is Consistent with IGRA

The history of IGRA makes it clear that states may enact laws such as Proposition 5, affirming tribal-state compacts that arguably allow only tribes to conduct forms of Class III gaming. The language of §2710(d)(1) was intended to protect states that did *not* want to enter into tribal-state compacts from being forced to do so. Congress had no reason whatsoever to preclude states from making compacts that they wished to make. Yet petitioners' reading of §2710(d)(1) would have precisely that disabling effect. For that reason, it should be rejected.

The precipitating event for the enactment of IGRA was the 1987 United States Supreme Court decision in *Cabazon Tribe of Indians* v. *California*, 480

US 202 (1987). In this decision, which referenced an article by amicus Professor Carole Goldberg, the Court determined that the Cabazon tribe could conduct high-stakes bingo games on reservation land notwithstanding such games were illegal under California law. To reach this conclusion, the Court applied a three-part balancing test, which considered tribal, federal, and state interests. In analyzing the state's interest, the Court took account of two facts: first, that bingo was regulated rather than absolutely prohibited by the state; and second, that the state authorized various other forms of gaming, such as pari-mutuel horse-racing and a state lottery. Under these circumstances, the Court found that the state lacked a strong interest in preventing high-stakes tribal bingo.

Section 2710(d)(1) was adopted against the background of the *Cabazon* decision. *Senate Report* at 2 Following *Cabazon*, states were alarmed by the possibility that the decision had rendered them powerless to limit any form of tribal gaming, at least where the state ran a lottery or permitted gaming of any type. Under these circumstances, the purpose of §2710(d)(1) was to empower states to refuse to negotiate tribal-state compacts under some circumstances. Regardless of one's view of the soundness of the ninth circuit's opinion in *Rumsey*, *supra*, it is clear that §2710(d)(1) enables states to block tribal gaming in some cases even if the state otherwise has no jurisdiction to regulate the gaming directly. The legislative history of IGRA confirms that this section was designed as a limited form of state veto over tribal gaming, *Senate Report* at 5–6; 134 *Congressional Record* S12650 (September 15, 1988): (Senator Inouye: "Tribes that do not want any State jurisdiction on their lands are precluded from operation of what the bill refers to as class III gaming").

Petitioners' argument turns the purpose of this section on its head, completely subverting its intent. If, as we have demonstrated, the purpose of §2710(d)(1) was to protect states against *unwanted* forms of tribal gaming, there is no reason to use that language to prevent states from "permitting" *desired* tribal gaming. As Senator Inouye pointed out during the floor debate on IGRA, the statute was "intended to provide a means by which tribal and State governments can realize their unique and individual governmental objectives...." 134 *Congressional Record* 12650 (September 15, 1988). When a state's objectives include fostering tribal economic development, there is no reason for IGRA to stand in the way. In the present case, the overwhelming passage of Proposition 5 reflects the voters' judgment that tribes have special claims to carry on such economic development activity. Thus, the state's "interest" (to use the terminology of the *Cabazon* opinion) supports rather than resists tribal gaming. The legislative history of IGRA is devoid of any language that suggests Congress wanted to curb state authorization for tribal gaming. Indeed, Congress was careful to couch IGRA as a "limited intrusion on the right of tribal self-government...." Statement of Senator Daniel Evans, 134 *Congressional Record* S12651 (September 15, 1988). (Senator Evans was the Republican manager of the legislation.)

The only possible source of support for petitioners' reading of §2710(b)(1) is the language in the legislative history expressing concern about regulation of tribal gaming. Although IGRA created the National Indian Gaming Commission to oversee tribal gaming, and tribes possess the power to regulate their own on-reservation gaming, the legislative history of IGRA reflects some expectation that states might play a role in regulating tribal gaming through the compacting process, *Senate Report* at 13-14; 134 *Congressional Record* S12650 (September 15, 1988): (Statement of Senator Daniel Inouye) If that is true, it may be reasonable to believe that states would function more effectively in regulating tribal gaming if they already possessed the apparatus for such regulation due to the existence of "permitted" off-reservation gaming.

Although this argument has some surface appeal, it is ultimately unhelpful for two distinct reasons. First, there is nothing in IGRA that *requires* state regulation of tribal gaming through the compacting process. Thus, a state with elaborate regulatory machinery for off-reservation gaming could enter into a valid tribal-state compact whether or not the compact specified that the state regulatory apparatus would be employed for tribal gaming. Indeed, the legislative history of IGRA is replete with statements that Congress did not want to dictate state regulation of tribal gaming, 134 *Congressional Record* 12651 (September 15, 1988): (Statements of Senators Evans and Inouye) As Senator Evans indicated, "I wish to ... make clear that when a tribe and a State negotiate a compact, there need be no imposition of state jurisdiction whatsoever."

Second, just because a state "permits" a form of Class III gaming off the reservation is no guaranty that the state has regulatory machinery for that form of gaming that would be useful in managing tribal enterprises. For example, several states, such as Oregon and Connecticut, "permit" Class III gaming off the reservations, but they do so only[6] for charitable organizations that hold occasional "casino nights" where imitation money is used, Ore. Rev. Stat. §167.117 et seq.; Conn. Gen. Stat. Ann. §7–186a. In these states, there are tribal-state compacts authorizing a wide variety of Class III games, because of a broad reading of §2710(d)(1) that says the states "permit" such gaming, *Mashantucket Pequot Tribe v. Connecticut*, 913 F.2d 1024 (2d Cir. 1990). But the regulatory institutions that the states established for the charitable "casino nights" were in no way suited to management of the much larger, cash-intensive, and for-profit operations of the tribes. Thus, reading §2710(d)(1) to require that states "permit" Class III gaming off the reservation would not necessarily promote any congressional interest in effective regulation of tribal gaming.

In sum, the context and overall objectives of IGRA demonstrate the consistency between Proposition 5 and the federal act. Congress, through IGRA, wanted to protect states from the tribes, not from themselves. Where the voters of the state approve tribal gaming, it does not matter, for purposes of IGRA, whether the voters also approve of off-reservation gaming.

C. Any Ambiguity in §2710(d)(1) Should Be Resolved in Favor of Tribal Gaming

Amici are convinced that the text, legislative history, and context of §2710(d)(1) render that section consistent with Proposition 5. Subdivision (B)'s requirement is satisfied so long as the tribal-state compact, as enshrined in state law, "permits" the tribe to engage in Class III gaming.

If this Court is nonetheless uncertain about the proper reading of IGRA, the canons of construction prescribe an interpretation that favors tribal self-government. See *Rumsey, supra,* 64 F.3d at 1257; Senate Report at 15 ("The Committee ... trusts that courts will interpret any ambiguities [in IGRA] in a manner that will be most favorable to tribal interests consistent with the legal standard used by the courts for over 150 years in deciding cases involving Indian tribes"). According to these canons, the petitioners' proposed interpretation may be chosen only if it is clearly manifest from the language or the circumstances surrounding its passage. As neither of these conditions is satisfied, this Court should decline to find that Proposition 5 is preempted by federal law.

III. IGRA IS CONSTITUTIONAL IF CONSTRUED TO ALLOW TRIBAL-STATE COMPACTS FOR GAMING THAT IS NOT ALLOWED ELSEWHERE IN THE STATE

Petitioners contend that if IGRA is construed to allow Proposition 5, IGRA may be unconstitutional. Although their constitutional argument is not fully developed, it seems to focus on the fact that tribes could secure a "monopoly" on forms of Class III gaming that are allowed via tribal-state compacts but not otherwise within the state. Their argument appears to be that exclusive tribal rights to carry on Class III gaming would violate the equal protection clause of the Fifth Amendment.

In making this argument, petitioners implicate—and misapply—a distinctive body of federal constitutional law. This constitutional doctrine supplies a special standard for evaluating constitutional challenges to federal statutes affecting tribal interests. Because of the unique government-to-government trust relationship between the United States and Indian tribes, federal Indian legislation will be upheld in the face of due process or equal protection challenges so long as the legislation "can be tied rationally to the fulfillment of Congress' unique obligation toward the Indians,..." *Morton* v. *Mancari,* 417 US 535, 555 (1974). The Supreme Court has declined to treat the hundreds of special benefits for tribes as discrimination based on race, finding instead that the classifications involved are "political," id. See also *Cohen* at 654–658. These holdings find strong support in Article I of the Constitution, which singles out "commerce with ... the Indian Tribes" as a separate basis for congressional legislation. See Carole Goldberg-Ambrose, "Not 'Strictly' Racial: A Response to 'Indians as Peoples,'" 39 *UCLA Law Review* 169, 174 (1991). It is difficult to imagine how Congress could exercise this power without making classifications based on tribal status.

Indeed, the very jurisdictional scheme that the United States Supreme Court has established for Indian Country—and derived from Article I's Indian Commerce Clause—practically guarantees that there will be circumstances where tribes may carry out economic activity that is otherwise unlawful within their states. The Court has held, for example, that states may not regulate hunting and fishing by Indians or non-Indians within Indian Country, *New Mexico* v. *Mescalero Apache Tribe,* 462 US 324 (1983). Accordingly, any tribe that prescribes more liberal hunting and fishing rules than the surrounding state will enjoy an economic advantage. Likewise, tribal lands are not subject to state regulation regarding waste disposal, *Washington Department of Ecology* v. *EPA*, 752 F.2d 1465 (9th Cir. 1985). As a result, tribes have an economic advantage over off-reservation landowners in competing to provide waste disposal sites. It is this very jurisdictional scheme that gave rise to the *Cabazon* decision and to gaming as a form of tribal economic development.

If IGRA allows tribal-state compacts regarding games that are prohibited elsewhere within the state, the law will easily survive constitutional challenge under the doctrine described above. Congress has declared in IGRA that tribal gaming on Indian land advances tribal economic development and self-government. Although IGRA imposes restraints on such gaming, Congress sought to keep the intrusion into tribal self-government a limited one. Indeed, it is arguable that without IGRA, tribes in most states would have been able to conduct Class III gaming regardless of state prohibitions on many forms of such gaming elsewhere within the state. Under these circumstances, IGRA promotes the federal government's trust responsibility by authorizing Class III tribal gaming under tribal-state compacts whenever the state is prepared to make such an agreement, regardless of state law applicable outside Indian lands.

In arguing to the contrary, petitioners rely on the ninth circuit's decision in *Williams* v. *Babbitt*, 115 F.3d 657 (9th Cir. 1997), which determined that the Reindeer Act of 1937, 25 USC §§500 et seq., did not prohibit reindeer herding by non-Natives in Alaska. Judge Kozinski's opinion for two of the judges arrived at this construction out of concern that a statewide federal ban on non-Native reindeer herding would be unconstitutional. In dictum, Judge Kozinski also expressed "serious doubt ... that Congress could give Indians a complete monopoly on the casino industry...." 115 F.3d at 31.

Judge Kozinski's constitutional analysis in *Williams* stretches existing authority such as *Morton* v. *Mancari* nearly to the breaking point. However, even if one agrees with the constitutional approach adopted in *Williams*, that case does not point to constitutional problems with IGRA. IGRA and the Reindeer Act are fundamentally different—the Reindeer Act is concerned with what non-Indians can do on non-Indian land, and IGRA is concerned with what tribes can do on tribal land. More particularly, both the Reindeer Act and Judge Kozinski's hypothetical "complete monopoly on the casino industry" posed the dilemma of Congress prohibiting commercial activity by non-Indians *both within and outside Indian lands* in order to give tribes a commercial advantage. IGRA, in contrast, does not even address gaming outside of Indian lands. It is intended to support tribal self-government by establishing a framework for tribal-state cooperation with respect to on-reservation tribal gaming only. Furthermore, IGRA does not prescribe any tribal monopoly at all, even as interpreted to allow for Proposition 5. IGRA merely enables states to choose to compact with tribes for forms of gaming that state law does not permit elsewhere within the state. Under §2710(d)(1) of IGRA, states are likewise free to decline to make compacts for Class III gaming that is barred elsewhere in the state; alternatively, states could choose to legalize on a statewide basis the forms of Class III gaming that are the subject of tribal-state compacts.

In his opinion in the *Williams* case, Judge Alex Kozinski was careful to distinguish complete federal prohibitions of off-reservation non-Indian activity from more "narrowly tailored" federal preferences for tribal activities on Indian lands. He stated, for example, that "[l]egislation that relates to Indian land, tribal status, self-government or culture passes *Mancari*'s rational relation test.... As 'a separate people,' Indians have a right to expect some special protection for their land, political institutions..., and culture," 115 F.3d at 30. Judge Kozinski also quoted language from the United States Supreme Court's opinion in *United States* v. *Antelope*, 430 US 641, 646 (1977), to support federal preferences "directly promoting Indian interests in self-government...."

IGRA is precisely the kind of statute that meets Judge Kozinski's own test for a statute that directly promotes tribal self-government and facilitates tribal control over use of tribal lands. The statute's Declaration of Policy mentions the objective of promoting tribal self-government; and the gaming it allows is confined to Indian lands. For purposes of this analysis, it is irrelevant whether gaming was or was not a traditional tribal activity. The nexus to tribal self-government and tribal control over economic development of tribal lands is sufficient to sustain IGRA, even as interpreted to allow compacts for Class III gaming that is prohibited elsewhere within the state.[7]

CONCLUSION

There is no constitutional basis for choosing a construction of IGRA that would confine tribal-state compacts to forms of gaming that are permissible outside Indian lands. The text, legislative history, and circumstances of enactment of IGRA all point to an interpretation that would sustain Proposition 5. The canons of construction that federal Indian law applies to statutes such as IGRA further reinforce this reading of the act. To maintain the coherence and consistency of basic principles of federal Indian law, IGRA should be interpreted to allow Proposition 5.

NOTES

1. See Rennard F. Strickland and Charles F. Wilkerson, eds., *Felix S. Cohen's Handbook of Federal Indian Law* (Charlottesville: LEXIS Publishing Company, 1982), 207 for an explanation of this power.

2. "Did these [European] adventurers, by sailing along the coast, and occasionally landing on it, acquire for the several governments to whom they belonged ... rightful dominion over the numerous people who occupied it?... But power, war, conquest, give rights, which, after possession, are conceded by the world; and which can never be controverted by those on whom they descend. We proceed, then, to the actual state of things, having glanced at their origin; because holding it in our recollection might shed some light on existing pretensions."

3. Class III gaming is defined under the act as all games other than traditional Indian games and various forms of bingo, 25 USC 2703(8). The games authorized for tribes in Proposition 5 are Class III games.

4. The highest courts in several states have adhered to this principle. See, e.g., *Salt*

River Pima-Maricopa Community v *Hull*, 945 P.2d 818 (Ariz. 1997); *State ex rel. Clark* v *Johnson*, 904 P.2d 11, 22-25 (NM 1995); *State ex rel. Stephan* v *Finney*, 836 P.2d 1169, 1178-80 (KS 1992); *Narragansett Indian Tribe of Rhode Island* v *State of Rhode Island*, 667 A.2d 280 (RI 1995). See also William Thompson, in *Indian Gaming and the Law* 29, ed. William Eadington (Reno: University of Nevada Press, 1989), 40–41.

5.   Petitioners' claim that states have no jurisdiction over reservation gaming reflects an admirable regard for the general principle of tribal sovereignty. But it misstates the scope of that principle as it has been developed by the United States Supreme Court and the Congress. In *Cabazon Tribe* v *California*, 480 US 202 (1987), the Supreme Court established no absolute bar to state regulation of tribal gaming within Indian Country. Rather, it applied a three-part balancing test, assessing federal, tribal, and state interests. Although the facts in *Cabazon* led the Court to conclude that California could not bar high-stakes tribal bingo games, the Court left open the possibility that stronger state interests opposing tribal gaming might produce the opposite result. For example, a state which completely prohibited gaming throughout the state might be able to mount a much stronger case against tribal gaming. Any state that could put forward such a case against tribal gaming would also be in a position to drop its objections to tribal gaming, and thereby "permit" such gaming. IGRA's use of the word "permit" makes sense in light of this possibility.

6.   In Oregon, the state has also allowed video poker to be played in commercial taverns.

7.   If IGRA itself is constitutional, any state legislation, such as Proposition 5, that is enacted in order to promote the purposes of IGRA is likewise constitutional under the Fourteenth Amendment. *Washington* v *Fishing Vessel Ass'n*, 443 US 658, 673 n.20 (1979); *Peyote Way Church of God, Inc.* v *Thornburgh*, 922 F.2d 1210 (5th Cir. 1991); see *Cohen* at 658–660.

♠

Cabazon and Its Implications for Indian Gaming

Alexander Tallchief Skibine

There are a few points I want to make in regard to the 1987 Supreme Court decision in *California* v. *Cabazon Band of Mission Indians*, 480 US 202 (1987), because I think it is sometimes misunderstood. In *Cabazon,* California was attempting to regulate gaming on Indian reservations under two legal theories. First, the state claimed that its gaming regulations were criminal/prohibitory and therefore applicable to tribes because California is a PL 280 state. PL 280 is a federal law allowing some states to apply their criminal laws to Indian reservations. The Supreme Court in *Cabazon* held that California could not use PL 280 to apply its gaming regulations on Indian reservations because they were civil/prohibitory and not criminal/prohibitory laws. Second, California asserted that even if its gaming regulations were considered civil/regulatory and not criminal/prohibitory, these laws should still apply to Indian reservations under the so-called preemption doctrine, because the state had an overriding interest in controlling organized crime on Indian reservations. Under the federal preemption doctrine, state law is not applicable on Indian reservations if it has been preempted by federal law. Whether state law has been preempted depends on: (1) whether it is incompatible with federal law or (2) whether tribal interest in self-government as reflected in federal law is stronger than the state's interest in applying its laws. Federal courts have stated that this type of test lends to a check-and-balance system, weighing the federal and tribal interests against state interests. In *Cabazon,* California did not make a good argument. The state could not prove that organized crime had infiltrated Indian gaming facilities. As a result, the balance of interest went in the tribe's favor.

But this does not mean that tribal interests will always prevail over those of the states. *Cabazon* was a six to three decision in which Chief Justice William Rehnquist sided with the majority. To make a long story short, I think that the Supreme Court has been slowly but surely eroding tribes' rights to be free of state jurisdiction. When comparing the 1832 Supreme Court case of *Worcester* v. *Georgia*, 31 US 515(1832), with the recent decision of *Cotton Petroleum* v. *New Mexico*, 490 US 163 (1989), it is clear that the balance between tribes and states has shifted. In the former case, the Court ruled that states have no jurisdiction whatsoever over Indian Country; in the latter, the justices held that states can tax non-Indians who are leasing tribal lands for the purpose of producing oil. It seems to me that, of late, states have won 90 percent of the time.

I was working on Capitol Hill for Congressman Moe Udall in the early 1980s and, faced with this erosion of tribal rights concerning state jurisdiction, we thought that perhaps *Cabazon* was going to be decided against Indian gaming interests. So Udall introduced the first version of what was to become eventually the Indian Gaming Regulatory Act (IGRA). At that time it was a very simple bill. Its only purpose was to ensure that gaming would be authorized as long as it was conducted pursuant to a tribal ordinance approved by the secretary of the Interior. The purpose of the bill was to secure a federal law that would preempt any state attempt to impose its gaming laws on Indian reservations. I think the Nevada delegation, however, put a hold on Udall's bill once it reached the Senate, thus preventing its enactment.

Then 1988 came around and the Court ruled in favor of the Indians in *Cabazon*. Suddenly, the anti-Indian-gaming constituent, who were initially against any gaming bill, became supportive of some kind of Indian gaming legislation. The Senate went into high gear to pass the bill. Of course, by then, many tribes were against it. In fact, some of them did not want the act to begin with. The gaming bill, which eventually became IGRA, passed through the Senate in 1988. The Senate bill sped through the House of Representatives without referral to any committee. Consequently, it passed the House without any amendments.

There is a reason we on the House side agreed to IGRA. As some people say, "In Congress, money talks." At that time, the lobbying interests against Indian gaming were very powerful and we did not think we had the votes to improve the Senate bill in the House. That's why Udall agreed to a procedure through which the Senate bill was not referred to any House committee, but was "stopped at the Speaker's desk," agreed to by the House, and sent to the president for his signature.

I am recounting all this because I think that tribes need to understand that the legislative forum may not be as favorable as it appears. This is why I have been concentrating not on legislative solutions, but on administrative resolutions. That, of course, means pursuing the secretary of the Interior and convincing him or her to issue the "gaming procedures" provided under IGRA. I want to make several points about getting the secretary to issue these gaming procedures.

As some of you may know, under IGRA, a state's failure to negotiate a Class III gaming compact in good faith with a tribe may lead to a tribal lawsuit against the state in federal court. If the federal judge finds that the state has indeed failed to negotiate in good faith, he can appoint a mediator who can recommend a compact. If the state refuses to accept the mediator's compact, the matter is referred to the secretary of the Interior who has to issue gaming procedures for the conduct of gaming on that reservation.

However, in *Seminole Tribe* v. *Florida*, 116 S. Ct. 1114 (1996), the Supreme Court held that because of the Eleventh Amendment of the Constitution, Congress could not abrogate the states' sovereign immunity so as to allow tribes to sue states in federal court. The first problem, therefore, is one related to the so-called severability doctrine. In other words, if the Court declares one part of a congressional act unconstitutional, this part may be severed from the remainder of the act or, in some cases, the whole act may be declared unconstitutional. The question then remains, can the secretary of the Interior still issue gaming procedures at a tribe's request despite the fact that the tribes can no longer sue the states in federal court?

The severability test devised by the Supreme Court is a two-part test. First, any unconstitutional part of an act may be severed from the rest of the act as long as the remaining portion of that act is "functionally independent" from the stricken provision. The second portion of the test consists of figuring whether or not Congress would have enacted the remainder of the section without the unconstitutional portion. This requires that courts do a lot of mental gymnastics in regard to congressional intent.

The secretary of the Interior was troubled with this issue and issued an advance notice of proposed rule-making asking for the public's opinion. I read this record. Most if not all of the tribes took the position that they could go directly to the secretary of the Interior and ask for the gaming procedures. Most if not all of the state attorney generals said that the secretary could not issue such procedures and that, if the states invoke their sovereign immunity, the tribes are just out of luck. The states' position is that the *Seminole* decision did not sever anything from IGRA. The only thing it did was deprive the tribes of one major solution: the right to sue the states in federal court.

There is a third position not advocated by anyone in particular but suggested by Justice Ruth Bader Ginsberg during the oral argument in the *Seminole* case. This position is that, as a result of *Seminole,* all parts of IGRA dealing with tribal-state compacts and Class III gaming should be severed from the act. This would mean that when it comes to Class III gaming—everything but bingo and certain card games—we would revert back to the law under the *Cabazon* decision. This is why *Cabazon* is still important. While I think *Cabazon* is a favorable decision for tribes, I am not sure whether this particular Court would decide this case the same way today. The attempt to balance state and federal/tribal interests under the preemption doctrine could lead to some very unpredictable results.

A return to *Cabazon* also means that slot machines would again be prohibited. This was one of the hidden or lesser known benefits of IGRA. It waived the Johnson Act's prohibition on slot machines. Some tribes' gaming operations are not financially possible without the slots. This is why very few tribal gaming advocates suggest a return to *Cabazon.*

I've written an article for the *Arizona State University Law Review* suggesting that the secretary does have the authority to issue these gaming regulations despite *Seminole.* I argue that he possesses such authority under IGRA supplemented by sections 2 and 9 of Title 25.

Under Section 2, the commissioner of Indian affairs shall, under the direction of the secretary of the Interior, manage all Indian affairs and matters arising from Indian relations. Section 9 basically states that the president may prescribe such regulations as he sees fit for carrying into effect the various provisions of any act relating to Indian affairs and for the settlement of the accounts of Indian affairs.

The fact that some states may invoke sovereign immunity does not mean that they are abiding by federal law. Under federal law, the tribes have a right to negotiate a Class III gaming compact with the state in good faith. In order to enforce this right, the secretary should be able to issue gaming procedures so that tribes can conduct gaming on their reservations when a state has failed to negotiate in good faith but will not allow itself to be sued in federal court. Of course, this is not a sure thing—the law of severability is complicated.

The last part of my paper takes the position that the secretary not only can issue those regulations, but also has a duty to do it in order to protect the tribes' rights to Class III gaming on their reservations. I know that this position presents an uphill battle because it involves many laws that invest a considerable amount of discretion in the secretary to remain inactive. In other words, it is very hard when an agency refuses to do anything to make the agency move. I think, however, that when you look at the law, there is some sound argument that can and should be made by the tribes in order to force the secretary to issue these gaming procedures in the event he is reluctant to do so.

Let me mention one last thing concerning what I believe to be the best way to resolve the dilemma tribes face in the wake of *Seminole*. The best solution would be for Attorney General Janet Reno and the Justice Department to agree to sue the states on behalf of the tribes in federal district court whenever the states are guilty of not negotiating with the tribes in good faith. I do not believe that legislation is necessary to allow her to sue states on behalf of tribes. Legislation may be necessary, however, to force her to litigate on behalf of the tribes if she does not want to do it willingly. This is so because her decision to undertake litigation or not is almost plenary. So this is the problem with that particular solution.

I also want to mention that the secretary's decision to issue those gaming procedures does not mean that the gaming tribes will be automatically pleased with these procedures. Most people who have dealt with the Bureau of Indian Affairs and the secretary of Interior know that they do not always do what you want them to do. When I went over all of the records in the advance notice of proposed rule-making, I found that the states' attorney generals believe that the secretary of the Interior cannot be trusted because he will always be biased in favor of the tribes since he is the tribes' trustee. In effect, the attorney generals took the position that the secretary was not going to respect their rights and interests. I think there is no reason to believe that this will be the case. I do not believe that the secretary of the Interior will come up with gaming procedures that allow tribes to do anything they want without taking into consideration the states' concerns and interests.

One of the things that the secretary may well decide to do is adopt a position on the "scope of gaming" issue that would be closer to the ninth circuit decision in *Rumsey* v. *Wilson*, 64 F.3d 1250 (Ninth Circuit, 1994) than the second circuit position in *Mashantucket Pequot* v. *Connecticut*, 913 F.2d 1024 (Second Circuit, 1990). If you'll recall, the *Rumsey* court took the position that a state can compact for some Class III gaming without having to allow all Class III games. The second circuit adopted a different position, holding that tribes had the right to negotiate with a state on any Class III game which, based on the same type of analysis the Court used in *Cabazon*, was not against the public policy of the state.

Contrary to what the *Rumsey* court stated, the law is ambiguous on this issue. People could go either way in regard to the scope of gaming issue and still not be wrong. I think there is some ambiguity in the act; both the *Mashantuckett* and the *Rumsey* decisions are reasonable.

Indian Gaming: The State's View

Thomas Gede

As a representative of the executive branch of the state of California, I have been the target of occasional criticism in regard to the Indian gaming question. A degree of criticism of the state of California by tribes may be warranted, given the state's fairly sordid history concerning the treatment of Indians for the past 150 years. I personally hope current state policy will overcome the historical record with more positive developments in tribal-state relations. Certainly, there are legislative means to improve these relations.

Some of the views I have expressed at previous tribal fora have been unpopular, and some of my comments here may fall into the same category. I disagree with the premise that resistance to Indian gaming in California is based on a perceived threat to tribal political power, cultural or racial antagonism, or an effort to thwart tribal economic development. Quite to the contrary, much of the dispute over Indian gaming turns on the question of what constitutes lawful gambling and its place in criminal law, rather than its role as an instrument of political power or economic development.

Resolving the question of the legal nature of gambling is no easy task. Gambling has occupied a unique niche in criminal law and law enforcement. It has always been at the crossroads between civil and criminal law. Unlike milling rice or making shoes, gambling does not resemble other kinds of economic activities. The only commodity in gambling is cash. The predominant role of cash in gambling activities presents problems that do not typically accompany other economic ventures. From the perspective of those in law enforcement, gambling presents problems that must be addressed by the legislative, executive, and judicial agencies throughout the state. Specifically, gambling activities carry a high risk of money laundering, loan sharking, tax evasion, and other sophisticated financial crimes. Drug traffickers, for example, may use gambling establishments in place of more regulated economic activities in order to avoid the reporting and record keeping requirements applicable to those activities.

Given the problematic nature of gambling, there are some very legitimate concerns that state and local governments may express in good faith—these concerns are not meant as attacks on tribal sovereignty. Both the federal and state legislatures have developed approaches to these concerns, and perhaps it is no surprise that a great deal of litigation has ensued.[1] Notwithstanding this plethora of litigation, however, certain issues have persisted. One of the most important is whether, under the Indian Gaming Regulatory Act of 1988 (IGRA), Indian gaming includes within its scope activity that is prohibited as a matter of criminal law within a state.[2]

This recurrent issue is driven by relevant case law, which tells us that the criminal jurisdiction of states that have assumed jurisdiction over Indian land to enforce their criminal laws on that land exceeds the civil jurisdiction over that land.[3] The issue thus becomes whether gambling laws are civil/regulatory or criminal/prohibitory.[4] This issue is particularly important for states such as California, Oklahoma, Washington, Alabama, Florida, and New Mexico, where there are clear criminal prohibitions against certain gambling activities. The real flash points in these states are over questions relating to those specific games and specific activities in the gambling field for which there is a state law criminal prohibition. This is complicated by how courts distinguish between criminal/prohibitory and civil/regulatory laws. Courts have held that the subject matter of criminal/prohibitory laws is that which runs afoul of public policy and is illegal under all circumstances.[5] The subject matter of civil/regulatory laws, on the other hand, does not plainly implicate such policy considerations, and is not all-inclusively illegal.[6] Therefore, much of the litigation has turned on what general public policy considerations are implicated by gambling activities, such as whether a state can prohibit certain gambling activities while allowing others, and thus whether the state regulates the field. These legal questions ultimately brought Indian gaming issues into federal court.

This development was unfortunate. Neither the tribes nor the states wanted to watch their resources disappear as lawyers endlessly went before the courts filing appeals while these issues slowly progressed through the judiciary. By 1993, the governors of the several states passed by a vote of forty-nine to one a resolution that urged Congress to consider modifying IGRA with certain key amendments.[7] The amendment principally urged by the National Governors Association was a "game-specific" rule.[8] Under this rule, tribal-state negotiations would follow the state's law with respect to *each* game. Thus, if the state criminalizes a particular gambling activity, that criminal prohibition would be respected in negotiations. The fact that the state permits a state lottery would not necessarily open the door to banking or casino style games. This was particularly important for those states that ran a state lottery, but did not permit casino gambling. Senator John McCain himself openly asked at a 1993 session of the Indian Affairs Committee: if a state operated a state lottery, would that open the door to all casino type games? At the time, the question could not be answered.

By 1993, Senator Daniel K. Inouye, chair of the Indian Affairs Committee, and Senator McCain, the vice chairperson, formed a task force to develop a consensus on IGRA amendments. This began a process of negotiations that dragged through all of 1993. I served as one of the states' representatives in the negotiations. During the course of these talks, which occurred in several locations ranging from Albuquerque to Washington, DC, we drafted many proposals that we thought would overcome diverse concerns, such as the implications of the Tenth and Eleventh Amendments[9] and issues of retroactivity.[10] Still other concerns appeared, such as questions regarding the effect of contemporaneous changes in state law.

These negotiations proved difficult and, at times, grueling. Nonetheless, the process was initially fruitful, and Inouye and McCain indicated that they looked forward to further progress. Such optimism was short-lived. By the end of 1993, the negotiations slowed over the issue of electronic gambling devices. This issue was critical to the states that prohibited slot machines and electronic or video gambling. We could not come to a resolution on the issue. Simply put, the tribes wanted to have gambling devices in states that prohibited them. Ultimately, this blocked further progress, and the negotiations came to a halt by the beginning of 1994.

Despite the stalemate, several drafts of legislation were developed by the task force.[11] In Congress, however, there was no consensus on the issue. By the time McCain became chairman of the Indian Affairs Committee following the November 1994 elections, the process of amending IGRA came to a standstill.

In March of 1996, Senate Bill 487 (S 487) was introduced by Senator McCain.[12] This bill essentially derived from earlier drafts that came out of the task force, although it rejected some of the state proposals. Since the bill was introduced shortly before the court's decision in *Seminole Tribe* v. *Florida,* it did not contemplate the issues raised by that case. At any rate, it failed to get to the Senate floor in September of 1996.[13]

S 487 did not make a change in the existing tribal-state compact process, which mandates state involvement in negotiations with a tribe upon the tribe's request.[14] This inaction was in distinct contrast to an earlier version of the bill that Senator Inouye had proposed, S 2230, which sought to use the compacting process as an incentive to the state to be involved in what would be an otherwise federal-tribal process.[15] The principal relationship under the Constitution is a federal-tribal one, and under S 2230, the process would have been essentially federal-tribal. If a state wanted to be involved, it could "opt in."[16] This approach avoided the Tenth and Eleventh Amendments problems inherent with mandating state involvement.[17] S 2230 faced strong tribal opposition and, in a surprise move, Inouye and McCain introduced a substitute amendment on 16 August 1994 that removed the scope of gaming clarifications, definitions, categories, and limitations. Governors expressed their disappointment in these developments.

By the time S 487 passed out of the Senate Indian Affairs Committee on 9 August 1995, the improved "opt-in" compacting proposal had been dropped and S 487 returned to the original compacting process. That process begins when the tribe makes a request for negotiations for a Class III gaming compact upon the state. The state is thereafter obligated to negotiate. IGRA permits a tribe to sue a state in federal court if it believes the state has failed to negotiate or has not done so in good faith. If the court finds the state did not negotiate in good faith, a federal mediator may require the state to accept the last best offer from the negotiations. If the state refuses, the secretary of the Interior ultimately shall intervene.[18] Now, in light of *Seminole,* if the state raises the Eleventh Amendment, the federal court process comes to an end.[19] Of course, if the state consents to suit in federal court, the process may proceed.[20]

Despite the absence of the opt-in compacting provisions, S 487 retained other key provisions of the earlier drafts. One of the governors' requests in the 1993 resolution retained in S 487 was that the good faith burden be equalized—both the tribes and the states should be expected to proceed in good faith.[21] Another provision retained in S 487 provided that the publication of a tribal-state compact would be conclusive evidence that the gaming activity was subject to negotiation.[22] The states opposed that provision because they were convinced that this still had to meet IGRA's scope of gaming requirement.[23]

The scope of gaming requirement in S 487 mirrored the existing requirement under IGRA, except for one additional provision, namely that the scope of gaming provision in IGRA follow the rule established in *California* v. *Cabazon Band of Mission Indians*.[24] Under this rule, the public policy of the state regarding gambling would be examined. If a state criminalizes any type of gambling, the courts would look to see if gambling is illegal throughout the entire state or, on the other hand, if the state permitted some gambling and, therefore, "regulates" the field of gambling.[25] The states had long opposed introducing that standard into IGRA, and instead favored a "game specific" standard. Under such a standard, if state law places a clear criminal prohibition on any specific gaming activity, that prohibition would not be eviscerated by the fact that the state permitted, in other forms, different gaming activities.[26]

The gubernatorial concurrence requirement for secretarial approval of off-reservation gambling on newly acquired lands was another key issue in S 487. The governors were very concerned by the IGRA provision allowing gaming on lands acquired after the effective date of the act—1988—if the land is off, and not contiguous to, the reservation. As a response, S 487 requires the state governor to concur with the secretary that such land be subject to tribal gaming activities.[27]

In fact, IGRA, as currently written, gives the governor power to effectively veto the secretary's determinations regarding gaming activities on after-acquired land off the reservation. Specifically, the secretary must find that the gaming on that land would further the purposes of the tribe, not be detrimental to a neighboring tribe, and not be detrimental to the surrounding community.[28] The governor must then concur in this latter finding.[29] If the governor does not concur with the secretary's finding that the gaming would not be detrimental to the surrounding community, the law will not authorize gaming and the tribe is prohibited from using those after-acquired lands for gaming.[30]

The federal district court for the district of Oregon found the gubernatorial concurrence provision unconstitutional under the Appointments Clause and Separation of Powers principles.[31] The ninth circuit court of appeals in *Confederated Tribe of Siletz Indians* v. *United States*[32] reversed the Oregon District Court's decision, finding the gubernatorial concurrence requirement merely a condition to be met under federal law.[33] Thus, the gubernatorial concurrence provision of IGRA is valid, and the coordinate provision of S 487 does not appear necessary.

There are currently two bills before the House of Representatives that would amend the provisions of IGRA. HR 334, Gerald B. H. Solomon's bill, is generally viewed as the pro-state bill.[34] Esteban E. Torres' bill, HR 452, is generally viewed as the pro-tribal bill.[35] However, neither of these bills, nor any similar bill, will likely pass. Any pro-tribal bill that does not respect the concerns of the governors and the states will face insurmountable opposition on the floor. Conversely, given the tribes' considerable political power and respect from the Senate Indian Affairs Committee, any pro-state bill that does not accord sufficient respect to the tribes also will not survive. Indeed, the relationship of the powers and the interest groups in the House is such that neither a completely pro-tribal bill nor a completely pro-state bill would likely succeed. To put it simply, it is doubtful anything significant will emerge from the House.

As to developments in California law, if state law governs the question of the state's obligation to negotiate for a compact, California is under an obligation to negotiate only for lottery games.[36] Further, the California Supreme Court has made it clear that lottery games and banking games are mutually exclusive.[37] Whether electronic technology can be used for the purpose of a lottery is unresolved. On the one hand, the state prohibits slot machines, and a slot machine is very broadly defined so that a lottery could be played on a prohibited device such as a slot machine.[38] Conversely, some lottery vending devices arguably may not be prohibited gambling devices.[39] The question thus arises, where an electronic device could play a lottery, would that device be a slot machine in violation of state law? Negotiations have continued to deal with this question.

The legislature has the opportunity to examine these questions as well. It could, with the governor's signature, enact laws that allow the lottery to use devices that would otherwise be in violation of the slot machine prohibition, as long as they play lotteries. Because the California State Supreme Court held that a banking game and a lottery are mutually exclusive, a slot machine that operates as a banking game cannot be the subject of negotiations. However, a slot machine that plays a lottery under state legislation that authorizes such a machine may be on the table as a permitted game. State law that permits a lottery to be played in a certain way would then govern the subject of negotiations, and that would carry forth in a compact.[40]

Perhaps the most critical issue in California is whether a compact actually requires legislative approval or whether state law governs on the question of who speaks for the state in Indian gaming negotiations. The state, as unpopular as it is with the Indian tribes, is a sovereign and a partner with the federal sovereign. Somebody must speak for the state, and, in California, the governor represents the supreme executive power of the state. It would be wise to clarify that the governor speaks for the state in tribal-state negotiations under IGRA. Such legislation would forestall litigation and foster considerable progress on this question.

However, this question, like all the questions I have discussed, is the subject of considerable debate and is by no means settled. As we seek answers to these questions, our duty to discuss these issues sincerely rises to a level of unquestionable importance. It is for this reason that I am grateful for this opportunity, and encourage similar dialogue in the future.

NOTES

1. See Conference of Western Attorneys General, ed., *American Indian Law Deskbook*, second ed. (Boulder: University of Colorado, 1994), 338–376.

2. See Public Law No. 100–497, 102d sess., 102 Stat. 2467 (1988) (codified at 18 USC sections 1166–1168 and 25 USC sections 2701–2721).

3. The relevant jurisdictional statute is Public Law 280, Act of 15 August 1953, Public Law No. 90–280, 67 Stat 588 (codified at 18 USC section 1162, 25 USC sections

1321–1325 and 28 USC section 1360), which establishes state jurisdiction over Indian Country. This jurisdiction is mandatory for six states, including California, and is voluntary for all additional states. As interpreted, a state exercising Public Law 280 jurisdiction may enforce state laws that are "criminal prohibitory," but not ones that are "civil regulatory." See *California v Cabazon Band of Mission Indians*, 480 US 202, 213–14 (1987) (holding that Congress did not intend to grant state jurisdiction over civil matters within Indian Country); see also *United States v Cook*, 922 F.2d 1026, 1034 (Second Circuit, 1991) (applying civil/regulatory and criminal/prohibitory distinction in prosecution).

4. 480 US, 214.

5. See, for example, *Seminole Tribe v Butterworth*, 658 F.2d 310, 314 (Second Circuit, 1991):

> Although the inclusion of penal sanctions makes it tempting at first glance to classify the statute as prohibitory, the statute cannot be automatically classified as such. A simplistic rule depending on whether the statute includes penal sanctions could result in the conversion of every regulatory statute into a prohibitory one. The classification of the statute is more complex, and requires a consideration of the public policy of the state on the issue of bingo and the intent of the legislature in enacting the bingo statute.

6. Ibid.

7. See National Governors Association (NGA) Policy on Indian Gaming, 2 February 1993.

8. Ibid.

9. Potential Tenth Amendment problems are created by IGRA's provision mandating the state to negotiate upon the tribe's request. See *New York v United States*, 505 US 144, 162 (1992). Further, the fact that the tribe may bring a suit in federal court against the state, based on the state's noncompliance with IGRA, raises Eleventh Amendment problems. See *Seminole Tribe v Florida*, 116 S.Ct 1114, 1116 (1996).

10. US Constitution, Art. 1, section 9.

11. US Senate bill number 1035, introduced 19 April 1993; US Senate bill number 2230, introduced 7 June 1994; HR 1512, introduced 7 April 1995.

12. See US Senate bill number 487, the Indian Gaming Regulatory Act Amendments of 1995, introduced 2 March 1995 by Senator McCain.

13. 116 S.Ct. 1114 (1996).

14. See Public Law No. 100–497, 102d sess., 102 Stat. 2467 (1988) (codified at 18 USC sections 1166-1168 and 25 USC sections 2701-2721).

15. S 2230, introduced by Senator Inouye 22 June 1994, the "Indian Gaming Regulatory Act Amendments Act of 1994."

16. US Constitution, Art. IV, section 3.

17. See *New York v United States*, 505 US 144, 162 (1992) (federal government cannot compel state action) and *Seminole Tribe v Florida*, 116 S.Ct 1114, 1116 (1996) (Congress may only abrogate Eleventh Amendment pursuant to Section 5 of Fourteenth Amendment).

18. See 25 USC section 2710(d)(8).

19. *Seminole Tribe* holds that the Eleventh Amendment bar to suits against the state

in federal court cannot be abrogated by Congress under the Commerce Clause of the US Constitution. Ibid., 1116. Since IGRA was enacted pursuant to Congress' federal commerce power (25 USC section 2703), the state may invoke the Eleventh Amendment as a defense to federal jurisdiction, thus defeating the mandatory negotiation provision of IGRA.

20.   Contrary to the views of some commentators, *Seminole Tribe* did not undo the federal court process. Under *Seminole Tribe*, if the state raises the Eleventh Amendment as a jurisdictional defense to a suit by a tribe in federal court, the process is barred only in that case. See 116 S.Ct. at 1119. Thus, the Eleventh Amendment issue is relevant only when the state invokes it. The state may consent to the lawsuit and submit itself to federal jurisdiction, which empowers the federal court to rule on whether the state negotiated in good faith. Ibid., 1121.

21.   See US Senate bill number 487, The Indian Gaming Regulatory Act Amendments of 1995, introduced 3 March 1995 by Senator McCain.

22.   Ibid.

23.   See *Rumsey Indian Rancheria of Wintun Indians* v *Wilson*, 41 F.3d 421, 429 (Ninth Circuit, 1994) (discussing scope of gaming).

24.   480 US 202 (1987).

25.   Ibid., 213–214.

26.   Ultimately, this standard was adopted as a clear reading of the existing law under IGRA, first by the eighth circuit court of appeals in *Cheyenne River Sioux* v *South Dakota*, 3 F.3d 273, 278 (Eighth Circuit, 1993) ("IGRA does not require the state to negotiate with respect to forms of gaming it does not presently permit"). By 1994, the ninth circuit court of appeals agreed in *Rumsey Indian Rancheria of Wintun Indians* v *Wilson, supra*, 1258 n.22. cert. denied sub. nom. *Sycuan Band of Mission Indians* v *Wilson*, 521 US 1118, 117 S. Ct. 2508 (1997) ("IGRA does not require a state to negotiate over one form of gaming activity simply because it legalized another, albeit similar form of gaming"; "[A] state need only allow Indian tribes to operate games that others can operate, but need not give tribes what others cannot have").

27.   Ibid.

28.   See 25 USC section 2703. See also *Policy for Placing Lands Trust Status for American Indians*, Memo. From Secretary of Interior to Assistant Secretary of Interior Indian Affairs dated 19 July 1990; see also *Off Reservation Land Acquisitions for Indian Tribes*, 56 Fed. Reg. 32,278 (1991).

29.   See 25 USC section 2703.

30.   Ibid.

31.   *See Confederated Tribe of Siletz* v *United States*, 841 F.Supp 1479 (D. Oregon 1995).

32.   110 F.3d 688 (Ninth Circuit, 1997).

33.   See ibid., 692. In an opinion authored by Chief Judge Hug, the court held that the governors' authority does not rise to an unconstitutional level, is exercised only episodically, and, as an exercise of state authority, derives from state law. In IGRA, held the court of appeals, Congress fashioned conditional legislation, with consent to gaming on newly acquired lands dependent on various events including gubernatorial approval (ibid).

34.   See House of Representatives bill number 452, 105th session, introduced 21 January 1997 by Representative Torres.

35. See House of Representatives bill number 334, 105th session, introduced 7 January 1997 by Representative Solomon.

36. In *Western Telecon, Inc.* v *California State Lottery*, the California Supreme Court invalidated the then-operating California Keno game as an unlawful banking game. The court held that, as a matter of state law, the state lottery could operate only lottery games and that lottery games and banking games are mutually exclusive under statutory law and well-understood definitions, 917 P.2d 651, 657 (Cal. 1996). In *Rumsey Indian Rancheria of Wintun Indians* v *Wilson*, the Ninth Circuit held that IGRA requires states only to allow the tribes to operate games that others can operate, 41 F.3d 421, 427 (Ninth Circuit, 1994), amended, 64 F.3d 1250 (Ninth Circuit, 1994).

37. See *Western Telecon*, 917 P.2d at 657. See generally William E. Horwitz, Note, *Scope of Gaming Under the Indian Gaming Regulatory Act of 1988 After* Rumsey v. Wilson: *White Buffalo or Brown Cow?* 14 Cardozo Arts & Entertainment L.J. 153 (1996) (summarizing decisional authority).

38. See Cal. Pen. Code section 330a, prohibiting "any slot or card machine,… or mechanical device, [in which] money or other valuable thing is staked."

39. See Cal. Pen. Code section 319, defining a "lottery" as:

> any scheme for the disposal or distribution of property by chance, among persons who have paid or promised to pay any valuable consideration for the chance of obtaining such property or a portion of it,… upon any agreement … that it is to be distributed or disposed of by lot or chance.

40. A bill by Senator Polanco, currently before the state senate, would achieve this result (Cal. Senate Bill 1067, introduced 27 February 1997). Senator Polanco has another bill that would amend the state constitution to allow casino gambling for the purposes of Indian gaming only (Cal. Senate Const. Amend. 21, introduced 13 September 1997). The constitutional amendment requires a two-thirds vote by both the Senate and Assembly, and then majority vote by the people of the State. (See Cal. Const., Art. XVIII, section 1.) Another relevant bill was introduced by Cruz Bustamante and Curt Pringle in the state assembly. This bill simply authorized the governor to speak for the state in Indian gaming negotiations (A.B. 1442, introduced 28 February 1997 by Representative Bustamante and Representative Pringle).

♠

Community Prospects

Educating Local Non-Indian Communities About Indian Nation Governmental Gaming: Messages and Methods[1]

Katherine A. Spilde

In his recent novel, *Tropical Depression*, Laurence Shames utilizes popular stereotypes about Indian nation gaming and identity to tell the story of Tommy Tarpon, the only surviving member of the fictional Matalatchee tribe in Florida.[2] Shames' book reads like a laundry list of Indian gaming stereotypes, complete with dirty politicians, Mafia gangsters, bug-infested tribal land, federal recognition scams (including a field representative from the Bureau of Indian Affairs wearing khaki pants and a pith helmet), and tax-free business opportunities. This array of characters and characterizations frames the novel's plot, in which a state senator and his mob friend exploit Tommy's tribal identity and his tribal claim to a small island.

The non-Indians in Shames' book offer Tommy federal acknowledgement for his one-person tribe. These crooks persuade Tommy to seek federal recognition so that he may reclaim his ancestral homeland, an island off the coast of Key West. There, the senator and his friends plan to open a casino and put Tommy to work. He grudgingly goes along with the plan but later sets the crooks up by exposing them to a newspaper reporter who reveals the scam to the public.

In addition to those mentioned above, the book plays into non-Native assumptions regarding Indian nation gaming, including beliefs that tribal people are a front for Mafia-run businesses, that they do not pay taxes, and that their identity is often manipulated for political purpose (by both Indians and non-Indians). The most insidious stereotype, however, is the insinuation that tribal people cannot handle the intricacies of federal recognition, land management, and casinos on their own.

These popular images of tribal government gaming and Native American identity constitute the most difficult hurdles to jump in educating local non-Indian communities about Indian nation gaming and economic development. Because of their proximity to Native communities, non-Indians living near Indian casinos often feel that they understand the realities of Native American life. Unlike the majority of Americans, whose perceptions of contemporary Native American realities are shaped primarily by feature films, frontier ideology, and "vanishing Indian" narratives, non-Indians living on or near reservations have frequent, firsthand interaction with Native people. These interactions often produce a sense of common ground. Non-Indians feel that they know about reservation life. However, what they know about Indian nation governmental gaming is often embedded in their own cultural background, economic class, and public discourses.

On 23 May 1992, the Shooting Star Casino opened its doors in Mahnomen, Minnesota, less than one-half mile from my childhood home. By most accounts, this event was a joyful moment for residents in and around this small community (population 1,200) on the White Earth Reservation in northwestern Minnesota. Residents of Mahnomen and the surrounding communities watched in anticipation as the White Earth Nation, along with a management company, Gaming World International, erected a $16 million gambling facility on the south side of town.

Six months prior to the grand opening, a temporary casino was established in the Golden Eagle Bingo Lodge in South Mahnomen, giving the community a small taste of what was to come. Limousines and tour buses were a new sight in town. A housing shortage resulted from an influx of new and potential employees. Lights glowed in and near the building twenty-four hours a day, seven days a week.

Local newspapers followed the construction of the permanent casino closely. The grand opening event was covered by most newspapers within a one-hundred-mile radius. The new casino promised jobs, entertainment, tourism, and increased revenue for city and county governments and businesses. Tribal leaders hired local contractors, purchased supplies from community businesses, and moved the tribal council from White Earth Village (twenty miles away) to a new building in downtown Mahnomen.

However, in spite of all the press about the casino's promise of economic development and jobs, there was no local public discourse regarding Native sovereignty issues. Furthermore, there was no analysis of the broader context in which Indian nation governmental gaming developed in the United States, the state of Minnesota, or the region. Such a local emphasis on the Shooting Star Casino's impact on Mahnomen overlooked the national debates surrounding Indian nation sovereignty, the federal trust relationship, and the Indian Gaming Regulatory Act. This public oversight still exists at the local and regional levels.

I returned home to Minnesota in 1996 as a graduate student in anthropology to document the many changes that have occurred in Mahnomen and other reservation communities on the White Earth Reservation. I was particularly interested in potential changes in the relationship between the Indian and non-Indian communities at White Earth given the shift in economic power brought by the casino.

As part of my ethnographic research, I interviewed a spectrum of individuals, including casino employees, patrons, and management as well as tribal government officials, long-term community residents, returning and new residents, city and county government officials, school personnel, law enforcement, and local business owners. I also kept in daily contact with a wide range of community members since I had grown up in Mahnomen and people were curious about my research. However, as I asked questions about the casino, I was in turn questioned in patterned ways. Many non-Indians I talked with wanted to know if I supported the Indians' "right" to have a casino. I found a lot of interest in gaming and the controversies surrounding it.

In contrast to the myriad articles and editorials published locally about the 1996 White Earth trial, in which three tribal council members were convicted by a federal court for embezzlement, there was a profound lack of discussion regarding the particulars of Indian nation governmental gaming, including its history and social context. Local newspapers, especially *The Fargo Forum*, were the main source of information on gaming and tribal issues for most people. The state-wide fascination with the White Earth trial left an informational gap in regard to the basic context of Indian nation gaming and fueled misconceptions about the integrity of Indian nation governmental gaming.

Throughout the course of my fieldwork, I was questioned routinely about my view of the casino. Over time, I came to realize that people were searching for more than my personal opinion; they wanted to understand why and how the local tribal government secured the "right" to build a casino in Mahnomen. There was a profound lack of understanding regarding federal Indian policy, tribal history, or any of the basics of the trust relationship.[3] This knowledge gap should not have surprised me, given my experiences there as a child. Despite having grown up and attended school on the reservation, I did not learn about Indian removal policies, reservation allotment swindles, tribal government reorganization schemes, and coercive relocation programs until I was in college. Many area residents did not have the luxury or interest to immerse themselves in federal Indian policy or tribal history. Local reactions to the tribal casino were grounded in a lack of understanding at best, and a deliberate misunderstanding at worst.

In order to bridge this gap, I found myself explaining the basics of sovereignty, the Indian Gaming Regulatory Act, the compact process, and other information about Indian nation governmental gaming that I had come to take for granted. Most of my information-sharing was with non-Indians living on or near the reservation. This process of education started casually on a one-on-one basis. Over time, I organized public discussions to answer people's questions and concerns on a group level. It is from this position, then, that I offer an outline of information that I think the public wants and needs to know in order to better discuss, debate, and vote on Indian nation governmental gaming issues. In some states, such as Nebraska and Florida, public support is crucial for the future of gaming. While gaming is not at a crossroads in Minnesota at this time, I believe there is a clear correlation between knowledge about the history and impacts of Indian nation governmental gaming and public support of gaming. This overview represents what I see as a basic foundation of knowledge about gaming that is essential for local communities with Indian nation governmental gaming facilities. I hope that better neighbors, more informed voters, and discriminating opinions will emerge.

MESSAGES

This outline contains the basic information local non-Indian communities want and deserve to know before they make decisions about Indian nation governmental gaming. Based on personal experiences in my home community, I can safely say that many non-Indians want to know more. Presenting this information in an outline format allows the reader to scan headings for major themes, and provides potential educators with a specific text from which to tailor presentations for other communities. I have labeled sections with provocative questions that could provide possible titles for public discussions.

What Are the Differences Between Indian Nation Governmental Gaming and Commercial Gaming?

It is important to distinguish between Indian nation governmental gaming and commercial gaming in order to clarify two major points and to introduce the rest of the presentation. The first point is that tribal casinos are run by Tribal governments in order to raise funds for tribal projects benefiting tribal members. Much like state governments use revenue from state lotteries to fund state projects, tribal governments invest their gaming proceeds into community projects. The 1988 Indian Gaming Regulatory Act stipulates that profits from casinos be used for five specific purposes, including economic development, social services, health care, and contributions to surrounding local governments.[4] This basic point is often lost in rhetoric that identifies Indians as an ethnic, racial, or special rights group, overlooking the fact that they are governments. The public perception continues to lean toward an emphasis on per capita payments and/or individual enrichment based on identity. The fact is that gaming is the exclusive right of tribal governments, not individual tribal members, and that proceeds are specifically geared toward economic development. Commercial gaming enterprises, on the other hand, benefit private investors and individuals. In addition, commercial gaming profits are not earmarked for specific causes or expenses, and can be freely invested by individuals.

The second distinction between tribal governments and commercial gaming businesses is that tribal governments have sovereign rights while commercial enterprises do not. However, making this point does not explain sovereign rights or how Indian nation governmental gaming fits into the history of tribal sovereignty. Emphasizing that a tribal government is the primary beneficiary of casino profits does not clarify why Native American nations are governments or what those governments do.

What Is Sovereignty? Why Does It Matter?

I usually start a discussion of sovereignty by talking about treaties specific to the local tribal community (in one case, I explained several Chippewa treaties involved with what came to be known as the White Earth Band). Treaties signed with European nations and later the United States guaranteed the tribes continued recognition and treatment as sovereigns. Many people do not know that the US Constitution institutionalized the political, or government-to-government, relationship between the federal government and Indian nations, and made that relationship distinct from that between the federal government and states or foreign nations.

I also provide an overview of the Marshall Trilogy in order to emphasize that the US Supreme Court has repeatedly recognized tribal sovereignty in court decisions for more than 160 years. A cursory understanding of the Marshall Trilogy provides a necessary foundation for understanding Indian nation sovereignty because these three cases clarified the relationship of Indian tribes vis-à-vis the federal government and states. For example, in 1831, the Supreme Court decided in *Cherokee Nation* v. *Georgia* that Indian nations had the full legal right to manage their own affairs, govern themselves internally, and engage in legal and political relationships with the federal government and its subdivisions.

My focus in defining the basic history of the federal trust relationship is political rights. Taking this approach is a deliberate attempt to avoid discussions of authenticity or modernism as it relates to Native identity. There is a peculiar form of racism that insists on certain appearances or behaviors as markers of Indianness. I do not want to enter into this type of debate, so I emphasize political and legal identity for these presentations and discussions.

This historical and legal information can be quite dense. My reason for providing a rich historical perspective is to emphasize that sovereign rights did not begin with gaming rights. Because Minnesota is a Public Law 280 state—meaning that the state could apply its criminal laws to Indian reservations—many people I speak with are unaware of the long history of a primarily federal-tribal relationship. Even the local newspaper printed an editorial asking the state of Minnesota to honor its treaties with tribes.[5] This lack of historical and legal context results in a misinformed public that is not able to fully comprehend the range of impacts generated by Indian nation gaming. In addition to the political context of gaming, most non-Indians are surprised to learn that the White Earth Nation has a formal constitution dating to 1913.

What Is the Indian Gaming Regulatory Act? Why Is It Controversial?

Starting with the 1987 decision in *California* v. *Cabazon*, in which the Supreme Court decided that California could not use PL 280 to apply its gaming regulations in Indian Country, I am able to provide perspective on the reactionary nature of the 1988 Indian Gaming Regulatory Act (IGRA). I emphasize that IGRA actually required tribes to surrender some measure of sovereignty to the states in order to exercise their federal right to run gaming establishments. The idea that tribes surrendered sovereignty, rather than the popular notion that IGRA granted special gaming rights to tribes, represents a major ideological shift for many people with whom I speak. The erosion of sovereignty encoded in IGRA is often lost in special rights rhetoric, wherein the historical basis of the federal trust relationship outlined above disappears and is replaced by an emphasis on contemporary racial or ethnic politics.

In the context of IGRA, I discuss the tribe's historical relationship with the state (including the regulatory/prohibitory distinction) and outline the compacting process. In addition, I talk about the three classes of gaming outlined in IGRA and the various levels of regulation associated with each class.

At White Earth, for the first five years, the Shooting Star Casino was managed by an outside management company from Pennsylvania. This company, along with the men who arrived in limousines to oversee the casino, were a great source of local speculation. A discussion of management contracts as codified in IGRA also led to an overview of the secretary of the Interior's role in Indian affairs, as well as a discussion of the National Indian Gaming Commission. I also discussed the levels of regulation required under IGRA. Many people worried about rumors that tribal casinos were unregulated. I assured them that no entity has a greater interest in protecting the integrity of Indian nation gaming than tribal governments. Indian gaming is subject to more stringent regulation and security controls than any other type of gaming in the United States. Indian nation gaming operations are regulated at three distinct levels: federal (through the National Indian Gaming Commission and federal government agencies such as the US Justice Department, the Treasury Department, and the Department of the Interior), state (through tribal-state compacts), and Indian nation (the Indian Gaming Regulatory Commissions).

What Are Common Myths and Misunderstandings about Indian Nation Governmental Gaming?

I find that, after an in-depth discussion of sovereignty and IGRA, many misunderstandings (for example, the idea that tribes have special rights or that tribal government gaming is unregulated) are already addressed. However, one of the most pervasive myths, and one not limited to gaming debates, is that Indians do not pay taxes. This notion is a particular sore point among non-Indian community members. For instance, most were shocked to learn that the White Earth Nation has paid nearly $850,000 annually in property taxes on the casino property, despite the fact that it is located within original reservation boundaries. In addressing the taxation issue, I outlined all the levels of taxes paid by the non-Indian casino employees, including federal income tax, Federal Insurance Contribution Act (FICA) payments, and unemployment insurance, among others. In addition, people did not know that all Indian people pay federal income, FICA, and social security taxes. It was not widely known that only the small percentage of Indians who live and work on their own federally recognized reservations—not unlike soldiers and their families living on military installations—are exempt from paying state income and property taxes. However, they still pay sales tax such and all other special and excise taxes.

Another myth (and one not limited to Minnesota communities) is that Indian nations are rich now that they run casinos. While White Earth community members, along with a scandal-hungry Minnesota public, had just witnessed the conviction and imprisonment of three White Earth tribal leaders for embezzlement and other charges, many non-Indians continued to believe that the tribal government had a surplus of earnings. It is important that the public know that less than one-third of the federally recognized tribes in the United States have some form of gaming operation (only 185 of 558 federally recognized tribes). In addition, the success of gaming establishments varies widely according to location, among other factors. For example, twenty Indian gaming facilities account for over 50 percent of the total Indian gaming revenue. Even with a total estimated revenue of $7.4 billion per year, Indian nation gaming revenues amount to only 10 percent of the entire gaming industry.

In addition to the notion that tribal governments are wealthy, there was a misconception that individual tribal members were receiving per capita payments from the tribal government.[6] This was not the case at White Earth and, in fact, out of the 185 tribal governments that have governmental gaming, only forty-seven have revenue allocation programs in place. Under the provisions of IGRA, tribal governments can only use gaming profits to give out per capita payments after it has been established by the Bureau of Indian Affairs that the five areas outlined in IGRA have been met and that they shall continue to be covered for the length of time that the tribe has asked to give out the per capita payments.[7]

Finally, there was a certain amount of discussion about the false idea that Indian culture would be destroyed by gaming. This was a popular concern in northern Minnesota, where some local newspapers and individuals disguised anti-Indian sentiments as anti-gambling morality or as concern for traditional tribal values. I normally address the question of tribal values with another question: "Why was no one concerned about the impact of poverty on Indian culture?"[8] I also emphasize that questions about the impact of casinos on tribal cultures should be answered by tribal members, not by concerned non-Indians.

Who Benefits from Tribal Government Gaming?

One major assumption in discussions of Indian nation governmental gaming is that only tribal members benefit from their casinos. The emphasis on tribal governments or tribal membership detracts from the numerous opportunities these casinos provide non-Indians. The most obvious benefit to White Earth communities, especially Mahnomen, has been jobs. For various historical and economic reasons, only 3,000 of White Earth's 22,000 enrolled members live on the reservation. Many of those 3,000 residents do not live near Mahnomen, the casino's site. Therefore, many jobs at the Shooting Star Casino are held by local non-Indians. While the ratio changes periodically, the casino employs approximately 60 percent non-Indians.[9] In Mahnomen, this means approximately six hundred new jobs were available to non-Indians once the casino opened.

In addition to jobs, tax revenues benefit Indians and non-Indians alike. In 1997, casino property taxes were projected to constitute 27 percent of the local school tax base, 41 percent of the city tax base, and 20 percent of the total tax base for Mahnomen County. This support is on top of the sales tax paid by casino patrons. Because of the Mahnomen area's new tourist industry, there has been a healthy increase in goods and services purchased locally. This influx of outsiders benefits business owners in the area, most of whom are non-Indian. Not only tourists spend their money in Mahnomen, however. Goods and services needed for the casino are purchased locally whenever possible and casino employees spend their paychecks in town. Interviews with local business owners were overwhelmingly positive. The mayor of Mahnomen, who owns a NAPA auto parts store in town, stated, "I can always tell when it is casino pay day. The drawer is stacked with fifties and hundreds."[10] Local examples, in particular, were helpful to local community understanding since everyone knew the person to whom I was referring.

I also pointed out the ways in which the tribal government at White Earth contributed to local charities and offered support for local causes. Again, the press did not cover these philanthropic stories faithfully, so this information was new to many people. This type of generosity is invaluable in gaining public support. However, it is imperative that the community know about it. For example, the tribal council presented a check for $148,000 to the Mahnomen hospital for the purchase of new equipment. They also sponsored events at the casino for the

Special Olympics, held fundraisers for local snowmobile clubs, and donated money towards food plots for feeding deer through the harsh winter months. Tribal money was invested in maintaining and improving the municipal golf course. During the 1997 flood in Grand Forks and surrounding communities, the Shooting Star Casino offered free lodging for flood victims. In addition, funding was provided for city and county workers whose work increased because of casino business.

Most people were interested in hearing about the impact of casino profits on their taxes. I emphasized that taxpayer burdens have gone down due to a decrease in welfare rolls in the state. The fact is that social service costs are reduced if tribal governments are allowed to be self-sufficient.

Where Do Proceeds Go and Why?

Many non-Indians (as well as many tribal members) in the White Earth area focused on one major question: where does the money go? While I did not feel I had the authority to answer this question fully, I did outline some of the more obvious costs and responsibilities of the tribal government.[11] For example, the tribal government produces and edits its own newspaper, *Anishinaabeg Today*, which is distributed free to all enrolled members. Copies of this paper are distributed to all post office boxes in Mahnomen as well, so most non-Indian community members are familiar with it. The tribal government pays management and administrative costs as well as personnel and payroll. In addition, it is funding new health care and community centers. Many of these projects were unfolding in nearby towns where tribal members constitute the majority of the population. This explains why many non-Indians were unaware of the new structures.

Finally, I emphasize that most casino proceeds go back into the casino as either winnings or as payroll, upkeep, maintenance, administration, or the like. I find that many people do not consider that a large percentage of money wagered is given back to customers as winnings. A large number of people I speak with do not think of the casino as redistributing money, but as merely taking in money. Finally, a discussion of profits reinforces the distinction between tribal government gaming and commercial gaming. While commercial gaming provides profits for individuals to invest as they wish, tribal governments are the primary beneficiaries of gaming profits that are meant to benefit all tribal members.

Are There Any Gaming Success Stories?

The message I convey at White Earth is that tribal success benefits everyone in the community. For example, the White Earth tribe held a ribbon-cutting ceremony at the opening of the new health clinic and invited city government officials. When it opened a new community center, city government participated in the event in order to highlight its cooperation with the tribe in job creation on the reservation. The city and tribe both invested in a new industrial park in Mahnomen with hopes of drawing new business to the reservation and expanding job options for all community members. These cooperative endeavors provide important reminders that tribal government gaming benefits everyone—not just tribal members. Proximity to tribal communities does not ensure participation in tribal social or community events by Indians or non-Indians. I often encourage non-Indians to attend the tribal events advertised in their paper.

What Are Common Community Concerns about Gaming?

National and local people often raise concerns regarding the relationship between Indian nation governmental gaming and problem, or pathological, gambling. While this concern is often used to make anti-Indian statements under the guise of morality arguments, pointing out this correlation is not always useful for educational purposes.[12] When this concern was raised at White Earth, I tried to point out that casinos are not to blame for gambling addiction any more than bars are to blame for alcoholism. In assigning blame for addictions to tribal gaming facilities, many people overlook the way addictions travel. Before the casino was built five years ago, potential gambling addicts used other available outlets for addictive behavior. This connection highlights the fact that gambling addiction is a symptom of addictive behavior, not the addict's only problem. Another main point to make here is that gambling addiction is not widespread despite heavy media coverage. Most tribal governments are sensitive to charges of corrupting the local population and have policies restricting credit lines or monitoring patrons who are known to wager beyond their means.

Another concern relating to Indian nation governmental gaming is the issue of trust status for the land housing casinos. Tribal leaders had recently applied for trust status for the lands housing the casino in Mahnomen. The property was within the original boundaries of the reservation but had been allotted in the early part of the century. There was a public outcry among non-Indians at White Earth over the tribe's petition to put the casino property into trust status. This move would remove the land from the tax roles and would potentially raise the burden on current taxpayers to maintain the current level of service. Mahnomen County government officials were adamant about relying on the tribe's tax payments to maintain a basic infrastructure. However, most non-Indians were surprised to learn that while the tribal government would continue to pursue trust status, they had no intention of cutting off either the city or county. Rather, alternate agreements would be made in order to reimburse local governments for goods and services rendered. While this payment would not be in the form of a tax and, therefore, not required of the tribe, it would be paid nonetheless. Many people did not realize that increased county and city law enforcement and administrative support staff were financed solely by tribal funds before the trust application was filed.

Again, it is helpful to clarify that Section 20 of IGRA outlined the process whereby tribal governments could take off-reservation land into trust for gaming purposes. This section gave the states an active role in the decision-making process. In 25 USC section 2719 (a) and (b), IGRA clearly states how to handle tribal lands not acquired by tribes prior to IGRA's passage. This provision, which limits the power of the secretary of the Interior to take land into trust off-reservation lands for gaming purposes after 1988, was inserted into IGRA in response to state demands. Federal courts have interpreted this provision to give state governors effective veto power over secretarial decisions regarding gaming on lands taken into trust after 1988. Since then, only eighteen parcels of land have been acquired by tribal communities for gaming purposes. Of those eighteen parcels, only two were on off-reservation lands.

The third major concern raised by the community was that of increased criminal activity in the area. The county attorney and sheriff were vocal about the rising cost of law enforcement in Mahnomen County and this concerned local residents.[13] While no one I interviewed or spoke with had been the victim of a casino-related crime, this concern was on many people's minds. I shared what I had learned through my interviews with the county attorney: the majority of casino-related crimes were bad checks. The increase in the actual number of crimes in the county reflected the large number of insufficient funds checks written at the casino. While the prosecution of this type of crime demands time, money, and paperwork, these crimes do not represent increased danger to local residents. In addition, when vandalism or other property crimes occur near or in the casino, there is nothing casino-related about them. In other words, car theft or other crimes that had occurred in the area recently were not related specifically to gambling, but rather were related to the fact that there was an increase in the number of cars left unattended in Mahnomen County. Some anecdotal evidence suggests that crime actually decreases with tribal government gaming due to the availability of jobs and the increase in the standard of living.

METHODS: IDENTIFYING AND ATTRACTING YOUR AUDIENCE

In my experiences on the White Earth Reservation, the audience was limited, local, and relatively homogenous in terms of class and cultural background. I met with most people face-to-face and attracted people to talks through fliers or word-of-mouth advertising. However, gambling surveys are available in many states and can be helpful in delimiting an audience as well as identifying gaps in public education. For example, the State Advisory Council on Gambling did a survey in Minnesota in 1995. Some of its findings pointed to obvious gaps in education that I felt could be filled with pro-gaming perspectives. This particular survey found that, generally, Minnesotans were uncertain about gambling's economic benefits. In addition, they wanted gambling profits to go to a good cause. While these vague answers may reflect problems with the survey, they also highlight opportunities for education and public discussion. Highlighting the theme that Indian nation governmental gaming benefits everyone leads to an analysis of gambling's benefits for Minnesota's Indian and non-Indian residents. This theme of sharing also addresses the public's desire for the money to go to a good cause; in other words, profits will benefit tribal members and those who work in casinos or live nearby.

Learning what the public is ambivalent about often allows for an opportunity to promote the adoption of concrete opinions. It seemed important to me to talk back to the generalizations outlined in newspaper stories about gaming and to raise new questions before public discourses had been adopted by community residents as the only available ones.

COMMUNICATING WITH YOUR AUDIENCE:
STRATEGIES FOR MESSAGE-MAKING

Letters to the Editor

Write letters to newspaper editors when their gaming story has an anti-Indian slant or casts tribal government gaming as immoral. Expose illogical or racist thinking—for example, the notion that financial success is a threat to Native American culture. Letters of support can be written at any time. Write letters praising charitable donations by the tribal government. Open up a discussion of Indian nation sovereignty in the paper's opinion section.

Public Forums

One way to control the spin on the gaming story is to hold public lectures on a given topic. Expect a higher turnout when you tailor talks to issues of local speculation and concern. In Minnesota, that interest translated into talks entitled "Are Native Americans Gaming Away Their Future?" and "Will Gambling Destroy or Save Native American Culture?" Some communities have existing community education facilities and/or forums—take advantage of them. Local colleges and universities also provide receptive and enthusiastic audiences. Contact departments that might offer classes into which a discussion of tribal government gaming might fit: anthropology, sociology, economics, American studies, and political science are all potential sites for gambling forums. Some professors offer special lectures to which the public are invited.

Radio

Promote your public forum through radio ads. Ask about doing an on-air interview in order to publicize your talk. Suggest a phone-in show or other types of surveys about gaming attitudes. Discuss the ways in which the casino has affected people's lives locally. Many people are eager to make their opinions known.

Handouts

Provide handouts on the basics of gaming so that people can read them on their own time. Get information from the National Indian Gaming Association or other scholars and researchers in your area on gaming data. The local county extension officer in Mahnomen had compiled an extensive database of articles and readings on gambling from the social work perspective. Locate items such as these and distribute them at appropriate locations, including libraries, schools, and public forums.

Television

Invite television crews to cover celebrations associated with gaming successes. If the tribal government is building a new health facility, new homes, or a museum, get the word out. Invite local celebrities or government officials. Positive visual images can impact attitudes more quickly than increased knowledge about the particulars of Indian nation gaming's legality or the inherent rights of sovereignty.

CONCLUSION: DISCUSSIONS OF GAMING CAN RESULT IN BETTER COMMUNITY RELATIONS

One major goal in this type of education is the promotion of relationships between the tribal community and the local non-Indian community. Talking about the casino, economy, community concerns, or other related topics opens up a line of communication that allows people to meet each other and ask questions in a structured environment. Before the casino opened in Mahnomen, there was an assumption that tribal issues were of interest only to tribal members, while issues affecting the town of Mahnomen were of interest primarily to non-Indians. Talking about Indian nation governmental gaming provides an opportunity for all members of the community to see themselves as interconnected. If the casinos are shut down, hundreds of non-Indians and Indians will lose their jobs. If the tribal government continues to prosper, it will invest in the local economy and continue its generosity towards community projects and joint endeavors.

By highlighting the benefits to all community residents, it becomes clear that Indian nation governmental gaming is not simply a tribal issue. Its effects and benefits do not recognize enrollment criteria. Therefore, it is important for everyone to recognize the potential gaming holds for economic development and job creation for the entire community, regardless of its identity. With Indian nation governmental gaming, everyone wins.

NOTES

1. This article emerged from the author's research and work at her home in Minnesota from 1996 to 1997. While many of the concerns of the local communities remain the same, the article has been updated to reflect the passage of time. It is striking that the issues raised by the local communities at White Earth in 1996 and 1997 continue to dominate the political debates surrounding Indian nation governmental gaming across the United States well into the year 2000.

2. Laurence Shames, *Tropical Depression* (New York: Hyperion, 1996).

3. The education projects I was involved in at White Earth attracted interested Indian and non-Indians. However, the outline that I routinely presented (and which I outline here) is geared toward the non-Indian population. Not surprisingly, most tribal members had a clear sense of sovereignty.

4. 25 USC 2710 (b)(2).

5. This editorial was in the context of hunting and fishing rights. This example highlights a lack of historical perspective when it comes to tribal-federal relationships. The 1837 treaty that was the subject of the editorial was signed before Minnesota received statehood.

6. While some tribal governments do make payments directly to tribal members, White Earth's huge enrollment of 22,000 does not allow for individual payments.

7. 25 USC 2710 (b)(3) (A)–(D).

8.   The concern about Indian culture resulted in two major public forums dedicated to that issue. Both were well-attended. For those presentations, at least one tribal member always presented with me to provide a tribal perspective.

9.   This number is not uncommon among tribal casinos nationwide. The Minnesota Indian Gaming Association estimates that the ratio of non-Indians to Indians working in state casinos is closer to 73 to 27 percent.

10.   Darvin Shoenborn, mayor of Mahnomen, interview by author, 28 February 1997.

11.   Usually I would refer people to the tribal newspaper where the secretary/treasurer wrote a regular report about the casino's financial affairs. Here I raise the question because most people I encountered were curious but did not consider the day-to-day expenses of supporting a tribal government.

12   Information on pathological gambling was not widely available in 1996 and 1997, so I spoke mostly from my own knowledge, experience, and intuition. Since then a number of studies have shown that pathological gambling is not as widespread as it is commonly feared to be. Despite the overwhelming growth of gambling opportunities over the last twenty-five years, the prevalence of pathological gambling among Americans has remained essentially unchanged. For example, the results of a Harvard University study on pathological gambling found that 1.1 percent of the American public experienced symptoms of pathological gambling in the past year, while 1.6 percent experienced these symptoms at some point during their lifetime. A 1998 study estimated .8 percent for the past year and .1 percent for lifetime. These figures are quite low when compared to the incidence of drug dependence (6.2 percent), alcohol dependence (13.8 percent), and major depression (6.4 percent) (Howard J. Shaffer, Matthew N. Hall, and Joni Vander Bilt, *Estimating the Prevalence of Disordered Gambling Behavior in the United States and Canada: A Meta-analysis* [Cambridge: Harvard Medical School Division on Addictions, 15 December 1997]).

13.   This vocalization of rising crime rates was part of a campaign to stop the petition for trust status recently filed by the tribal government. The county wanted to show their reliance on tribal funds to prosecute crimes directly related to the casino. Many locals did not know the political nature of this campaign. Therefore, these numbers were frightening to some.

♣

Gaming and Recent American Indian Economic Development

Joseph G. Jorgensen

In 1994 in Tulsa, Oklahoma a knowledgeable group of American Indians and scholars of American Indian topics gathered to forecast the future of American Indian sovereignty, economics, relations with governments, and general well-being.[1] With far too much temerity I stood in front of the gathering to forecast American Indian economic development. As was my wont after nearly forty years of observation and analysis of Indian economic ventures, particularly agriculture, but also recreation, industrial park, mining, energy, and sundry smaller business activities, I assumed that the future of economic developments among America's Indian tribes would be similar to past attempts to develop Indian economies. Indeed, I argued that it was wise to accept David Hume's proposition that the past is the best predictor of the future for social phenomena.[2] Hence, I foresaw nothing but failures, the exception being the maquiladora-like assembly operations owned and managed by the Mississippi Choctaw.[3]

I argued that reservation subjugation brought with it not domination alone, but expropriation of resources from which Indians gained their livelihoods, in some instances and in some places exploitation of Indian labor, and everywhere the dole. Tribal domination was made complete by the plenary powers over Indian affairs invested in Congress. Expropriation was made complete by the Cherokee decisions in regard to the impaired title to Indian land. The dole is not complete, but when it is forthcoming its source is the federal government.

Nearly a full decade before the great stock market crash of 1929, the United States experienced its first agriculture market glut. Indian agricultural production was not a significant factor in causing that glut, and it has only lost ground in agricultural production since that time as centralization of crops and livestock, transformation from intensive labor to intensive capital, lack of access to capital, lack of political influence, long distances from market, generally arid and unproductive land, and modest education and technical skills have coalesced to eliminate agriculture as a viable means for Indian economic development.

In 1994 I argued that a spate of legislation enacted since 1887 so as to rectify Indian economic problems as defined by Congress or its lobbies (or both) had been unsuccessful in rectifying those problems. My list, well known to Indian scholars, includes the pieces in the history that define the swings back and forth between policies that prompted individual, competitive behavior in the market and those that made some provisions for collective, tribal economic affairs.[4] The General Allotment Act of 1887 (individual), Indian Reorganization Act of 1934 (collective), Indian Claims Commission Act of 1946 and subsequent specific termination acts (individual), and the Indian Self-Determination and Education Act (collective) marked the swings in my view. In retrospect, the last mentioned is especially interesting because I recognized it as the most significant piece of legislation that offered some possibility to assist Indian economic development. I think I was half right. Whereas the Self-Determination Act laid the groundwork, I completely missed the significance of the Indian Gaming Regulatory Act (IGRA), although it had been enacted in 1988, six years prior to the occasion of the Tulsa symposium. As a matter of fact, when asked by one participant why I was so pessimistic about Indian development when Indian gaming operations were opening and, apparently, succeeding, my response was, in short, ignorant.

I responded that Foxwoods, the Pequot casino in Connecticut, was a success, as was Mystic Lake, the Chippewa casino in Minnesota. Yet off the top of my head I foresaw a host of financial, management, ownership, location, seasonal, governmental, and legal problems that would sink most Indian gaming operations—operations that Indians would seldom own or control. The more obvious problems were saturation (several casinos within modest proximity would compete for a limited patron pool, as in San Diego and Riverside counties, California); long distances from population centers and from major highways (poor marketing and bad locations would operate against most Indian casinos in the mountain and Plains states); seasonal fluctuation (casinos in the mountain and Plains states and others within proximity of vacation destinations would wither from fall through spring); non-Indian capital and control, often from organized crime, would deny Indians anything beyond employment (non-Indians, as in many bingo operations of the 1970s, would build and operate the casinos and maintain the books); paucity of acumen about gaming and the gaming business; lack of access to capital; and legal problems with state and federal governments.

Although each of the foregoing factors, often in combinations of three or four, have caused some problems, the more remarkable outcome at this stage is that Indian gaming operations have been so successful. Since passage of the IGRA of 1988, legalized gambling on Indian lands has provided revenues for tribes that I forecast to be impossible. Access to capital and control of the casino I considered to be insurmountable problems. Yet one of the features of the act is intended to deny the control of casinos by non-Indian corporations, the mob, and outside firms in general. Outside firms can invest in casinos, even manage casinos, but they cannot gain more than 30 percent of profits, and they can do so for only the first five years of operations. After that, the IGRA requires that operations be turned back totally to the tribe. Hence, the tribe must learn to manage its own casino, or if it chooses to hire outside management, the tribe retains full control over that management.

A symposium at the California Indian Conference for 1995 (held at the University of California, Los Angeles) brought together participants from several tribes that have gaming operations within California. These representatives discussed the poignant issues of the day, including the obstacles they were encountering in seeking a compact with the state of California to operate their casinos within the legal parameters established by IGRA; the inability to purchase electronic gambling machines (one-armed bandits and the like) because of pressures put on suppliers by Nevada hoteliers and gaming operators; and the threat of raids by state police intended to close casinos because of illegal (machine) gambling on the premises.

Discussions also turned toward the economic successes, if marginal, of some of the smallest and most disadvantageously located casinos; the managerial help contracted by tribes of leading casino operators, such as Caesar's Palace and Full House (contracts that had explicit termination dates, which required merit review and so forth); the employment provided for all local Indians willing to work and for many non-Indian locals as well; and the distribution of revenues as benefits to elders, and to health, education, recreation, and culture-historical projects, including tribal museums.

The early evidence from the testimony of the participants was that gaming was an economic development in and of itself and, as a multiplier, a source for further economic developments in areas surrounding the tribe which owned the casino. The revenues were being used to enrich Indian lives and to nourish Indian culture.

Research on Indian gaming operations is extremely meager, but analyses of the IGRA; a major suit spawned by that act, *Seminole Tribe* v. *Florida*;[5] and the questions of taxation, termination, and social consequences that are anticipated as consequences of the IGRA were presented at a symposium hosted by the Arizona State University College of Law's Indian Legal Program in Tempe, 11–12 October 1996. In the publication of symposium papers, Eric Henderson—a Ph.D. in anthropology as well as a J.D.—provides a magisterial treatment of what is known and what is not known about the social and cultural consequences of Indian gaming.[6] There are more learned questions than answers about Indian gaming and its consequences for families and individuals, problem gambling for Indians and non-Indians, intratribal social and political arrangements, economic benefits, factionalism, and other pressing topics, undoubtedly because of the recency of Indian gaming. There is much to learn and much to study. We are looking at Indian gaming through a very dark glass.

SELF-DETERMINATION

So let us recall the Self-Determination Act and related legislation enacted a quarter of a century ago which, collectively, sought to provide Indian tribal governments with some controls over various aspects of their private and public economic affairs. Forty years prior to the Self-Determination Act, the Indian Reorganization Act of 1934 was envisaged as self-determination legislation for tribes. Yet in this 1930s form of self-determination, Congress vested the secretary of Interior with veto authority over tribal decisions. A bit later, realizing that the reorganized tribes had no money to drive their new corporations, Congress provided a minuscule revolving credit fund for which tribes could compete to fund development projects—such as livestock or farm operations. The Self-Determination Act of 1975 enabled tribes to exert control over public sector services and to compete for public sector grants and programs. In a replay of the 1930s, a separate act created another minuscule revolving credit fund for economic development available to the nation's federally recognized tribes (more than 275 in 1975) on a competitive basis.[7]

The Reagan Administration did not add one penny to the revolving credit fund, yet it managed to decrease the federal budget for Indian programs in each of the administration's eight years. Reagan's administration replaced dollars with encouragement to Indians to nourish their entrepreneurial activities and to seek independence from the federal dole.

Indian economic development is closely tied to self-determination, while Indian economic *un*development is tied to the structure of the nation's political economy and to the unique niche that tribes occupy by law and by context in that economy (see note 4). The extinguishing of Eskimo, Aleut, and Indian claims to aboriginal hunting, fishing, and land rights in Alaska in 1971, the Arab oil embargo of 1973, and actions of Congress and of successive administrations over the past three decades have regularly turned scholarly attention to the political economic structure of dependency. Impartial observers can no more easily deny that structure than can tribes, through some formula, generate sustainable and growing economies in which they do *not* exercise ownership and control of production.

About fifty years ago the nation's total agricultural products were produced by about 25 percent of the work force. The nation's manufactured goods were produced by about 50 percent of the work force. In 1998, the nation's total agricultural products, including exports, were produced by less than 2 percent of the work force, while the nation's manufactured goods were produced by about 15 percent of the work force. Given the incentives for capitalists to reduce costs while seeking maximum profits, coupled with the technological advances which increase production while displacing labor, fewer jobs and fewer manufacturing sites in the United States appear to be in the offing. If the future is to be like the past, it is a reasonable bet that total production of goods in the United States will be manufactured by 2 percent of the population in the not too distant future.

The structure of contemporary capitalism, nested in worldwide competition, is recognizable. Businesses seek government assistance through tax incentives and through the development and maintenance of roads, sewers, airports, docks, communication systems, and security, while eschewing the burdens of environmental, safety, health, minimum wage, and equal employment laws and the regulatory compliance red tape that has grown from those laws.

GAMING: ECONOMIC DEVELOPMENT AND SOVEREIGNTY

Indian sovereignty was limited with the ratification of the First Article of the Constitution which gave Congress plenary powers over tribes. With several important exceptions in which the Supreme Court has stepped up to define and restrict tribal sovereignty, Congress has defined what Indians own and control. Lenders have been more willing to offer advice than to lend capital. Title to trust land, after all, is impaired, so it doesn't provide good collateral for loans from, say, a megabank such as NationsBank-BankAmerica for deals that must be approved by Congress to proceed.

The obstacles to Indian economic development are structural: tribes are domestic dependent nations whose decisions can be vetoed, whose title to land and resources are impaired. Until the advent of Indian gaming operations, recognized tribes in the United States have had extremely limited access to capital, and have suffered disadvantages in access to and control of information pertinent to their own resources as well as to the market. Most recognized tribes are located long distances from markets of all kinds, and because the interests and obligations of most tribal governments focus on the nourishment of the well-being of tribal members—whose needs are endless—decisions to use scarce resources to benefit many as soon as possible have dominated decisions to allocate tribal funds. When engaged in business ventures—whether joint with non-Indian corporations or whether as rentiers to lessees of land and resources— almost all tribal corporations have watched profits generated from reservation resources drain from reservations to the coffers of corporations in distant metropolises. And members of almost all reservation societies suffer from discriminatory words and acts from their nearest non-Indian neighbors, themselves situated in struggling rural areas.

With such a tiny proportion of the nation's population producing all of the nation's agricultural and manufactured goods, what, possibly, is the future of the economic development of Indian tribes? While it is the case that most reservations are located in marginal areas long distances from manufacturing and agricultural markets and suffer unique political constraints, their access to capital and to information has been dramatically altered in the past five years. Indian tribes have some options not available heretofore. It is no longer the case that non-tribal-owned companies and corporations whose offices are located long distances from reservations own or control all of the businesses operating on reservations, draining the profits from the reservation to their corporate headquarters, keeping the books, and dribbling back to Indian tribes some crumbs in the form of royalties, a few jobs, or lease income.

The Pequot of southern Connecticut have been uniquely successful in the gaming business. The Pequot, whose capital to build Foxwoods casino came from a federal judgment, have not required infusions of federal capital to maintain the casino and its work force. Rather, the casino has flourished, causing alarm to casino operators in Atlantic City who claim that the proximity of the Pequot operation to the densely populated region from Boston to New York City has throttled their own operations.

The successes of the Pequot's Foxwoods Casino and the Chippewa's Mystic Lake Casino have not been lost on the nation's recognized and unrecognized tribes. In mid-1997 there were 273 Indian-owned casinos. Among these, 145 tribes located in twenty-four states had entered into compacts (161 in all) with the governments of the states in which their casinos are located.[8] The gross revenues of all Indian gaming operations in mid-1997 have been estimated at $6 billion annually. The 128 tribal casino owners who have not arrived at agreements with the states in which they operate are seeking to do so, often against considerable obstacles.

For example, tribes operating forty-one limited gaming facilities in California—in which 13,000 video slot machines are the principal source of revenues[9]—had been thwarted for more than four years in their attempts to agree to a compact with the state. On March 7, 1998, Governor Pete Wilson's administration signed a compact with one of those forty-one tribes, the Pala Band of Mission Indians in northern San Diego County, allowing video lottery games in all California Indian casinos. Wilson's administration envisaged the compact as comprehensive, the formula for all compacts with California's tribes. Those compacts would restrict each tribe currently operating casinos to 199 video lottery machines[10] and all other federally recognized tribes in California to that same number of video machines, if and when they open casinos. There are 106 federally recognized tribes in California and dozens more unacknowledged tribes that are seeking federal recognition. Governor Wilson's comprehensive formula would reduce the number of machines now in use by about 5,000 (38 percent). The government-to-government agreement did not proceed in "good faith" according to thirty-nine California tribal governments currently operating casinos.

California's casino operating tribes responded quickly to the Pala compact. They gained sufficient signatures to place an initiative on the November 1998 statewide ballot in California: the Tribal Government Gaming and Economic Self-Sufficiency Act. The initiative, known as Proposition 5, sought to ensure California tribes that their gaming operations shall continue to operate on tribal lands to support Indian economic self-sufficiency.[11] The gaming tribes estimated that their forty-one casinos directly provided 15,000 jobs in the state, and they provided evidence that Indian gaming operations will not impact California's $2.3 billion non-Indian gaming industry (bingo, card rooms, horse racing, lottery).

The measure was approved by 63 percent of California voters in November 1998 following a campaign waged by supporters and detractors in which over $100 million was spent. It was the most expensive ballot measure of its type in United States history. Within days of Proposition 5's passage, groups of homeowners living near casinos and a labor union, financially assisted by Nevada casinos, raised the stakes again, bringing suits contending that Proposition 5 violated both federal and state law. Both federal and state governments, they argued, prohibited Nevada and New Jersey style casinos where the house is the bank. The Supreme Court of the State of California blocked enforcement of Proposition 5 while it considered the claims.

In the fall of 1999 the California State Supreme Court rendered the proposition unconstitutional. The gaming tribes, in response, wrote a new initiative to rectify flaws in Proposition 5 and began circulating petitions to get it on the statewide ballot in March 2000. The new initiative, Proposition 1A, passed in California, again reinforcing tribal self-sufficiency.

The stakes are high. The claims that casinos are crucial to the development of self-sufficient tribal economies, although not without some negative effects and some business failures, appear to be measured. Because of a paucity of research on Indian gaming nationwide, I must rely on anecdotal evidence in the following assessment of the successes of and the problems associated with Indian gaming.

Let us begin with Oregon's Grande Ronde Confederated Tribes, in part because they had so little and so few prospects when they opened a casino, and in part because the consequences to the tribe and to the local area from their casino's short history is similar to so many tribal casinos from Connecticut to California. Oregon's Grande Ronde Confederated Tribes were terminated from federal services and stripped of federal recognition. Twenty-three years later the Confederated Tribes successfully sought Congress to restore federal recognition to them, and the Grande Ronde were awarded a reservation of about 10,000 acres located about sixty miles from Portland. When the timber industry in which they were engaged for more than a decade faltered, the tribe voted to avail itself of the IGRA. According to Michael Killeen, the tribe sought to create jobs for Natives and non-Natives while building an income base that would allow them to invest in education, the environment, and the arts, while also becoming a multiplier for the local area.[12] They intended as well to implement measures to avert gambling addiction and crime, and to create treatment centers for gamblers with problems.

In 1996, Grande Ronde established the Spirit Mountain Casino, hired a tribal member and attorney as CEO, and in its first year of operation generated a profit of $30 million.[13] Killeen points out that the tribe hired 1,200 people, only 200 of whom were Indians. And of the new hires, 46 percent had been out of work, 35 percent had been on welfare, and 42 percent lacked health insurance. In the first year alone, $8 million in gambling profits were used to build and improve highways, the water and sewer system, and a new medical facility (for Natives and non-Natives), while $335,000 was invested in studies on the negative impacts of gaming, rescue helicopters for Portland hospitals, and to an exhibition of Native American Art at the Portland Art Museum.[14] The $335,000 represents 6 percent of net revenues. This proportion is committed to a community fund for non-tribal causes.

The San Manuel Serrano Indians, located near San Bernardino, California, opened a bingo parlor in 1986, expanding their types of games following passage of the federal gaming act. The tribe encountered opposition from the city and county of San Bernardino which they overcame by agreeing to finance road and traffic improvements for seven years (through 1993). They also overcame opposition from home owners in the area adjacent to the casino by agreeing in federal court to compensate them up to $300,000 total for devaluation of property.[15] In 1988 about 75 percent of the tribe's work-eligible population was unemployed and about the same proportion of tribal members received welfare benefits. In 1993, according to Mark Henry,[16] the casino embarked on an energetic advertising program and soon began drawing 100,000 gamblers per month. In short order the casino eliminated tribal unemployment and welfare. Any member who seeks work obtains it so long as he or she passes the background check and drug test required of all applicants. In 1996 the casino had a $26-million payroll, providing jobs for 25 percent of the tribe's total population and 1,400 jobs total. Employees come from a five-county area; most are non-Natives. As is the case for Grande Ronde, the San Manuel Serranos used casino profits to donate about $600,000 to charities in 1996; build a new water system, roads, and homes for tribal members; and provide per-capita distributions among tribal members. The tribe offers to pay the cost of college educations for any member who wishes to attend. In 1997 one person had accepted the offer.

Three bands in San Diego County, California—Barona, Viejas, Sycuan— totaling about 700 members, were mired in poverty a decade ago. Each opened casinos on their reservations following passage of the federal gaming act. "Barona closed three times between 1988 and 1991 when management companies failed to make it profitable."[17] Troubles were frequent: video games were confiscated by San Diego County law enforcement officers at the direction of the state attorney general (only to have them returned by a federal court judge). By 1994, following Barona's lead, Viejas and Sycuan had become successful running high-stakes bingo games, off-track betting, Indian blackjack (cards), and video poker. By 1995 high-stakes bingo gave way to high-jackpot video poker (up to $100,000 payoffs).[18] Video machines account for 70 percent or more of profits. Currently. the three casinos have about 2,500 video games (total) and draw about 15,000 gamblers daily (5.5 million per year), mostly from within San Diego County. The aggregate revenues for the three casinos are estimated at well over $1 billion annually. The San Diego casinos have restaurants, snack bars, and stores, but no alcohol.

All tribal members who desire employment are employed by the casinos. But of the 1,600 employees at one casino, only sixteen are tribal members. If but one person per household is employed, about 30 percent of the households have a casino employee. Inasmuch as all tribal members receive per-capita distributions from profits (about $4,500 per month for Barona tribal members), the modest number of casino employees per Indian household is not surprising. Per capitas are distributed each month only after basic services, improvements, and investments are determined by the tribal governments. Within the bands, improvements and public investments include gymnasiums, college funds, trust funds for all persons eighteen years of age with high school diplomas, libraries, computer centers, Head Start programs, homes. Outside the bands, contributions totaling more than $2.4 million in 1995 and 1996 were made to San Diego area charities, symphonies, community centers, and the like. And as for investments in the area economy, Viejas purchased a controlling interest in a local bank, and is building a discount outlet shopping center/entertainment complex. Barona operates a gas station that cost the band $600,000 to build and that employs sixteen people. Sycuan runs a regional health clinic.[19]

Many of the personal problems associated with Indian gaming are similar to problems associated with non-Indian gaming, namely, gambling addiction, the setting and occasions for crime, and the stresses that can occur within families because of gambling habits. Tribes have sought to counter these problems through the ways in which they advertise (some downplay enormous payoffs), prohibiting the sale and use of alcohol, prohibiting the use of checks or credit cards, prohibiting the development of tabs (credit) for regular customers, and educating persons against gambling addiction.

Problems of other kinds emerge as well. Former non-Indian managers and investors in Indian casinos have been convicted of operating illegal gambling operations and sentenced to prison terms and fines (while having charges dropped for skimming millions of dollars from one tribe).[20] Small casinos located in close proximity to large and successful casinos, such as the Cahuilla Creek casino in the little town of Anza near the profitable Indian casinos of the Palm Springs area, struggle to maintain a work force of seventy-five people, down from 150 in 1992. It draws no more than two hundred customers on a good night. The casino is unable to donate money to the community or to tribal services, nor is it able to invest in other businesses.[21] The National Indian Gaming Commission, established by the IGRA, requires all Indian casinos to submit annual audits and background investigations of key employees. In 1997 the commission found that nearly half of the 273 tribal casinos failed to submit either audits or background investigations of their key employees.[22]

And finally I call to attention problems that have been created within and between tribes as a direct consequence of the Indian Gaming Regulatory Act. The Juaneño Band of Mission Indians in Orange County, California, is not recognized by the federal government. In 1978 the Juaneño Band sought to be recognized through provisions of the Federal Acknowledgment Process. A list of tribal membership and a petition responding to the requirements of the acknowledgment process were submitted. The Federal Acknowledgment Process, administered by the Bureau of Indian Affairs (BIA) has had a hoary history. Not until 1994 was the Juaneño Band's petition close to being decided by the BIA. Between 1990 and 1994, however, the tribal leaders responsible for filing the petition were approached by Nevada gaming investors who offered to invest in a casino when the tribe gained recognition, established a sovereign government, and received land on which the casino could be placed. Soon an anti-gambling faction formed and filed a second petition with a different, but overlapping, list of tribal members and new responses to the questions posed in the BIA petition guidelines. By 1998 the person who had been the chairman when the original petition was prepared, but who did not stand for reelection, returned to re-present the original petition, bringing with him several persons. Yet the faction that had stuck with the original petition had elected a new chairman. Thus, the original petition was claimed by two factions, while the second petition retained a faction and chair of its own. The confusion of petitions and petitioners has not been resolved by the BIA's Branch of Acknowledgment Research, but if and when it recognizes the Juaneño Band, it will be only one of the petitions, hence only one of the tribal membership lists will be approved as enrolled members.[23]

A second problem pitted the Torrez-Martinez tribe against several casino-operating tribes in the Palm Springs area of California. Half of the Torrez-Martinez reservation was flooded in 1905 by a famous accident in which a Colorado River canal burst, causing the formation of the Salton Sea. The Salton Sea has inundated Torrez-Martinez land ever since. Recently the Torrez-Martinez received $14 million from Congress to purchase new land farther north in the Palm Springs-Palm Desert-Coachella Valley area (approved by the Department of Interior), and sought the assistance of Full House Resorts to help them establish and manage a casino. The casino has not gone forward because of intense lobbying by established Indian-owned casinos in the area that do not want to see their own revenues reduced by another casino in their vicinity.[24]

The problems in starting and maintaining successful gaming operations are many. Gaming offers, however, the most likely source of sustained economic successes for impoverished tribes, and is a remarkable employer and multiplier for moribund rural areas.

In conjunction with successful gaming operations made possible by the IGRA and agreed to in good faith compacts struck with state governments, the Self-Determination Act can be used by tribes to gain (and in some instances, regain) control over the federal services they now receive. If they are careful, obtain good advice, and are situated within good transportation networks, they may be able to create assembly firms similar to those of the Mississippi Choctaw as well, further lifting local economies. The obstacles to the smallest tribes located the longest distances from markets and population centers are, as in the past, structural and many. Yet the initiative placed on the ballot by California gaming tribes goes a long way to sharing wealth among tribes that do not have gaming operations and would not enjoy success if they had them.

NOTES

1. "Native America: Faces of the Future," Conference held at the University of Tulsa, Tulsa, Oklahoma (April 15–16, 1994).

2. For a full development of Hume's position, which is much richer and much more cautious than my claim about it, see Frederick L. Will, "Will the Future Be Like the Past," *Mind* (1956) for the most widely accepted critique of Hume's position.

3. About twenty years ago the Choctaw of Philadelphia, Mississippi successfully penetrated the automobile industry in the United States by installing cassette decks into the baskets which were hung in Ford, General Motors, and Chrysler cars and trucks for a lower price than any of those corporations could match should they install the cassettes in-house. Choctaw labor was eager and the price was right. Hours for employees were flexible, health benefits for Indians were covered by the Indian Health Service, and jobs were provided for non-Indians in the community as well. The Mississippi Choctaw recognized the niche and the competition posed by businesses that fled across the border to Mexico. Manufacturers sought lower costs and higher profits. For more than twenty years the Choctaw have been successful in acquiring new contracts to assemble a wide variety of products; hiring more local whites, blacks, and Indians; and building more buildings to assemble the items that come to them. The future of the Choctaw enterprise is surely bound to the future of manufacturing and to their ability to provide high-quality assembly at low cost to the manufacturers. Their competition is *maquilladore* operations along the US-Mexico border.

4. These issues have been addressed in detail from various perspectives in the past. My view has undergone only modest change in the past thirty-five years. See Joseph G. Jorgensen, "The Ethnohistory and Acculturation of the Northern Ute" (Ph.D. diss., Indiana University, 1964); "Indians and the Metropolis," in *The American Indian in Urban Society*, eds. Jack O. Waddell and O. Michael Watson (Boston: Little Brown, 1971), 67–113; *The Sun Dance Religion. Power for the Powerless* (Chicago: University of Chicago Press, 1972); "A Century of Political Economic Effects on American Indian Society," *Journal of Ethnic Studies* 6:3 (1978a): 1–82; "Energy, Agriculture, and Social Science in the American West," in *Native Americans and Energy Development*, eds. Joseph G. Jorgensen, et al. (Cambridge: Anthropology Resource Center, 1978b), 3–16;

"Energy Development in the Arid West: Consequences for Native Americans," in *Paradoxes in Western Energy Development*, American Association for the Advancement of Sciences, ed. Cyrus McKell (Boulder: Westview Press, 1984a), 297–322; "The Political Economy of the Native American Energy Business," in *Native Americans and Energy Developments II*, ed. Joseph G. Jorgensen (Boston: Anthropology Resource Center, 1984b), 10–51; "Federal Policies, American Indian Polities and the 'New Federalism,'" *American Indian Culture and Research Journal* 10:2 (1986a): 1–13; "Sovereignty and the Structure of Dependency at Northern Ute," *American Indian Culture and Research Journal* 10:2 (1986b): 75–94; *Oil Age Eskimos* (Berkeley: University of California Press, 1990). Differences are rather slight between my view and those expressed by several recent contributors to the analysis of American Indian economic development, including David F. Aberle, "Navajo Economic Development," in *Southwest*, vol. 10, ed. Alfonso Ortiz, gen. ed., William Sturtevant, *Handbook of North American Indians* (Washington, DC: Smithsonian Institution, 1983), 641–658; Matthew C. Snipp, "The Changing Political and Economic Status of the American Indians: From Captive Nations to Internal Colonies," *American Journal of Economics and Sociology* 45:2 (1986): 145–158; Irene Castle McLaughlin, "Colonialism, Cattle, and Class: A Century of Ranching on the Fort Berthold Indian Reservation" (Ph.D. diss., Columbia University, 1993); Sandra Faiman-Silva, "Multinational Corporate Development in the American Hinterland: The Case of the Oklahoma Choctaws," in *The Political Economy of North American Indians*, ed. John H. Moore (Norman: University of Oklahoma Press, 1993), 214–239; Thomas D. Hall, "Northwest New Spain," in *American Indians and Economic Dependency*, ed. Matthew C. Snipp (Norman: University of Oklahoma Press, 1998); and Shepard Krech, "Dependency Among the Northern Cree," in *American Indians and Economic Dependency*, ed. Matthew C. Snipp (Norman: University of Oklahoma Press, 1998).

5.   "Symposium, Indian Gaming," *Arizona State Law Journal* 29:1 (Spring 1997).

6.   Eric Henderson, "Indian Gaming: Social Consequences," *Arizona State Law Journal* 29:1 (1997): 205–50.

7.   If every tribe had equal access to the $10 million at the same time, each would receive about $36,000—an amount that may not have been sufficient to buy a McDonald's franchise in 1980. Another contrast of rich and poor will give perspective to that $10-million revolving credit fund in 1995: the CEO of the Walt Disney Corporation received about twenty-three times the amount of the total revolving credit fund as his annual compensation in 1995.

8.   I skirt the details of tribal-state compacts here except to point out that under federal law the regulation of certain types of games—called Class III gaming—must be governed by an agreement between the tribe that establishes a casino and the state in which it is located. The state must negotiate these agreements with tribes in good faith (see Henderson, "Indian Gaming: Social Consequences," 1997).

9.   Eleven tribes from northern Santa Barbara County to southern Riverside County gain more than 75 percent of their revenues from video games.

10.   The Pala compact allows a tribe to operate a maximum of 975 video machines if they buy allocations from other tribes. Several Indian casinos in the Palm Springs-Indio area (southern California desert) currently operate more than 1,000 electronic games.

11.   The measure seeks to extend the benefits of tribal gaming to tribes that do not have gaming facilities by dedicating part of the net revenues from Indian gaming to non-gaming tribes for health care, education, economic development, and cultural preservation programs. It will direct part of the net winnings to supplement emergency medical resources in each county in California and to a local benefits grant fund for cities and counties where Indian gaming facilities are located. It also puts into law strict gaming limitations, regulations, and public health, safety, and environmental standards.

12.   Michael Killeen, "Prosperity in the Cards," *Hemisphere* (1997): 41–45.

13.   Killeen, "Prosperity in the Cards," 42.

14.   Killeen, "Prosperity in the Cards," 44.

15.   Mark Henry, "Gamble Pays Off," *The Press-Enterprise*, reprinted in *Indian Times* (Spring 1997): 6.

16.   Henry, "Gamble Pays Off," 1, 5.

17.   Henry Garfield, "Casinos Deal County Indians a Winning Hand," *City Magazine* (San Diego, February 1997), reprinted in *Indian Times* (Spring 1997): 4–6.

18.   Garfield, "Casinos Deal County Indians a Winning Hand," 4.

19.   Ibid.

20.   George Ramos, "4 Plead Guilty to Running Illegal Reservation Casino," *Los Angeles Times*, 7 November 1996, A32.

21.   Stephanie Simon, "Legal Dispute Simmers in Remote Casino," *Los Angeles Times*, 27 May 1997, A24–5.

22.   "N.M. Tribe Casinos Fail Fed Standards," *The Albuquerque Tribune*, 9 April 1997.

23.   Yoriko Ogawa, "Honors Paper in Social Science" (School of Social Sciences, University of California, Irvine, June 1998).

24.   Tom Gorman, "Dispute Stalls Land Deal for Impoverished Tribe," *Los Angeles Times*, 23 September 1996, A3, A15.

♣

Traditional and Modern Perspectives on Indian Gaming: The Struggle for Sovereignty

James V. Fenelon

The key issues upon which all Indian gaming is predicated are Indian sovereignty, economic development and employment, and distribution of the proceeds as means for redress of historical and contemporary injustices and inequalities.[1] Central to all justification and defense of a separate legislation and system for Indian gaming is the complex notion of sovereignty.[2] Connected to evolving discussions and practices of Indian sovereignty are jurisdiction, divisional tensions among competing reservations,[3] economic development strategies, representations at National Indian Gaming Association (NIGA) negotiations, political governance, state governments opposed to tribal goals,[4] traditional social structures, and notions of justice and social control.

Gaming's effects on traditional cultures and social systems are particularly sensitive issues on most reservations. As this analysis shows, traditional identity, while critical to understanding social change mechanisms, varies greatly among reservations and gaming trust lands.[5] The question of form and practice of traditional culture ranges from the destruction of the Pequots'[6] culture to strongly traditional cultures such as the Lakota on the Pine Ridge Reservation or the Navajo located in the Four Corners.[7]

Notions of sovereignty[8] are prone to influence by the same forces that gave rise to Indian gaming policies.[9] The case studies used in this work demonstrate that ideologies and definitions associated with being or becoming a nation with sovereign rights are linked to a strengthened economic position when negotiating with state and federal agencies. Standing Rock is an example underlining such political problems[10] as a nation rather than a reservation.[11]

Traditionalists, those people from Native societies with the most knowledge of their indigenous culture, also participate in conflicting notions of identity and nationhood. Grey Eagles at Pine Ridge opposes tribal councils, while Lakota and Dakota traditionals are at odds with the governing bodies overseeing the casino operations and profit distribution.[12] The politically recognized form of limited sovereignty that originated in the United States Congress, the Bureau of Indian Affairs (BIA), and individual states differs markedly from traditional understandings, as is underscored in one hundred years of internecine conflict with the Lakota over these definitions.[13] Among other issues, these conflicts include different interpretations of terms such as *Sioux Nation* or *tribal treaty rights*.[14]

INDIAN GAMING AND SOVEREIGNTY

Sovereignty serves at least three manifest and latent purposes with Indian gaming enterprises on most reservations: (1) it is the primary legal rationale for Indian gaming casinos separate from non-Indian society; (2) it is both strengthening and weakening historical claims and notions of autonomy, nationality, and self-determination; and (3) it is fueling an ongoing controversy between traditional people and some tribal councils in regard to cultural representation, profit distribution, and treaty-based sovereignty.[15]

Social scientists have posed ineffective, even misdirected, questions about the effects of Indian gaming on traditional social structures. The metaphysical, cross-cultural, and methodological domains of this problem are found in a primary if not singular focus on traditionals, without observing how gaming institutions and resulting social change occurs in the mainstream society.[16] The mainstream or dominant society includes both development and distribution of gambling enterprises, as well as concerns among American conservative groups that see themselves as guardians of the moral and philosophical values of the larger society, including Native peoples.

Moving from an analytical discussion of conflict with traditional lifestyles to an analysis of conflict within the internal colonial administrators of tribal councils, it is easier to uncover the source of tensions associated with Indian gaming. In this respect, the problem is not gambling itself, but rather the practices of economic institutions and their ensuing social change.

For instance, note the following interchange that occurs when asking a traditional woman elder about gaming:[17]

> **Interviewer:** Are some traditionals against gambling?
> **Number Seven:** I never heard that.... When you go to Prairie Island ... to their casino Treasure Island, or to Prairie Knights [on Standing Rock], or the new casinos up around Fort Berthold, lots of elders will be there ... but there was nothing against gambling or gaming in traditional societies.
> **Interviewer:** What ideas about gaming do most traditionals express?
> **Number Seven:** I still use gambling paraphernalia in some of my demonstrations of traditional life.... The Dakota practiced hampa ape' achunjpi [hitting the bones hand game] for a kind of gambling.... These games could go on for three days and nights.
> **Interviewer:** Were these games mostly for entertainment or leisure time?
> **Number Seven:** Not at all.... One could or would put pressure on somebody to cause them to lose.... Besides the hand game, there was a kind of a dice game, which used carved plum pits, sometimes elk, sometimes buffalo.... People could bet a great deal on these.... There were other purposes ... they might want to know something, about the future for instance ... and there were mystical aspects, ways of knowing that were mysterious, wakan [spiritual power].... These [games] might be sponsored by a family with a sick person, hoping to benefit from it....[18]

We find ample evidence of gambling throughout traditional Native American societies, showing that gambling itself provokes little direct conflict with traditional lifestyles.[19] This is specifically true for the Dakota and Lakota peoples.

Because of the above noted social functions of gambling, including wealth redistribution, decision-making, philosophy, and even healing, I believe that other traditional social practices might contribute to these tensions surrounding gaming.

Interviewee Number Seven described how traditional society required a series of tests before appointing someone to a powerful leadership role, such as today's equivalent of heading up a casino, as well as processes for removing someone who did not represent the desires or values of the people.[20] Based on these observations, it becomes clear that some conflict between traditionals and moderns comes from the destructive cultural domination of BIA administration.[21] Many traditionals view the current tribal councils as an outgrowth of these internalized forces.

Therefore, the evidence collected from interviews for this study indicates that research should consider historical tensions, internal conflicts, and ongoing systems of domination as potential sources for gaming's effects on traditionals. In addition, however difficult some issues may become, the Indian casinos have to (at least in name) distribute profits or spend proceeds on tribal programs, but not as individual or business profits.

Bringing casino institutions and their resultant effects to the reservation are not much different than bringing those to any mainstream American community. In many of these towns, decisions and debates over the positive and negative effects of gaming are also under consideration. A recent headline in the Ohio magazine *Cleveland*, for example, reads: "The BIG GAMBLE—Casinos will bring Ohio millions of dollars and hundreds of jobs. Or they will bring crime, broken businesses and families torn apart by gambling addiction. In Iowa and Missouri, they may have done both."[22] However, two additional concerns are almost always present on American Indian reservations that may not be factors in non-Native communities. One is the need for economic development in the community or reservation, including mandates that gaming profits be directed toward the whole group—tribe, trust community, nation, reservation—rather than individual investors or businesses. The second difference is the concern over the effects of gaming on traditional social structures or cultural practices still used by the tribe.

In order to focus on traditional and modern perspectives on Indian gaming and casinos, the social research problem must be reframed.[23] The question becomes: How do Indian gaming and casinos differ from similar activities in dominant American society? From this question come two more tightly framed questions: (1) In terms of modernization, what kind of effects do full-scale casinos on Indian lands have on economic development and various illegal opportunity structures? and (2) In terms of traditional people's perspectives, what kinds of effects do full-scale casinos have on the continuation of traditional life and reservation social practices still in place?

While attempting to explain situational conflicts over reservation gaming may be complicated, making comparative statements is more so. For instance, in the reservation-less state of Ohio, one major Native American organization in the Miami Valley region was approached to verify claims made by various groups and individuals for status as recognized Native Americans. Similarly, the remnant Wyandot band in Kansas, removed from Ohio during the Indian-removal period of the nineteenth century, won recognition for burial grounds in Kansas City to be classified as trust lands open to gaming against protest by the Potawotamie of Kansas, who have been negotiating with the state.

In fact, Ohio state recently defeated a well-backed referendum on riverboat gambling, with proponents making the same appeal as Indians—"jobs ... helps the economy.... More jobs."[24] Thus we observe that the same structural effects and issues involving gaming are found in non-Indian states and communities, and between competing interests of Native peoples. Likewise, Oneida gaming interests are fending off attempted returns from their removed Wisconsin bands, reflecting structural competition that supersedes internal conflicts.[25] Using van Willigen's dictum, "studying up" applied anthropology to the dominant society, most gaming institutions appear remarkably similar whether from Indian or non-Indian social origins.[26]

COMPARATIVE PERSPECTIVES

Throughout the United States, there are multiple examples of competition over gaming profits, including the successful riverboat gambling in Iowa that is in direct competition with regional and local Native interests, as well as proposed gaming on the Nebraska border. Donald Trump has attempted to criticize and hamper Indian gaming enterprises that appear to compete with his own powerful holdings. With an ironic tone, Trump complains about "corruption" and even "organized crime" that are the very legacy of Las Vegas and Atlantic City.[27] Thus, mainstream gaming operations inform us that competition and conflict over financial resources, profits distribution, and group or individual ownership are consistent across cultures.

The most renowned and profitable Indian gaming operations at Foxwoods Casino demonstrate these relations between modern institutional life with a resurrected "traditional" identity and federal recognition. The Pequots of Connecticut were considered eliminated for over three hundred years, with an ever smaller yet persistent group maintaining descent by oral history until they remarkably won BIA recognition. Immense profits from their huge operation have allowed the Pequots to sponsor the largest powwow in North America and support some traditional practices from Native peoples who have not lost most of their traditions.[28] Conversely, the Oglala Lakota from Pine Ridge in South Dakota, with the highest poverty rates by county in the United States, are running a new, relatively tiny gambling house near the border of the reservation road leading to Hot Springs. The Prairie Winds Casino generates very small profits so far, and remains highly controversial among the people who have resisted assimilation more than most Indian nations. Thus comparative analysis between these gaming casinos is ineffective in terms of effects on and perspectives from traditional culture.

The M'deWakantowan Dakota of Prairie Island's very profitable casino, Treasure Island, makes a more intermediary case of such effects. Although technically similar to remnant bands, many Prairie Island people maintain knowledge of their language and traditional culture, much of which is shared with the more traditional Lakota living near the rural Prairie Winds casino on Pine Ridge.

Atlantic City's and Las Vegas' gaming appear to be diametrically opposed to Indian gaming and are rarely considered in the same research agendas.[29] Foxwoods Casino is in some ways similar. It has become a cultural icon, separated from the broader Native world.[30] Cultural representations are surface level, even stereotypical, yet have a major impact on the rest of Native America and Indian Country.[31] And, as leaders in the Indian gaming industry, they influence policy decisions on a national level.

A final comparative statement needs to be made more on the local level, and preferably with close proximity to Indian reservations and gaming operations. The Black Hills casino, Deadwood, stands out in this respect, sitting in the 1868 Fort Laramie Treaty lands, which belong to the Lakota, who are considered the Great Sioux Nation of Indians. Virtually all the casino gambling available elsewhere exists in the many halls of Deadwood, under advertising banners about Wild Bill Hickock and the Dead Man's Hand, or film images from Kevin Costner's romantic *Dances With Wolves*.

Interviews collected from both Natives and non-Natives while gambling in Deadwood stand out in contrast to one another. Note the cultural contestations stated by both parties below.

> **Number Twenty-Seven:** I'm just really glad to have the jobs. I worked here for two years after I got laid off.... Never really occurred to me about those Indian casinos now that you mention it.... Guess they can make their money, too, long as it don't interfere with ours.... (Non-Indian)[32]

> **Number Nineteen:** I really like the great buffet and the prime rib. It's even better than on Standing Rock. But there's no way I'm going into that casino run by Costner. And I'm never gonna visit that 'Dunbar' development, no matter how good it is. We taught him Lakota and made him famous, and now he sets his family to compete with our casinos.... (Native)[33]

Clearly, gambling is an individual issue first with these interviewees, usually associated with jobs, food, and good times. Yet differences lie in each person's loyalty to cultural issues connected to different histories and objectives.

SOVEREIGNTY PERSPECTIVES

Discussion of sovereignty as a central legitimating issue of Indian gaming and the ways in which it both strengthens and weakens practices and interpretation of Indian nations and tribes is complicated. Sovereignty existed among "treaty tribes" long before Indian gaming exploded and is supported in terms of economic power by most if not all tribal councils. Sovereignty, however, is seriously questioned by federally recognized tribes as potentially hampering government-to-government relations.[34]

> IGRA's [the Indian Gaming Regulatory Act's] passage in 1988 compromised those governmental rights to the extent that it allowed states, through the compact process, to negotiate a regulatory role in certain

forms of tribal gaming.... IGRA's grant to the states was opposed by tribes as an intrusion on their sovereignty, but was ultimately accepted as a necessary compromise to meet states' concerns while protecting this important economic resource to tribes.[35]

The same compact negotiations with states, as determined by federal law and the Congress, also threaten Indian nation sovereignty as determined by historical treaties with the United States. For example, the Oglala Lakota Nation stands out in large letters on the tribal flag of the Oglala (Sioux) Lakota from the Pine Ridge Reservation. Both in name and political practice, the tribe notes its cultural autonomy as the Oglala Lakota who participated in the 1868 treaty with the Sioux Nation of Indians. Chairman John Steele views the protection of sovereignty as critical to all Indian nations, tribes, and peoples.

> The Congress wants to move general assistance down to [the] tribal agencies level.... This will be a disaster.... Tribal Shares is [also] fraught with extreme danger, as Secretary Babbit agrees.... This is the same as the Termination Era.... Those of us without treaties need to support the treaty tribes ... treaty rights—we have to keep it that way.[36]

Standing Rock, with a more dubious claim to nation status but a more successful casino than Pine Ridge, has also moved its political identification to nation status.[37] This leads to another set of problems for traditionals: the nature of Lakota and Dakota identity constructs and their opposition in terms of an *oyate* (national or social grouping) as a people, since membership in a nation is determined by an Indian agency's federal enrollment lists.[38] Economic empowerment associated with gaming has allowed tribal councils to make claims that may threaten traditional identity and federal enrollment laws based on Indian reservations with or without treaties.

Again, primary conflict is not between modern and traditional forces on the reservation, but rather how they feed and fractionate historical differences that result from the "administrative technologies" of the BIA.[39] From this perspective, the government tries to control, dominate, and suppress the Lakota using divisional tactics, especially those with cultural sovereignty claims, and therefore the Black Hills and the Treaty of 1868.

Another set of examples demonstrates the jurisdictional fights between state governments, Indian Nations with casinos based on sovereignty rather than tribal-state compacts, and the National Indian Gaming Regulatory Act (NIGRA) in terms of the declaration and practice of sovereignty. Discussing Initiative 671, which provides for limited state oversight of Indian gaming, Tim Giago, editor of *Indian Country Today*, sees support by Colville and Spokane tribes as "trampling on their own objectives of sovereignty":

> The Indian nations of Washington must never surrender their inherent right to decide for themselves what is best for the people. They must never allow foreign government [the state] to infringe upon their status as a sovereign people. When the Indian nations of Washington were barely surviving as the poorest of the poor, where was the state government?[40]

Both state government and regional non-Indian newspapers accuse gaming enterprises of having "illegal gambling devices" that were "smuggled in the dark" unto the reservations.[41] Thus jurisdictional issues take on the rhetoric of crime and punishment between state and tribe, negotiated with the federal government over sovereignty. Many leaders, activists, and Indian journalists view federal negotiations as potential sources for a breakdown of sovereignty.

> I'm going back to 1988 when two very concerned tribal leaders, Roger Jourdain of the Red Lake Band of Chippewa and Wendell Chino of the Mescalero Apache, tried to warn all of the Indian nations in this land that the National Indian Gaming Regulatory Act was illegal. They were particularly concerned about the clause that gave state governments jurisdiction where they had none.[42]

Similar to earlier discussion on the reframing of research around differences and similarities, contrasts between the United States' handling of gaming casinos, such as in Nevada, and periodic attacks on Indian gaming, such as described herein, demonstrate continued cultural domination with insistent and invasive attempts to reduce Native sovereignty and increase US jurisdiction. The US Justice Department supports just such reductions and increases:

> "The [Justice] department has stated repeatedly to this and other congressional committees that, in the absence of adequate regulatory oversight, large-scale gaming potentially is subject to targeting by organized crime families or criminal entrepreneurs, corrupt managers and dishonest employees," [said] deputy assistant attorney general DiGregory, in the criminal division of the Department of Justice.[43]

Moreover, these pressures either to eliminate Indian gaming or subordinate it entirely to federal and state authorities, thereby diluting any practice of sovereignty associated with gaming, are also found in congressional annals.

> "Today, the distinctions between Indian gaming and traditional (American state) gaming are becoming increasingly obscured,"... Senator Reid said.... Senator Reid has been accused of attempting to protect the Nevada gaming industry by the National Indian Gaming Association. He is a former chairman of the Nevada gaming commission and overtly pats himself on the back for removing organized crime from Nevada gaming.[44]

Even if he did get rid of the overt connection to organized crime, suspect as that claim may be, the United States and Nevada commissions did nothing about long-term investments by crime syndicates, which is only a possibility with Indian gaming, as noted by the Justice Department. Moreover, allegations or actual incidents leading to small-scale violence has led to "the most severe penalties" being imposed, including "Closure orders issued against casinos in Minnesota, Texas, Oklahoma, Washington, New York, North Dakota, California, Idaho and Wisconsin."[45]

Clearly, if the United States hesitates or refuses to intervene in quieting violence on reservations stemming from other social issues, for instance Pine Ridge in the 1970s, and historically ignores extremely high negative indicators rates such as poverty on Pine Ridge, in the Four Corners, and elsewhere, then questions of sovereignty must be playing a part in their inaction. The two-edged sword of sovereignty as defended by traditional peoples and some tribal councils remains indicative of the historical domination of Native peoples. Senator Daniel Inouye, a democrat from Hawaii, put it bluntly:

> "Perhaps if the federal and state governments could point to a proud record of accomplishments in assisting Indian governments to survive the devastating conditions of poverty that have been thrust upon them, we would not have a reason to be here today, [Senate Committee on Indian Affairs hearings on Indian Gaming]. But our record, sadly, is not a proud one, nor even one of measured success, and whether we may like it or not, the conduct of gaming on Indian lands has begun, in a few areas, to effect a change in these conditions to some degree."[46]

The interplay between modernization and economic development from casino profits, and historic tensions and conflicts over sovereignty, jurisdiction, and exploitation, works itself out in the same social milieu as that of the traditionals and the tribal councils, noted in the opening discussion. To that arena we now turn to the Prairie Island case, a Dakota reservation just southeast of the Twin Cities in Minnesota.

MODERN PERSPECTIVES

The direct financial benefits from a successful casino for a small reservation population, such as at the profitable Treasure Island at the M'deWakantowan's reconstructed Prairie Island, are well documented and even touted by the proponents of gaming.[47] However, traditional-minded people evaluating their own social change fixate upon demographic and cultural make-up of their Indian identity and culture. Inevitably, blood quantum and enrollment are critical issues.

> **Number Ten:** More and more families are marrying non-Indians who immediately start to have children. Some of the white women who have these children are collecting their benefits, and they scream the loudest to have direct per-capita payments [per child per household]. This is causing a real problem for us. What about the future generations?[48]

The economic issue and financial gains emanating from casino gaming near metropolitan areas, cause further social change from both outside the "tribal structures" of a society that has resisted total assimilation for more than one hundred years, and from inside the "tribal identity" that historically had been whittled down with dissolution of full-bloods and traditionals through an increase in intermarriage with non-Indians and a continuing absorption of Indian culture and society.[49]

Outsiders marrying into family structures, possibly in hopes of considerable financial gain, along with shifting power and political issues within tribal councils controlling more monetary decisions, have led to internal corruption and negligence of cultural survival, the very thing that enabled claims for federal recognition and limited sovereignty in the first place. However, cultural decay is not inevitable, as is evident in some tribal members' concerns for future generations. Similar to the Pequots, but with more history and cultural integrity, the Prairie Island Dakota have adapted to needs and changes in a modern world, including economic life, with an eye toward resisting assimilation. The casino simply plays a part in ongoing survival measures of the people who have stayed.

> **Number Twenty-One:** The nuclear facility gave us jobs when we needed them. Now we have to fight the above ground storage of the radioactive waste. They made a deal without an agreement with us. The best way to resist that is through our council. We must use our sovereign rights to determine our own future, and to resist the destruction and exploitation of our lands. Casino profits give us more resources for that struggle, and less dependence on the nuclear power plant jobs and money.[50]

Complex interplay among resistance, survival, and economic betterment in both Indian and mainstream worlds has been disrupted by the sudden presence of profitable casinos. At Prairie Island these have provided economic development, potent threats to traditional life, individual and group financial gains, and a modicum of independence for ongoing resistance. Nowhere is this more evident than in a recent restoration of an important traditional ceremony called the Sun Dance among a small group. The summer solstice of 1993 saw some twenty participants, all M'deWakantowan descendants, participating in the Sun Dance less than two miles from the nuclear power plant and the huge casino that had played such large roles in the Prairie Island Dakota's ongoing struggle.

Resources, social empowerment, and cultural resurgence are additional factors growing out of Indian gaming in this case. Traditional people, who live and act in the modern world, utilize the potent forces of casino profits to maintain and resurrect their Dakota cultural values that are concomitantly threatened by the same modernization.

The Standing Rock (Sioux) Indian Reservation, more recently termed a nation, reflects these contradictory positions through the traditional culture of Hunkpapa Lakota and Yanktonai Dakota, and as the home of resistance leaders such as Sitting Bull, Gall, Running Antelope, and others.[51] The Prairie Knights Casino, just north of Fort Yates and south of Cannonball, has been operating for a few years with a high measure of financial success, considering its extremely rural location. Grand River Casino to the south, just over the river from Mobridge, South Dakota, followed shortly afterwards and has also turned a profit.

Initial changes in local socioeconomic situations include an increase in job opportunity. Unemployment in the area ran as high as 60 to 80 percent before the casino's opening and has seen a significant decrease since that time. In addition, there now is limited economic development in contrast to rations and BIA/federal dependence and an increase in the stature of the tribal council and other governmental agencies. This last set of changes, sociopolitical representations, has become crucial for many Dakota and Lakota traditionals having historical conflicts with and many criticisms of the tribal council. Suddenly, appointment to a gaming committee brings financial rewards and real social power. These appointments and political positioning, freed from the BIA systems of social control, empower those claims to sovereignty such as with the Oglala Lakota Nation from Pine Ridge. However, as noted, Standing Rock houses both Dakota and Lakota peoples.

> **Number Six:** The Standing Rock Nation gives rise to the oppression of some traditional people…. Standing Rock as this "nation" means that Big Horse's children are all half-breeds—aren't part of the "nation." That's not real.[52]

One set of problems arising from nation-status claims is that membership in an Indian nation, or Native "citizenship" enrollment as a Lakota, can be divided. Should Big Horse have dual citizenship in the Standing Rock and Cheyenne River nations or reservations? These very real policy implications remain unanswered by new leadership forms that are preoccupied with sovereignty questions relating to the development of profits from casinos and Indian gaming ventures that need protection from incursions by adjoining states. Real as those struggles may be, both traditionals and some tribal leaders have seen the potential weakness in allowing "national" claims to be based on compact negotiations with surrounding states that have formerly been their enemy.

TRADITIONAL PERSPECTIVES

Thus, the Standing Rock council, long resistant to forces of assimilation including the BIA, finds itself negotiating as a nation with a state in the United States that can revisit the proposed laws through its legislature. Ultimately, the traditionals are not finding problems with any particular form of gambling on Standing Rock, but rather with a general weakening of the cultural forms that have sustained resistance for more than one hundred years.

Cultural struggles with the Mohawk, Onondonga and Oneida, and a host of related Native nations and tribal peoples illustrate similar internal conflicts. With the Lakota on rural reservations in South Dakota, similar to the preceding discussion of the Dakota at Prairie Island, the sociocultural effects are most evident in the family systems.

Tiwaye, the family, and the historically disrupted *tiyospaye*, or extended relations, have been negatively influenced from the presence of the casinos, and will likely sustain further problems. These include the mundane but real effects of spending less time at home with children, spending more time traveling to and from the casinos, and the social production of a new cultural language revolving around gaming institutions. In fact, whole lifestyle changes are growing around casinos, evidenced at Standing Rock. With higher quality food, hotels, group facilities, and nightlife available, more Native people find the casinos to be a central gathering spot. This tends to cause less time or effort directed toward traditional life, including religious observation, Native language use, and formal or informal traditional gatherings. As Holy Rock of the Grey Eagle Society on Pine Ridge stated in an address to the National Indian Education Association about families:

> There was such an emphasis on absorbing our Indian people into American society, our cultural values have been lost.... Unless our young people can find balance, happy balance, they will remain in confusion ... and find themselves in conflict with the dominant society.[53]

Existing conflicts between societies, the dominant Euro-Americans and the subordinated, disrupted Native Americans, are exacerbated by the increased modernization resulting from casino gaming institutions. As noted earlier, these culturally destructive forces also carry the seed for their own resolution. Just as the family systems are experiencing stresses, they are also strengthened through increased employment and educational opportunities, both of which may yield much greater positive effects on the people.

> We should not be faulted as an inferior people—we have the capacity to live, and succeed, in the civilized world. Like doctors, in the field of medicine, educators work with the health of the people, reducing the confusion of our coming generations.[54]

All the evidence points to the observation that these same phenomena are occurring throughout Indian Country with nations and tribes that have casinos and a surviving traditional population. Furthermore, with the incredible mobility of Indian peoples partly established by the powwow circuit and partly strengthened through recent activist social movements, "supra-tribalism" helps to spread socioeconomic and cultural change rapidly, even from those locales without strongly surviving traditional ties.[55]

> **Number Four:** I see how the Foxwoods and Pequot sponsored "world-champion" powwow dancers, with huge prize money, has caused many dancers and even drums [drum-groups] to just focus on the big powwows.... Traditional powwows are fading away.[56]

Although certainly overstated, the perception among some dancers and singers that this phenomena is occurring, evidences a de-emphasis on traditional forms of supported social solidarity and cultural resistance. This particular Lakota dancer prides himself on creating cultural artifacts constructed with completely traditional materials. Yet his honesty and the presence of a pipe caused him to confess that his great desire was to win the big prize money at Foxwoods.

Dysfunctional lifestyles engendered by dependence on and domination by American society could be increased by ready access to the material source of such dysfunction—namely money. Traditional forms of resistance, for instance maintenance of the traditional O-inipi (Sweat Lodge) and Wi-Wang Wacipi (Sun Dance) of the Lakota may be weakened by easily accessible material comforts. Conversely, support and empowerment for these cultural forms may be increased because of heightened financial, social, and political resources now available. These value systems have already undergone considerable change, reflected in expressions from traditional people:

Number Fourteen: Sure, there are lots of problems. You know I am really angry about that Grand River Casino. I didn't win, lost all my nickels. So I'll never go back there again.... Seriously, though, the new Rosebud Casino, just south of Mission and near the Nebraska border, gets a lot of people from around here.... When the casino first opened, some of the more traditional people said they "saw the devil there...." He would sit by a person and they would win. I think this partly arises from an exposure to the white man's religion.[57]

Disentangling historic deculturation attempts by the United States becomes impossible in terms of local effects. Winning money is paramount in American society. There is no clear reason why Native Americans should not enjoy and be able to choose social activities similar to those of non-Indians.

Number Fourteen: Now, though, traditional people go there to eat, and go out [to casinos] with their friends who gamble.[58]

Another fundamental consideration arises from the choices individual Lakotas make in regard to their time and money. However, long-term neglect and oppression by the US government, including Individual Indian Money accounts and defining full-bloods as "incompetents" probably have at least as great an effect.[56]

Number Sixteen: The effect from Bingo is greater than the casinos. Some people would leave their children for hours and hours.... While, in a casino, if you don't have much money, you lose it quickly.... Many people only have money once a month, from GA [General Assistance], and so only one week is affected.... The long-term effects are they spend, lose their money on the wrong things [instead of spending on the family's needs].[60]

Earlier attempts at invasive, dominating forms of social control over everyday life produced deep dependence as well as devolution of existing traditional patterns of social values.[61] These incursions have resulted in the disappearance of normal cultural mechanisms that protect traditional peoples from the negative forces of modernity.

SOCIOECONOMIC PERSPECTIVES

Other related issues are the deleterious effects arising from the influx of readily disposable income and cash sources from casino profits. These appear to have negative, rather than positive, effects on social development, namely increased crime and drug and alcohol use. Related to these issues are connections to the forms of cultural retention and survival that enable resistance to cultural hegemony from the United States over traditional lifestyles and social institutions. If, as has been demonstrated, internal forms of cultural resistance have been strengthened by oppressive forces of domination, then they may well be weakened by the dependence and excess of modern lifestyles made easier through the access to money and social resources that once were limited.

These are, however, most likely short-term effects that were already on a gradual rise. More appropriate concerns might be the social changes arising from employment-related issues and employer-employee relations. Sources of tension and potential resolution are found in the relationships between Indian casino employees and casino management, and among community people, including many traditionals. On Rosebud, employees have grieved their treatment using modern negotiating language:

> Whirlwind Soldier presented a letter from "the majority of Rosebud Casino employees"… and said they "are being mistreated and neglected when we try to establish benefits through our chain of command." The employees voiced their concerns to the tribal council.[62]

Development related to building effective employment patterns, including grievance procedures, has proven extremely difficult for non-Indian companies and vocational education programs. Yet already employees are making claims to the justification of employer relations.

> Another concern is the contract punishment system. The employees said, "If we are excessively late and not working hard, we don't get fired. We have the option of working for minimum wage for 30 days. Our voices need to be heard and not ignored. We are not lazy or greedy Native Americans. We want to advance and have better opportunities for our casino and most importantly our families."[60]

The structural issues underlying economic and social development are tied to employment concerns of these Indian casino employees, leading to greater awareness of the familial, societal, and institutional effects. Improving the condition of the people, albeit in struggle with potential corrupting forces, also results from the economic growth of the casinos.

With the advent of modern economic structures on reservations historically lacking such institutions, other developments come into play. For instance, the tribal councils can be questioned as to responsibilities and rights to the people they represent. Contrary to predictions of increased tensions in these arenas, these structures may reduce the disparity between council members and community people, and increase the solidarity of reservation-nation residents as a whole. These are separate from tensions arising out of the previously identified factors: the distribution networks, corruption, and sharp increases in external and internal competition for profits and individual payouts.

The net effect of traditionals' perception of their benefits or losses, monetary as well as cultural, may reside in the amount and type of inclusion in, or exclusion from, the development strategies of their tribe or nation. These vary greatly by each Indian nation and by each reservation's situation.[64] These developments—economic, social, and political—will possibly assist the betterment of relations among the historically disenfranchised traditional Lakota people, their oftentimes employed offspring, and governing tribal councils.[65] Only time will tell if any developments will occur.

Modernization on contemporary Indian reservations with operating gambling casinos is not necessarily opposed to contemporary traditional life.

However, US government policy has not and is not pursuing methods of traditional or cultural preservation. Internecine divisions between traditionals and US governing institutions, and between Indian agents and tribal councils set up by Indian Reorganization Act (IRA) constitutions, have fostered assimilationist strategies that do not assist internal institutional development for the Native peoples they ostensibly serve.[66]

Additionally, cultural destruction and decay resulting from decades and even centuries of coercive assimilation policies may be better addressed through secondary institutions, such as labor unions, that profit from increased development of these economies of scale. However, traditional people living on the reservations are often excluded from primary participation. Moreover, the traditional value systems and cultural interaction patterns are further disturbed by the influx of capital, people, employment, and management from off the reservation.

These contrasting cultural systems engage existing tensions on American Indian reservations in northern midwestern states, including imposed BIA-IRA governing structures, depressed and even destroyed local economies, assimilation, sharp and conflicting ideas of progress and societal goals, ongoing debates on the per-capita/program distributions, and possibly threatened maintenance of indigenous lifestyles.[67]

INDIAN GAMING STRUGGLES

Political effects resulting from the presence and economic distributions of the casinos range from shifts in national politics to local changes in tribal council elections and appointments. Sovereignty issues command national politics, as discussed earlier in regard to Senator Reid, various gaming commissions, the IGRA, and NIGA.[68] National politics, clearly dominated by sovereignty issues, therefore shape the regional and local issues as well, especially the nature and practice of cultural autonomy and sovereignty. Traditional Dakota and Lakota people from "treaty tribes" maintain similar perspectives when analyzing these relations:

> **Number Twenty-Four:** [T]he system is not right, is corrupt. The BIA, the states, our own IRA councils.... We did not grow up with drugs, with gangs, we had our own good value system.... I am against these casinos. They destroy our ways of life.[69]

The powerful point here is that this traditional Dakota woman is clearly connecting tribal council activity and political structures with the advent of casinos and the destruction of traditional value systems. Two more important points are made herein. One is the view that financial distributions and democratic elections inappropriately personalize a tribal society and a collective identity. Another is that individualism as a natural outgrowth is woven through these structures. Individualism and unequal distributions are viewed as harmful to traditional life.

However, as discussed in the cultural and economic terms above, modernization can be linked to continued resistance and strengthening of cultural systems, including treaty right struggles.

Number Twenty-Four: Some of the treaties are still being broken, abrogated.... [T]raditional people, we honor all persons, even those with forked tongues. That has to stop ... we must band together.[70]

Modernization linked to economic development and political structures growing out of casinos threatens much traditional life, and is opposed to sociopolitical systems long suppressed. Ironically, these same structures might hold the key to continued resistance.

Current tensions are not only framed by these conflicts, but are also exacerbated by ongoing competition and conflict over existing tribal resources with the state governments. For example, one contested point in New Mexico with the Apache is over "shares for state revenue resources" that would be partly determined by the state of New Mexico's government.[71] Resource and profit-sharing can become influenced by surrounding states' laws, which may be in competition with the economic development initiatives of tribes or nations under review.

Moreover, the previously identified concerns over sovereignty are clearly evidenced: "The court declared these compacts were invalid because the state legislature had not approved them."[72] Therefore, the very issue that allowed for the rise of casino gaming, historically determined sovereignty, becomes threatened by the limited expression of those laws through the economic institutions of casinos.

Just as one highly educated Lakota educator finds casino gambling to be "devastating to the families" and social structures on the reservation, another Lakota language teacher believes that "yes, gambling is addictive, but [it is] similar to other modern addictions—alcohol and even welfare—we have to learn to adjust our behaviors."[73]

Traditional perspectives also vary depending on their emphasis and the local situation. Pine Ridge residents report that a majority of traditionals in southern Pine Ridge are very much against the Prairie Winds Casino just west of their community on the reservation border, seeing it as politically and culturally motivated.

Number Seventeen: Many people are wondering about that casino [Prairie Winds], and what will happen to the money.... [I]t's supposed to go to the districts for education and development. Now a lot is missing, but we can't find out where it went. People are worried that they [the government] will use this money as an excuse to cut down on GA [General Assistance].... "They" are already talking about that.
Interviewer: But at least some people have jobs, and that helps.
Number Seventeen: Yeah, well, many traditional people are against these casinos anyway. They worry about the problems that money brings.[74]

Again, there are observable tensions between the deleterious forces of modernization and those struggling to maintain traditional social relationships. While part of this discussion draws on situational sociology to study the direct impact on families, another part of this discourse presents a macro-analysis on the tribal, nation, and even pan-Indian levels.

Voting, in state, tribal, and local elections becomes another set of cultural adaptations. However, notions of sovereignty are linked to these negotiated social constructs. Tim Giago sees sovereignty as contested simply through relations with the state governments, evidenced in the Washington state referendums noted previously. The importance of these questions is found in the recent closings of the Mescalero Apache casinos in New Mexico and the sudden, devastating unemployment caused by the Pueblo casino's closings.[75]

Sociopolitical constructs arising from the negotiations with state governments are thus two-edged swords—on one side there are the potential threats to tribal sovereignty that may refer to treaty rights, and on the other is the strengthening of local economies and political power with possibilities of sudden closures that weaken and potentially devastate political and economic gains.

CONCLUSIONS

To some extent, opposing negative effects derive from the differing perspectives of the modern gambling and traditional institutions on most Indian reservations. However, in separating out the shared cultural decay and degradation handed down from non-Native dominant society, it is impossible to analytically separate the modernizing effects taking place along the way, from the massive social change arising out of gambling casinos.

Moreover, economic development from gaming itself cancels out dichotomous analysis, yielding negative and positive effects. Traditionals are on both sides of these ideological fences. Whereas they appear to agree that gambling was historically condoned and currently acceptable, they differ sharply about whether positive effects or further erosion of traditional lifeways may result from casino gaming profits.

Furthermore, drawing distinctions between these effects and any real or perceived dependency increase is artificial and discriminatory. The United States' policy institutions and their mechanisms of social control have created the high levels of socioeconomic dependence noted throughout the social science literature. The solution to reducing such dependence remains in the political arena of Native nations or reservations and in economic development itself. These are precisely the two major social institutions, political and economic, experiencing great gains and visibility from the presence of Indian gaming, especially in the more oppressed areas, such as with the Lakota. Therefore, net gain analysis from both the traditional and modern perspectives, irrespective of local situational dynamics such as those found at Pine Ridge and Saint Regis, demonstrates numerous benefits and overall strengthening as a result of the casinos.

Casinos and their economic development are prompting even more intensive social change throughout the communities on Standing Rock. It is a process that is welcomed for its income, but considered suspicious by most traditional elders who have observed cultural losses over the years.

This paper has relied on traditionals and elders as the primary cultural informants on the changing indigenous identities for the people on Standing Rock, Rosebud, and Pine Ridge reservations. Casino gaming has destabilized those identities, and introduced both good and bad modern forces. Political structures and economic relations are in flux in these situations, increasing the stresses already placed on Native families in these environments.

Indian gaming enterprises, especially in the guise of casinos on traditional reservations, have played major roles and will continue to influence ongoing developments of Native nations and traditional cultures. Cultural destruction and decay is better addressed through secondary institutions that profit from increased development of these economies of scale. However, traditional people living on the reservations have often been excluded from primary participation. Moreover, traditional value systems and cultural interaction patterns are further disturbed by an influx of capital, people, employment, and management from off the reservation. These structures amplify depressed local economies, complex levels of assimilation, sharp and conflicting ideas on "progress" and societal goals, ongoing debates on per-capita/program distributions, and the maintenance or loss of indigenous lifestyles.

While the Pequots have experienced forms of cultural revitalization from casino profits, other Native nations and tribal peoples have developed deep internal divisions, usually between traditionals and moderns who are historically at odds because of US systems of domination. The Dakota near the Twin Cities in Minnesota have adapted gaming systems, while the Lakota are experiencing painful developments and growing conflicts, even as the Seneca and Tuscarora (Iroquois) have voted down casino gaming developments.

I find that surviving systems of traditional life are often supported indirectly by sustained development resulting from gaming, albeit with tensions between moderns and traditionals. However, normal and already stressed family social structures are under added pressures from social life growing around gambling facilities. Further study is required to determine if these features will exacerbate a breakdown of Native families, or whether families and other social spheres will simply adapt to these forces. Both results contribute to previously highly stressed social systems that managed to survive centuries of genocide, cultural domination, and coercive assimilation.

Perhaps that should be the concluding message of this study. Native traditional peoples, whether from high-stakes profits at the Pequot's Foxwoods, or with meager financial rewards from the few casinos on rural Lakota reservations, live and interact in a modern American world. Their political, economic, and social institutions adjust and adapt to the changing conditions of life, guaranteeing a strong presence in the years to come, with or without casino gaming.

NOTES

1. See National Indian Gaming Association (NIGA), "Facts and Fiction of Indian Gaming," [http://www.indiangaming.org/], 1996.

2. Sharon O'Brien, *American Indian Tribal Governments* (Norman: University of Oklahoma Press, 1989); Philip J. Deloria, "The Twentieth Century and Beyond," in *The Native Americans*, eds. David H. Thomas, Jay Miller, Richard White, Peter Nabokov, and Philip J. Deloria (Atlanta: Turner Publishing Inc., 1993); Kirke Kickingbird, et al., *Indian Sovereignty* (Oklahoma City: Institute for the Development

of Indian Law, 1977).

3. Donald Lee Parman, *Indians and the American West in the Twentieth Century* (Bloomington: Indiana University Press, 1994); George P. Castile and Robert L. Bee, eds., *State and Reservation: New Perspectives on Federal Indian Policy* (Tucson: University of Arizona Press, 1992).

4. American Indian Lawyer Training Program (AILTP), *Indian Tribes as Sovereign Governments* (Oakland: American Indian Resources Institute, AIRI Press, 1988).

5. Michael K. Green, "Cultural Identities: Challenges for the Twenty-First Century" in *Issues in Native American Cultural Identity*, ed. Michael K. Green (New York: Peter Lang Publications, 1995).

6. William Apes, *On Our Own Ground* (Amherst: University of Massachusetts Press, 1992).

7. Severt Young Bear and R. D. Theisz, *Standing in the Light, a Lakota Way of Seeing* (Lincoln: University of Nebraska Press, 1994).

8. Rennard Strickland, "Native Americans," in *The Oxford Companion to the Supreme Court of the United States*, ed. Kermit Hall (New York: Oxford University Press, 1992), 577–581.

9. Keith Stack, "Sovereignty and Indian Gaming in the United States," *Cultural Survival Quarterly* (Summer/Fall 1994); see also Castile and Bee, *State and Reservation*.

10. Tribal Leaders, "American Indian Tribal Leaders—An Open Letter to the Members of the Congress of the United States, 1993" [http://www.nativeweb.org/] and [http://indy4.fdl.cc.mn.us/~isk/games/gaming.html], 1993; posted on Internet 1996.

11. See Wilkinson in AILTP, *Indian Tribes as Sovereign*.

12. See Young Bear and Theisz, *Standing in the Light*.

13. See Stack, "Sovereignty and Indian Gaming."

14. Thomas Biolsi, *Organizing the Lakota: The Political Economy of the New Deal on the Pine Ridge and Rosebud Reservations* (Tucson: University of Arizona Press, 1992); Frank Black Elk, "Observations on Marxism and Lakota tradition" in *Marxism and Native Americans*, ed. Ward Churchill (Boston: South End Press, 1983).

15. Tribal Leaders, "An Open Letter":

> We, the undersigned representatives of federally recognized Indian tribes of the United States, attending a meeting in Washington, D.C. on March 19, 1993, wish to clarify some of the current issues surrounding Indian gaming. We are concerned that there is a campaign underway by a few state officials and private gaming interests to amend the Indian Gaming Regulatory Act (IGRA) of 1988 in a manner that would be very detrimental to our tribal governments.... The Supreme Court recently reaffirmed tribal sovereignty in recognizing tribes' specific right to regulate and operate gaming projects for tribal governmental purposes in the 1987 Cabazon decision. IGRA's passage in 1988 compromised those governmental rights to the extent that it allowed states, through the compact process, to negotiate a regulatory role in certain forms of tribal gaming. IGRA thus permits tribes to retain the economic benefits of gaming recognized in Cabazon while providing states a government to government opportunity to participate in the regulatory process.... IGRA's grant to the states was opposed by tribes as an intrusion on their sovereignty, but was ultimately accepted as a neces-

sary compromise to meet states' concerns while protecting this important economic resource to tribes.... [List of sixty-nine tribal leaders, chairmen, and presidents, signatories attached]

16.   For metaphysical issues, see Vine Deloria, Jr., *The Metaphysics of Modern Existence* (San Francisco: Harper & Row, 1979); for cross cultural, see Edward W. Said, *Orientalism* (Vintage Books: New York, 1979); and for methodological, see Bruce Trigger, "Ethnohistory: The Unfinished Edifice," *Ethnohistory* 33:3 (Summer 1986): 253–267. For comparative analysis, see James V. Fenelon, *Culturicide, Resistance and Survival of the Lakota ("Sioux Nation")* (Garland Publishing: New York, 1998), 104–109.

17.   The author conducted more than one dozen interviews with Lakota and Dakota traditionalists and gaming employees in 1996 and 1997 in the Dakotas and Minnesota. These interviews focused on individuals indigenous perspectives on gaming and socioeconomic development. All interviewee quotations are from this time period.

18.   Interviewee Number Seven is a Dakota woman elder from Standing Rock. She is knowledgeable about Dakota and Lakota traditional culture and contemporary situations.

19.   Kathryn Gabriel, *Gambler Way* (Boulder: Johnson Books, 1996), 1–29; NIGA, 1996, n.1; Thomas E. Mails, *The Mystic Warriors of the Plains* (Garden City, NY: Doubleday, 1972).

20.   Interviewee Number Seven, see note 17.

21.   For social dysfunction on the reservation, see Robert Blauner, *Racial Oppression in America* (New York: Harper and Row, 1972); J. M. Blaut, "Colonialism and the Rise of Capitalism," *Science and Society* 53 (Fall 1989): 260–296; Discussion 54, Spring 1990; 55, Winter '91/'92; for BIA, see notes 13 and 14.

22.   Shari M. Sweeney, "The Big Gamble," in *Cleveland Magazine* 25 (October 1996), 10.

23 .   The research problem approach of social scientists has been mono-culturally focused on Native gaming situations at large, rather than comparative between societies.

24.   Sweeney, "The Big Gamble," 10.

25.   Oneida Indian Nation, "Message of Urgency from a Small Indian Nation" [http://oneida-nation.net/], posted on Internet 1996.

26.   For information on Willigen's dictum, see John van Willigen, "Applied Anthropology and Cultural Persistence," in *Persistent Peoples,* ed. George Castile (Tucson: University of Arizona Press, 1981).

27.   Stack, "Sovereignty and Indian Gaming."

28.   Francis X. Clines, "With Casino Profits, Indian Tribes Thrive," *New York Times* 31 January 1993, A18.; for history, see Apes, *On Our Own Ground.*

29.   Deloitte and Touche, Inc., "A Historical Review of Gaming in the United States" and "Case Studies of 8 American Indian Tribes" (Washington, DC: Tohmatsu International, NIGA, June 1995).

30.   Mike Epifiano, "The New Buffalo, How Indian Casinos Have Helped Impoverished Tribes Achieve New Levels of Self-Sufficiency" (Atlantic City: Casino Journal Publishing, December 1995).

31.   Annette M. Jaimes, "Federal Indian Identification Policy: A Usurpation of Indigenous Sovereignty in North America," *Policy Studies Journal* 16 (Summer 1988): 778–98.

32.   Interviewee Number Twenty-Seven is a middle-aged non-Indian man with

a wife and family. He was interviewed while gambling in Deadwood, South Dakota, where he had worked for two years.

33. When interviewee Number Nineteen, a Lakota woman educator from Rosebud, went to Deadwood with friends to gamble and socialize, she refused to go into a casino-club owned by Kevin Costner's brother, as it was funded by profits from *Dances With Wolves* and by Costner's Dunbar Estates. The casino is in direct competition with those of the Lakota.

34. John R. Wunder, *"Retained by the people": A History of American Indians and the Bill of Rights* (New York: Oxford University Press, 1994).

35. Tribal Leaders, "An Open Letter."

36. John Steele, "Tribal Leaders Day: Four Presidents Speak," 14 October 1996 address to the National Indian Education Association (NIEA) convention in Rapid City, South Dakota.

37. Standing Rock was an Indian agency turned into a Dakota and Lakota reservation, despite the fact that major treaties refer to the Lakota as a "Sioux Nation."

38. Jesse Taken Alive, "Tribal Leaders Day: Four Presidents Speak," 14 October 1996 address to NIEA convention in Rapid City, South Dakota.

39. Biolsi, *Organizing the Lakota.*

40. Tim Giago, "What Price Sovereignty," *Indian Country Today*, 14 October 1996, A4.

41. Ibid.

42. Ibid.

43. David Melmer, "Gaming commission regulation draws critics," *Indian Country Today*, 14 October 1996, A2.

44. Ibid.

45. Ibid.

46. Ibid.

47. See Deloitte and Touche, "A Historical Review of Gaming" and NIGA, "Facts and Fiction."

48. The testimony from this M'deWakantowan Dakota respondent, referred to here as interviewee Number Ten, is replicated in many interviews and testimony from a wide variety of respondents. The interviewee is a Dakota woman from Prairie Island M'deWakantowan who has worked for private companies and public agencies on and off the reservation. An ex-BIA superintendent (Native) for the Mesquakie in Iowa observed the conflict on that reservation as one of the greatest threats to internal social cohesion arising from casino gaming activity.

49. Matthew Snipp, "The Changing Political and Economic Status of American Indians: From Captive Nations to Internal Colonies," *American Journal of Economics and Sociology* 45:2 (April 1986): 145–157.

50. Interviewee Number Twenty-One is a gaming administrator from Prairie Island with long-term economic development perspectives.

51. Standing Rock was formed with two groups of the Lakota, the Hunkpapa, and the Blackfeet (Sihasapa), with the Yanktonai Dakota "given" the northern half in the 1890s.

52. Interviewee Number Six is a traditional Dakota educator and a sociopolitical organizer with connections to both tribal and national government groups. Here she is discussing the fact that Standing Rock does not recognize Cheyenne River blood quantum. Because of this, Big Horse's children will only be enrolled on their Standing Rock blood quantum, even though Big Horse is a full-blood Lakota married to a Lakota woman.

53. James Holy Rock, "Grey Eagle Society Message" to NIEA, unpublished proceedings from NIEA Conference, Rapid City, South Dakota.

54. Ibid.

55. Stephen Cornell, "The Transformations of Tribe: Organization and Self-Concept in Native Americans Ethnicities," *Ethnic and Racial Studies* 11 (January 1988): 27–47.

56. Interviewee Number Four is a traditional Lakota dancer and artisan and is knowledgeable about the tribe's culture, sociopolitical involvement, and history.

57. Interviewee Number Fourteen is a Lakota woman educator.

58. Ibid.

59. See Biolsi, *Organizing the Lakota.*

60. Interviewee Number Sixteen is a Lakota school administrator.

61. Biolsi, *Organizing the Lakota.*

62. Jean Roach, "Rosebud Casino Workers Voice Concerns Over Wages," *Indian Country Today*, 14 October 1996, B1 and B2.

63. Ibid.

64. Stephen Cornell and Joe Kalt, "Where Does Economic Development Really Come From? Constitutional Rule Among the Modern Sioux and Apache," *Harvard Project on American Indian Economic Development* (Cambridge: Malcolm Weiner Center for Social Policy, 1992).

65. See Biolsi, *Organizing the Lakota* and Parman, *Indians and the American West.*

66. See Young Bear, *Standing in the Light*; Duane Champagne, "Organizational Change and Conflict: A Case Study of the Bureau of Indian Affairs," in *Native Americans and Public Policy,* eds. Fremont Lyden and Lyman Legters (Pittsburgh: University of Pittsburgh Press, 1992).

67. Carolyn Reyer, *Cante Ohitika Win (Brave-hearted Women)* (Vermillion, SD: University of South Dakota Press, 1991).

68. See Tribal Leaders, "An Open Letter"; Melmer, "Gaming commission regulation"; and NIGA, "Facts and Fiction."

69. Interviewee Number Twenty-Four is an educator from Standing Rock.

70. Ibid.

71. Evelina Zuni Lucero, "New Mexcio Rides Gaming Roller Coaster," *Indian Country Today*, 21–28 October 1996, C1–C2.

72. Danica Tutush, "Apache Casino Employees Join the Unemployed," *Indian Country Today*, 14–21 October 1996, Section C.

73. Interviewee Number Nineteen is a Lakota woman who works in education and is involved in politics and reservation development with Rosebud and Pine Ridge groups.

74. Interviewee Number Seventeen is a Lakota man from Pine Ridge involved with grassroots development.

75. See Lucero, "New Mexico Rides Gaming Roller Coaster."

♣

The Gambler's Style

Contesting the Evil Gambler: Gambling, Choice, and Survival in American Indian Texts

Paul Pasquaretta

The dramatic rise of the tribal gambling industry has occasioned renewed interest in traditional Indian gambling practices and stories. As the fortunes of many tribal communities have been bound up with the economic, legal, and social implications of the gambling trade, Indian writers have exploited the dramatic and symbolic potential of traditional games and stories, weaving them into written performances as ideological touchstones and plot-shaping devices. While this is largely a contemporary phenomenon, it can be traced to Indian novelists writing almost a century and a half ago. An early example is provided in *The Life and Adventures of Joaquin Murieta*, an 1854 novel written by John Rollins Ridge, a Cherokee who published under the pen name Yellow Bird. In the early twentieth century, Hum-ishu-ma, a Salishan writer known to her readers as Mourning Dove, offered a more complex commentary on gambling in her allotment-era novel *Cogewea, the Half-Blood*, first published in 1927. Some of the best examples of the influence of traditional gambling practices are found in works published since the late 1970s, when high-stakes reservation gambling operations began to appear on tribal lands. One of the first of these was Leslie Marmon Silko's *Ceremony* (1977). In this text, Southwestern Indian gambling practices are integral parts of a healing ceremony undertaken by an American Indian World War II veteran. Gerald Vizenor, mining his own Chippewa/Anishinabe traditions, has written extensively about gambling in many of his works, including *Bearheart: The Heirship Chronicles* (1978), *Heirs of Columbus* (1991), and *Dead Voices* (1992). These texts reference woodland bowl games, moccasin games, and a card game identified as *wanaki* chance. Also of Chippewa descent, Louise Erdrich has featured gambling stories and scenarios in *Love Medicine* (1984, expanded and republished in 1993), *Tracks* (1988), and *The Bingo Palace* (1993). In these texts, tribal gambling traditions are reenacted through Euro-American games such as poker and bingo.

For each of these writers, traditional gambling stories, metaphors, and ceremonial practices provide an opportunity to comment upon tribal issues and controversies of all kinds. By suggesting strategies of resistance and survival to colonial domination and genocide, they function as ritual and narrative sites where the forces of assimilation and destruction are contested. In traditional Indian gambling stories, good gamblers are pitted against evil opponents associated with Euro-American culture, traditional social vices, and traditional tribal

131

enemies. The evil gambler might be a figure from tribal lore, a white man, or another Indian. Having multiple significations, the evil gambler provides a means to distinguish appropriate and inappropriate forms of behavior as well as healthy and unhealthy attitudes towards gambling itself. In addition to providing moral instruction and guidance, gambling stories establish the importance of ritual play in ensuring the long-term survival of individuals and groups. For Indian writers, the survival of traditional games and stories is necessary for the people's survival.

Indigenous gambling rites were among the first cultural practices criticized by the European colonists. From as early as the 1630s and the publication of William Wood's *New England's Prospect*, British colonists and their Anglo-American descendants treated Indian gambling as a sign of the Native's degeneracy and backwardness.[1] Although gambling had always been practiced by Euro-Americans themselves, it was considered detrimental to the progress of civilization, particularly when it was practiced by non-white others. Distinguishing the vicious gambling of others from their own virtuous speculations, government and business leaders worked to supress the gambling practices that they perceived to disrupt work patterns, limit productivity, and interfere with the proper accumulation of wealth and property.[2] Among other ill effects, this sentiment resulted in Native Americans being stereotyped as a game-playing people who stood in the way of progress. By helping to justify the takeover of Indian lands and the necessity of so-called reform efforts, this misconception contributed to the oppression of Indian peoples.

An important change in the way whites perceived Indian gambling practices occurred near the turn of the nineteenth century. In 1903, Stewart Culin published *Games of the North American Indians*. Writing for the Smithsonian's bureau of American ethnology, Culin included material on 229 different Native groups in North America and Mexico, and identified thirty-six different types of games, including both games of skills and dexterity and games of chance. Culin described games of chance as,

> rites pleasing to the gods to secure their favor, or as processes of sympathetic magic, to drive away sickness, avert other evil, or produce rain and the fertilization and reproduction of plants and animals, or other beneficial results.[3]

Culin wrote at a time when Indians were no longer a threat to the land expansion policies of the United States. Under the paternalistic guidance of American policymakers, Natives became the focus of intense scrutiny from a variety of outside observers. These developments contributed to a strain of American historicism that attempts to view the historical relations of Indians and whites from a cross-cultural perspective. Following in this tradition, Neal Salisbury describes the same gambling practices that the Puritans identified as signs of Indian vice as mechanisms of democracy and egalitarianism.[4]

Indian writers have also worked to counter the negative assumptions whites often make about traditional gambling practices. In his 1928 autobiography *My People the Sioux*, Luther Standing Bear describes *hanpa-pe-cunpi*, the moccasin or hand game of the Plains Indians. While commentators like Francis Parkman likened this practice to the "desperate gambling" that occurs in the "hells of Paris,"[5] Standing Bear emphasized the game as communal celebration and wholesome entertainment. "No drinks were observed," he stresses, "which took away the sense of our men and women, so no one grew boisterous. We had no bad words in our language, so none were used."[6]

Mourning Dove's description of the stick game of the Okanogans similiarly emphasizes the communal aspects of traditional gambling practices:

> In the evening, people made large bonfires in the open air and challenged other tribes to play the stick game. Lively songs were sung by both sides, and each team tried to distract the other while it was trying to hide the two bones. The object of the game was for the other side to guess which hand had a particular bone. Each side had a long pole stretched across in front and pounded on it with a short stick, keeping time with the songs. Bets of robes, blankets, coins and so forth were piled in the middle. Anyone could bet on a team, even women. Women also had their betting games, which could last for a few hours or several days.[7]

Mourning Dove identified good sportsmanship as a necessary attribute of the players. "It was shameful for poor losers to grieve," she wrote, "They would get no sympathy."[8]

In her analysis of Indian gambling practices, Schaghticoke writer Trudie Lamb has emphasized the ceremonial and spiritual significance of traditional games of chance. Among the Iroquois, she writes,

> Gus-ka-eh, the ancient peach stone game, is an important rite of the Midiwis or Mid-winter Ceremony … the Midiwis concludes the end of one cycle and marks the beginning of another. The Sacred Bowl Game is one of the Four Sacred Rituals of Mid-winter and symbolizes the struggle of the Twin Boys to win control over the earth. The Mid-winter is a time of praying and awaiting the rebirth, a renewal of life. It is a time of giving thanks to the spirit forces and to the Creator.[9]

The Twin Boys referred to by Lamb represent the competing forces of creation and destruction. According to Iroquois cosmology, the twins played the peach stone game to settle their differences. When played during the four-day mid-winter period, the game commemorates the good twin's victory, amuses the life-giving forces, pleases the plant and animal kingdoms, and makes the Creator laugh.[10]

While Indian texts celebrate traditional gambling practices, they also make distinctions between appropriate and inappropriate forms of gambling. Such distinctions are evident in *The Code of Handsome Lake*, an Iroquois text from the late eighteenth century. While the *Code* describes Gus-ka-eh as one of four divine amusements the Creator made for the happiness of the people, it traces the decline of Native peoples to the introduction of European playing cards. According to the *Code*, the time of trouble began when the Evil One duped a young European preacher into importing to North America five deadly objects: playing cards, money, fiddles, rum, and witchery. The preacher naively believed that these objects would be used for the betterment of the Indians: "Bring these to the people," he is told, "and make them as white men are."[11] At the preacher's request, the evil objects are brought to America by Christopher Columbus. Once this was accomplished, the Evil One laughed to himself over the destruction they would cause:

> These cards will made them gamble away their wealth and idle their time: this money will make them dishonest and covetous and they will forget their old laws; this fiddle will make them dance with their arms about their wives and bring about a time of tattling and idle gossip; this rum will turn their minds to foolishness and they will barter their country for baubles; then will this secret poison eat the life from their blood and crumble their bones."[12]

With this list of evil objects *Handsome Lake* identifies the European goods and practices that are most damaging to his people. Describing a casino-like environment in which gambling and drinking are prevalent, it demonstrates how a variety of outside influences contributes to the breakdown of Iroquois society. This breakdown leads directly to the loss of the land. *Handsome Lake* may refer to the type of atmosphere speculators created when they came to negotiate with Indians. In identifying this link between European gambling practices and the machinations of land speculators, the *Code* offers a traditional perspective on the role of gambling in Native society. When practiced within a traditional framework, games like Gus-ka-eh affirm Iroquois culture and support the long-term survival of the people; when practiced irresponsibly and in a nontraditional manner, games can lead to disaster.

The literary dimensions of traditional Indian gambling practices were first sketched out by John Rollins Ridge, a Cherokee who published under the pen name Yellow Bird. In his 1854 novel, *The Life and Adventures of Joaquin Murieta, the Celebrated California Bandit*, monte dealing is described as a legitimate means of employment for people denied access to mainstream sources of income. Yellow Bird first heard about the historical Joaquin Murieta in San Francisco. A scourge to white miners and settlers, Murieta had become something of a Robin Hood to Mexicans and Indians who found themselves increasingly oppressed and marginalized by the in-rushing Anglos. Yellow Bird understood the sources of Murieta's actions and sympathized with his crusade. The son of John Ridge and grandson of Major Ridge, the two principle leaders of the pro-removal party, he had firsthand experience with the violence that resulted from hostile colonial takeovers. Born in Oklahoma, or Indian territory, in 1827, he witnessed the murder of his father by other Cherokees who harbored resentment against those who had favored the move.[13] Thus, while white newspaper men emphasized Murieta's barbarity, Yellow Bird emphasized his humanity. In his novel, the youthful Joaquin is described as having a mild, peaceable, and generous disposition. Upon reaching adulthood, he cast his lot with the Americans, a people he admired, and joined the California Gold Rush. The well-intentioned young man soon discovered that the country was full of "lawless and desperate men" who looked upon "any and all Mexicans ... as no better than conquered subjects of the United States, having no rights which could stand before a haughtier and superior race."[14] Replaying the violence committed against the Cherokee some twenty years earlier, Murieta is confronted by Americans, who, "having the brute power to do as they please, visited [his] house and peremptorily bade him leave his claim, as they would allow no Mexicans to work in that region" (*JM* 10). Joaquin went on to establish a farm, from which he is again driven by Americans "with no other excuse than that he was 'an infernal Mexican intruder!'"(*JM* 10).

Cast upon his own devices the young man makes his livelihood dealing monte. While professional gamblers in the mid-nineteenth century were often characterized as social pariahs, the narrator contends that monte dealing "is considered by the Mexican in no manner a disreputable employment, and many well-raised young men from the Atlantic States have resorted to it as a profession in this land of luck and chances" (*JM* 11). Reflecting the characteristics of the gentleman gambler of western lore, Joaquin is known for playing the game on "very fair and honest principles"(*JM* 11). According to the narrator, he won others' money with such "skill and grace, or lost his own with such perfect good humor that he was considered by all the very beau ideal of a gambler and the prince of clever fellows" (*JM* 12). Insofar as his gambles are associated with efforts to resist colonial violence and oppression, Joaquin can also be read as a type of the good gambler of tribal tradition. Rather than being a victim in the land of luck and chances, he is able to beat the Anglos at their own game. As John Lowe points out, Joaquin boldly turns the tables on his colonial adversaries. Able to negotiate both a vast landscape and the "restricted space" of the saloon, Joaquin "is not content merely to penetrate this sanctum sanctorum of the patriarchs; the poker table, a doubled altar with the gods of money above and guns below, is literally trampled and profaned by [his] muddy boots."[15] Joaquin's supernatural abilities are also evident in his "magical luck"(*JM* 51). According to the narrator, the bandit's "extraordinary successes" lent credence to "the old Cherokee superstition that there were some men who bear charmed lives and whom nothing can kill but a silver bullet" (*JM* 139).

Mureita gives up on a law-abiding existence after he is falsely accused of horse stealing and whipped by an Anglo mob. Drawing back into the California landscape he becomes an agent of vengeance. Eventually his luck runs out and he is killed by agents of the law. While Joaquin's life has tragic overtones, he is not the victim of fate. Rather than being an inevitable defeat at the hands of a superior force, his death results from an "extreme carelessness" born of confidence in his own ability (*JM* 153). Although the emphasis on overconfidence provides the hero with a tragic flaw, *The Life and Adventures of Joaquin Murieta* expresses a profound if cautionary hopefulness and optimism that is characteristic of the gambler in tribal fiction. Although Joaquin does not survive, the story holds out the possibility of his survival, and by association, the survival of others who choose to resist social injustice.

If Yellow Bird introduced the tribal gambling metaphor to American Indian literature, Mourning Dove showed how it could provide more than an ideological touchstone. Written in collaboration with Lucullus Virgil McWhorter, a white writer and student of Native culture, her 1927 novel *Cogewea, the Half-Blood* is organized around a series of gambling rituals.

Among the games referred to in *Cogewea* are poker, monte, and traditional tribal games. At a box social the men bid on picnic baskets anonymously prepared by the women. For the single members of the community in search of husbands and wives, this ritual of courtship is a type of high-stakes guessing game. Betting on horse racing is also featured in the text. For the narrator, the excitement of the race provides an opportunity to reflect on the differences between Native and white gamblers. While the whites crowd to the judges' table, "disputing, in language more emphatic than elegant," there are no contentions among the tribal gamblers: "With them, winnings and losses alike were accepted with stoic indifference."[16] As in her autobiography, Mourning Dove here describes good sportsmanship as an important attribute of the Indian gambler. The perceived lack of sportsmanship among the white track bettors foreshadows the tactics of Alfred Densmore, a white man with whom the title character gambles.

The novel is set during the allotment period of American Indian history, a time when speculations on Indian lands and federal Indian policies combined to divest Native peoples of some 90 million acres, 60 percent of the lands they held prior to the passage of the General Allotment Act in 1887.[17] At the outset of the novel, Cogewea is described as a twenty-one-year-old mixed-blood woman and recent graduate from Pennsylvania's Carlisle Indian Industrial Arts School. She is now working on her sister's ranch, her white brother-in-law being a rancher who married into the community during allotment. Her Indian mother has long since passed away and her white father has abandoned her and her two sisters for the Alaskan gold rush. As the action begins, Cogewea faces choices involving lifestyle, work, and marriage. She describes these in terms of gambling and fishing metaphors. "Life is a gamble," she reflects, "a chance, a mere guess. Cast a line and reel in a splendid rainbow trout or a slippery eel" (*CHB* 21). This comment is repeated later in the novel when Cogewea is on the verge of making a near fatal guess.

As the novel's references to traditional tribal gambling practices suggest, the gambling metaphors in *Cogewea* are likely informed by the stick game ceremonials that Mourning Dove described in her autobiography. If life is a stick game, Cogewea must choose the correct hand. In this case, "hand" signifies a metaphorical hand in marriage. On the one hand is Alfred Densmore, a charming and sophisticated easterner who represents an opportunity for the young woman to travel the world and enjoy the refined lifestyle to which she was introduced during her boarding school days. On the other hand is James LaGrinder, a fellow mixed-blood, the most skilled cowboy on the ranch, and Cogewea's best fiend. Jim, however, lacks the romantic possibilities that Densmore seems to offer. Dismayed by her rebuffs, he takes solace in the idea that he might "yet have a chance" (*CHB* 30).

As the reader knows all along, Densmore is only interested in his own economic well-being. Having come west in search of the opportunities and adventures no longer available to him in the increasingly ossified business and social climates of the East, he views Cogewea as a potential source of income. By marrying her in what he sees as a bogus Indian marriage rite, he hopes to stake a claim to her allotment. Like the Indian agent who makes gestures of friendship only to rob the people blind, Densmore seduces the young woman in order to steal her tribal inheritance. His greedy, self-interested nature earns him the nickname Shoyahpee, an Indian word that is translated to mean "one who eats up everything he sights" (*CHB* 289). Densmore justifies his actions by denigrating Indians. His constant use of racial epithets to describe Cogewea and her friends demonstrates his total disregard for their rights as people. While Densmore is a type of the predatory white man, he can also be viewed as a tradtional tribal enemy. As a result of his deviousness he is frequently compared to Coyote (*CHB* 249, 278–79), the tribal trickster known as much for his cruelty as his compassion. As Martha L. Viehmann points out, Coyote shares a number of characteristics with Densmore. Both are driven by "insatiable desires" and distinguished by their "self-centered, greedy, and mendacious" personalities.[18]

Densmore's deception, disguised as courting, proceeds like a high stakes game of chance. Having come west to see the "painted and blanketed aborigines of history and romance," he finds himself on the H-B Ranch, where he plans to "rough it awhile among the Indians and cowboys" (*CHB* 44). The mixed-blood cowhands, doubtful that Densmore possesses the skills of which he boasts, trick him into riding a wild horse—Croppy—that only Jim, the most talented cowboy on the ranch, has been able to ride. Croppy throws Densmore, who breaks his arm on the fall. Accepting no responsibility for his misfortune, Densmore secretly vows revenge against the men. The injury allows him to pursue Cogewea, who nurses him through his rehabilitation. As foreshadowed by the fishing metaphor in Cogewea's opening speech, a later passage finds Cogewea and Densmore on the banks of a river and betting on who will land the first fish. Densmore hooks one first but it breaks the line before it can be reeled in. Cogewea lands her own fish and thus wins the first round. In jest Densmore ups the ante by betting five thousand dollars against her hand in marriage on the next fish. Cogewea promptly wins again. Densmore asks, "would you have been as prompt in delivering, had I won?" (*CHB* 158) Her response, expressing a cautious affection for the easterner, reminds Densmore of the moral implications of play: "An *honest* gambler is supposed to meet all obligations unequivocally" (*CHB* 158). What Cogewea fails to realize is that Densmore is operating under no similar set of beliefs; his only concern is winning. At his suggestion the ante is once again upped. Ten thousand dollars or Cogewea's hand is bet on the next fish. Again she wins, but only by a fraction. Densmore is willing to bet higher, as he has no intention of ever paying off his debt. The game only ends when she declares that betting is off.

While Densmore has lost the fishing bets, he is closer to his goal. Cogewea is falling for him, and his constant attentions are lowering her resistance and clouding her judgment. After much effort, he finally convinces her to elope. On this ill-fated ride into the night, he discovers that her rumored inheritance was much smaller than he supposed. Angry and frustrated in his desires for economic gain, he beats her and leaves her to perish in the woods. At the prompting of Cogewea's grandmother, the young woman is soon rescued by Jim and nursed back to health. Cogewea is severely demoralized by the realization that Densmore was playing her for a fool. Nonetheless, her story ends on an optimistic note. At the end of the novel, she receives a notice that her long-lost white father struck it rich before he died. Due to a technicality in the will, a sizable fortune is left to his Indian daughters. The last laugh is on Densmore, who can only read about Cogewea's good fortune in the papers (*CHB* 284). With this hopeful finish, the novel demonstrates how the community can provide a hedge against the schemes of the white trickster.

From a political and economic standpoint, *Cogewea* can be read as a critique of the federal allotment policy. By dramatizing the threat posed to Indian women by predacious white speculators masquerading as loving suitors, the novel highlights the effects of white laws that allowed for the cession of Indian land to white husbands of Indian brides. Because allotment defined Indians as the patentees of private lands, lands owned by an Indian woman became, upon marriage, the property of her white husband, a transfer that was not always possible before allotment when lands were held by treaty with the federal government. The new laws thus provided a motivation for white men to secure Indian brides. Rather than introducing them to the benefits of civilization, allotment made Indian women targets of white male speculators. Pursuing Mourning Dove's gambling metaphor, we can say that allotment was presented to the tribes as a rainbow trout; what they got was a slippery eel.

Mourning Dove's use of tribal gambling metaphors suggests the methods of later Native American writers like Silko, Vizenor, and Erdrich. In Silko, gambling metaphors can be traced to ancient Pueblo and Navajo cultures, as well as to the ruins of Chaco Canyon and other ancient sites. In *Gambler Way*, Kathryn Gabriel traces Indian gaming politics in Mexico and the Southwest to hundreds of years before the arrival of Europeans. In the late nineteenth century, archaeological excavations at Pueblo Bonito turned up hundreds of wooden and bone gambling sticks and dice chips.[19] At about the same time, folklorists recorded a Navajo origin story that describes a gambling temple being built in Chaco Canyon for a gambler god known as Noqo'ilpi, a figure carefully preserved in numerous folklore journals and excavation reports.[20] According to stories recorded from Navajo and Pueblo speakers, the region was once lorded over by a gambler of great power and wealth. Some archaeologists believe that Pueblo Alto, known to local Navajos as *niyiilbiihi bighan*, or "home of the one that wins (you) by gambling," was a center of gambling in the ancient Southwest.[21] This gambling lore is reflected in Keres stories that inform Silko's novel *Ceremony*.

In the Keres tradition games of chance are invented by Iyatiku, the Corn Woman or Earth Mother, during a time of drought to distract the people from their troubles. As reported by Paula Gunn Allen, this pastime soon became an obsession among the men of the community who now devoted all of their time to gambling. Angered by the neglect of their sacred duties and communal obligations, Corn Woman returns to the underworld; the town is soon destroyed by a flood and the people are forced to evacuate their homes. Out of compassion and pity for her people, Corn Woman leaves behind her power, the Irriaku or corn fetish, which she explains is her heart. She tells them to share the fruits of her body and to remain at peace in their hearts, as the rains come only to peaceful people.[22] In this story, gambling is presented as both a social entertainment and a vice to be controlled.

In another Keresan story collected by Elsie Clews Parson in the 1910s we read about the career of an evil gambler known as C'ky'o Kaup'a'ta who rises to great power through a combination of gambling skill and witchery.[23] An expert gambler, C'ky'o Kaup'a'ta increases his advantage by enchanting his mortal opponents with cornmeal seasoned with the blood of their own slain relatives. Under his spell, the people gamble away both possessions and lives. Not content to merely destroy the people through gambling, C'ky'o Kaup'a'ta steals the rain clouds. The ensuing drought causes all the earth to suffer. It is at this point in the story that Sun Man, in search of the clouds, comes forth to contest the gambler.

Before journeying to the gambler's lair, Sun Man is given instructions by Grandmother Spider. Also known as Thought Woman, Grandmother Spider symbolizes the creative life-creating force, which is also the generative source of tribal stories.[24] The Gambler, she tells him, will first engage him in a dice game. Sun Man will lose this contest. He will then be challenged to guess the contents of two bags hanging from the walls of the gambler's house. If Sun Man guesses correctly he will win the clouds; if he guesses wrongly, he will lose his life. Grandmother Spider knows that the bags contain the constellations Orion and the Pleides. Armed with this knowledge, the good gambler has an advantage over his evil opponent, but he is still at risk. His chance or gamble is not knowing the future as it has been foretold to him: "'Indeed?'" he remarks to the grandmother's plan; she responds with a challenge, "'Go ahead, be a man.'"[25] In the contest that ensues, Spider Woman's instructions, combined with his own courage and compassion, allow Sun Man to defeat the Gambler and release the clouds. The Gambler loses his eyes, but survives to play again.

As Gabriel argues, the evil gambler of tribal lore is continually transformed to embody the current dominating party.[26] Among Navajo and Pueblo peoples this figure is related to white incursions into the region by Spanish and Anglo colonists. The stories thus "grapple with the ebb and flow of power and fortune and to warn against hostile religious takeover."[27] We see this process at work in *Ceremony*. In the novel, C'ky'o Kaup'a'ta is associated with a variety of forces, including white men and white culture, that threaten the survival of Native peoples. The story of Sun Man's sacred gamble thus provides instruction and guidance for Tayo, a Native man living in the relocation era of American Indian history. In the course of the novel, the story gradually becomes a part of Tayo's mental framework as he negotiates a dangerous world of choices. These choices involve the possible engagement with two basic forces, described by Paula Gunn Allen as "the feminine life force of the universe and the mechanistic death force of the witchery."[28] Tayo's task is to recall the stories of the creative life force and reenact them in terms of his own life. As the storyteller explains in the beginning of the novel,

> ... stories
> ...aren't just entertainment.
> Don't be fooled.
> They are all we have, you see,
> all we have to fight off
> illness and death.[29]

At the beginning of the novel, Tayo is lost in grief and sadness. Having survived a Japanese prisoner of war camp, he has suffered the loss of his cousin, Rocky, who died in his arms, and of his beloved uncle, Josiah, who died while he was away. Tayo feels responsible for both deaths, as well as for the long drought that has persisted at home. Before the war, Tayo made prayer offerings to the rain. During the war, he cursed the rains that prevented his cousin's wounds from healing. As Louis Owens writes, by cursing the rain, Tayo has failed to see the "necessity for every thread in the web of the universe."[30]

Silko foreshadows the disastrous choices of Tayo and Rocky with a traditional story about a C'ky'o medicine man known as Pa'caya'nyi and two brothers, Ma'see'wi and Ou'yu'ye'wi, figures whom Allen identifies as the war twins of Keres tradition.[31] In this story Pa'caya'nyi convinces the brothers to practice a new and dazzling kind of magic. Obsessed with performing these tricks, they neglect their traditional responsibilities to the Corn Mother. As a reprimand to them, she collects the life-giving things, the plants and rain clouds, and retires to the world below. Drought and suffering are again visited upon the land (*C* 46–49). Unwittingly, Tayo and Rocky reenact this story, playing the part of the foolish brothers, while the role of the C'ky'o medicine man is played by the army recruiter, a would-be agent of assimilation. Tayo and Rocky enjoy their new way of life in the army and take full advantage of the status the uniform confers upon them. While Rocky loses his life for the uniform, Tayo has the chance to complete a redemptive journey that reenacts Sun Man's sacred gamble for the return of the rain clouds.

The Sun Man-Gambler story is introduced in the novel in the summer before Tayo joins the army. During a dry spell, he goes to a spring to make a prayer offering for rain. At the spring Tayo watches the animals, spiders, frogs, dragonflies, and hummingbirds drink. The spider reminds him of the Sun Man-Gambler story, and how Spider Woman had told Sun Man how to win the storm clouds back from the Ka't'sina's mountain prison. As Tayo watches the animals, he sees a world made of stories, "a world alive, always changing and moving" (*C* 95). Soon after he hears the rumble of thunder from Tse-pi'na (known as Mount Taylor to English speakers), the place where the Gambler imprisoned the clouds: "The wind came up from the west, smelling cool like wet clay. Then he could see the rain. It was spinning out of the thunderclouds like gray spider webs and tangling against the foothills of the mountain" (*C* 96). In this passage, Tayo's prayer offering coincides with the end of the dry spell. Later that same day, he makes love to Night Swan, a woman associated with the healing powers of the mountain rain.[32] Through these experiences, Tayo becomes aware of his own vital role in aiding the earth's regenerative cycles.

Tayo's development into a traditional person is interrupted by the war and the sickness it causes. His return to health begins when his grandmother suggests that he consult with traditional medicine people, as the white doctors have not been able to help him. Under Ku'osh and Betonie's care, Tayo takes part in healing ceremonies. Later, an encounter with a Ka't'sina woman known as Ts'eh continues the process they had begun. To complete the healing process, Tayo undertakes a vision quest which is also a ritual reenactment of the Sun Man-Gambler story. This phase of the novel is set in motion when Betonie envisions the signs that will guide Tayo to Tse-pi'na to retrieve Josiah's stolen cattle: a field of stars, a woman, and a mountain lion (C 152). Tayo encounters each of these signs as he replays the gambling story in terms of his own life. At first, he moves with uncertainty. But, as his journey proceeds, he becomes increasingly aware of the story and his role in it. The following passage, often quoted, epitomizes that transformation of time, space, and vision that occurs as Tayo completes the ceremony:

> The ride into the mountains had branched into all directions of time. He knew then why the old timers could only speak of yesterday and tomorrow in terms of the present moment: the only certainty; and this present sense of being was qualified with bare hints of yesterday or tomorrow, by saying, "I go up to the mountain yesterday or I go up to the mountain tomorrow." The C'ky'o Kaup'a'ta somewhere is stacking his gambling sticks and waiting for a visitor; Rocky and I are walking across the ridge in the moonlight; Josiah and Robert are waiting for us. This night is a single night; and there has never been any other. (C 192)

As sacred time merges with Tayo's own ritual actions, the journey becomes increasingly dangerous. As the white police force closes in on him, Tayo knows he will have only "one chance" to win the release of the cattle (C 190). In this context, Floyd Lee, the white rancher who has appropriated the mountain pastures for grazing rights, with the help of his security patrol, represents the forces of the evil gambler. Guided by the mountain lion foretold by Betonie, Tayo finds the cattle just before he is himself discovered. With the snow falling, he drives them through the fence. As the metaphorical counterparts to the rain clouds, the cattle, once returned to the Pueblo, signal an end to the drought.

Collectively, the stories of the Pueblo embody a cultural and spiritual identity that provides meaning and context to Tayo's ongoing struggle against the witchery, a force that Silko has described as a "metaphor for the destroyers or the counter force, that force which counters vitality and birth."[33] Tayo's continued survival will depend on his ability to avoid being subsumed into white stories that traditionally assign Indian peoples to isolation, despair, and death (C 231–232). As Ts'eh informs him, whites

> have their stories about us—Indian people who are only marking time and waiting for the end. And they would end this story right here, with you fighting to your death alone in these hills. (C 231–232)

With this speech Ts'eh warns Tayo against taking retributive action for the murder of his friend Harley. Reminding him that violence will only further evil's plans, she provides a moral for the story. For Tayo to contribute to the continuance of the earth and its people, he must control his rage and direct his energies in a positive manner. By modeling non-violent means of resistance and survival, gambling ceremonies and storytelling traditions provide means to teach this lesson.

In *Bearheart*, Gerald Vizenor reworks a Chippewa/Anishinabe story describing the trickster-creator Manabozho's sacred gamble against an evil gambler known as the Nita Ataged. The counterpart to Sun Man of the Keres gambling story, Manabozho is called upon to save the people from the clutches of the cannibalistic gambler. Before journeying to the Nita Ataged's lair, Manabozho consults with his grandmother, who warns him against undertaking such a dangerous mission. Manabozho does not take her advice: "the folk hero of the anishinabe felt that he was brave and should know no fear. The warning words of *nokomiss*, his grandmother, were unheeded."[34] Upon reaching the gambler's lodge, Manabozho is challenged to play a version of the woodland bowl game. In the bowl are four figures representing the four ages of man. The players will take turns tossing the pieces in the bowl. The winning player will be the one who makes the pieces stand on four successive tosses. The Nita Ataged wastes no time in demanding that Manabozho stake his life on the outcome of the contest:

> there is but one forfeit I demand of those who gamble with me and lose, and that forfeit is life. I keep the scalps and ears and hands, the rest of the body I give to my friend the wiindigo and their spirits I consign to *Niba Gisiss*.[35]

This speech, intended to frighten the Manabozho, elicits laughter instead. As Nora Barry explains, the evil gambler would destroy the comic yet sacred survival strategies that Vizenor's texts celebrate. A potentially tragic trope, the Nita Ataged is defeated by the comic trickster who balances the world with humor.[36] Defeat for the Nita Ataged, however, will not signal the end of the game. In one form or another, the gambler's spirit will survive to play again.

In *Bearheart*, Vizenor creates a futuristic version of the evil gambler in the figure of Sir Cecil Staples, the Monarch of Unleaded Gasoline. Sir Cecil is a type of the white confidence man/speculator who sets traps for people by disguising them as opportunities. A manifestation of the Nita Ataged, he is a trickster that tricks to enslave and destroy. In post-apocalyptic America, the gambler's talent for murder and destruction thrive. As Sir Cecil explains, "the plastic film known as social control hanging over the savage urge to kill was dissolved when the government failed and the economic world collapsed:"

> When the value of material possessions were useless ... there were no common values to bind people together and hold down their needs for violence and the experience of death.[37]

Through Sir Cecil's monologue Vizenor offers a critique of what Nora Barry describes as the "social and spiritual cannibalism of the dominant culture."[38] By emphasizing pathological behaviors evident in Euro-American society, he turns the tables on those who have described tribal gambling practices as evidence of the Native's wasteful and uncivilized ways.

Sir Cecil is contested by a group of cross-blood pilgrims led by Proude Cedarfair, the novel's counterpart to Manabozho. The pilgrims first encounter the gambler at What Cheer Trailer Ruins, where he is believed to have a hidden stockpile of gasoline. The pilgrims have come in hopes of acquiring enough fuel to continue their journey. Having no way to take the gasoline by force (and, as we later learn, unaware that no gasoline actually exists), they agree to gamble their lives against a chance to win five gallons of gas. First, they must decide on who will gamble for the group. Little Big Mouse argues that goodness must contest evil: "The most good person should be the gambler" (*BH* 110). In retrospect, her suggestion was a good one, but it is not seconded. Another member of the group, Belladonna Darwin-Winter Catcher, argues that the good gambler should be chosen by chance. This initiates a debate on the meaning of chance. "Nothing is chance," Proude argues, "there is no chance in chance.... Chances are terminal creeds" (*BH* 110–111):

> Fools praise chance to avoid the fear of death.... We must fear the living to leave so much death to chance.... We are fools with terminal creeds when we gamble with chance. (*BH* 112)

Elaborating on Proude's statement, Louis Owens writes that "a mere capitulation to chance would deny the emphasis upon our ultimate responsibility for ordering and sustaining the world we inhabit that is central to Native American ecosystemic cultures."[39] By contrast, Belladonna's understanding of chance seems to rely on a blind faith that goodness will overcome evil. Thus, in lieu of a volunteer, and in an attempt to choose the good gambler fairly, the pilgrims opt for a method of choosing the good gambler that is similar to the drawing of lots. In this way, Lilith Mae Farrier is selected to be the group's good gambler.

As they are defined in the novel, terminal creeds are simplistic mental and verbal conceits. By silencing questions and forcing agreement, they provide means to avoid, rather than engage, complex issues and problems. Changeless and unadaptive, they are often expressed as formulaic discourses that lead their bearers to isolation and death. In her gamble against Sir Cecil, Lilith Mae falls victim to terminal creeds. Terrified of facing the evil gambler, she sets her mind to "luck and chance" (*BH* 116). When she does win a round of the game, she takes "personal pleasure in winning." Her egocentric response causes her to lose her place in the "energies of sacred time" (*BH* 118). Sir Cecil immediately recognizes the weakness of his first opponent. "Chance and luck are the game of fools," he declares after winning her life (*BH* 119). In his later gamble with Proude, Sir Cecil is likewise defeated by a terminal creed. In this contest Proude takes the initiative when he announces to Sir Cecil that he has come to speak with him about "evil and death" (*BH* 129). As Sir Cecil points out, Proude's is not a simple game of death: "You would change minds and histories and reverse the unusual control of evil power" (*BH* 130). Sir Cecil is confident, however, that he will not be beaten by Proude and that the game will at least end in a draw. In this case, "evil will still be the winner because nothing changes when good and evil are tied in a strange balance.... We are equals at this game of good and evil mister proude. Nothing is lost between equals" (*BH* 131, 132). Proude rejects this reasoning:

> "But we are not equals. We are not bound in common experiences. We do not share a common vision. Your values and language come from evil. Your power is adverse to living. Your culture is death."

> "And so we are equal opposites."
> "Death is not the opposite of living.... Your evil is malignant. The energies that live are never malignant." (*BH* 132)

In this dialogue Proude exposes the narcissistic attitudes that informs the evil gambler's philosophy. The game follows the pattern of their speech. When Sir Cecil tosses the figures in the bowl, they fall into its cracked center. When Proude throws, the figures stand back-to-back, facing out towards the edge of the bowl, which is a symbol of the earth. The placement of the figures demonstrates his own outward-looking philosophy. Like Tayo in *Ceremony*, he does not gamble for sheer amusement, power, or gain, but for the sake of creation and the people.

In Louise Erdrich's *Love Medicine*, traditional gambling stories are reenacted among the trappings of contemporary reservation life. With no mention of evil gamblers or traditional games of chance, poker, a New Orleans card game with roots in European culture, provides the form of the sacred gamble. The contestants in *Love Medicine* are King and Lipsha, half brothers and the sons of June Kashpaw, a tribal woman who dies in the novel's opening pages. Their gamble is for her inheritance, as represented by a Pontiac Firebird that King, recognized by the courts as June's legitimate heir, has purchased with the money he collected from her life insurance policy. Self-centered, violent, and untrustworthy, King functions as the evil gambler of the stories. Compassionate, gentle, and honest, Lipsha represents the good gambler whose powers are associated with healing and growth. Presiding over the game is Gerry Nanapush, Lipsha's father and King's tribal nemesis.

The sacred gamble begins without apparent ceremony. In search of information about Gerry, Lipsha pays a visit to King's Minneapolis apartment, a location that functions as the symbolic lair of the evil gambler. Quite by chance, it seems, he discovers a deck of cards on the sill of the air shaft window. Later in the scene, Gerry, as the embodiment of the trickster/creator Nanapush, enters the apartment through this hole. To pass the time, the brothers begin an idle game of poker, betting on pieces of Lucky Charms cereal. King calls for a game of five-card stud; Lipsha designates deuces wild, because he liked that "puny little card becoming strategy."[40]

Unbeknownst to King, Lipsha is an expert gambler with inherited talents. In Erdrich's second novel, *Tracks*, we meet his great grandmother, Fleur Pillager, a tribal shaman who reveals the traces of the good gambler when she beats four white men at poker. Fleur's skill is inherited by her daughter Lulu, Lipsha's grandmother, who teaches Lipsha the art of card playing. The training includes lessons on keeping the odds in his favor. As Proude Cedarfair suggests, the good gambler must take the chance out of chance. Lipsha does this by marking the deck. By the time something of worth is staked on his game with King, the cards are virtually transparent in his hands.

The game reaches higher levels of significance when Gerry enters the scene. As his last name suggests, Gerry is an embodiment of the Great Hare, the compassionate trickster of the Chippewas. His power is demonstrated in a miraculous leap from a three-story hospital window, through which he squeezes himself like a "fat rabbit disappearing down a hole" (*LM* 169). He reappears in King's apartment in a similarly magical and mysterious fashion. In his presence, the game is continued, but the stakes have been increased dramatically:

"We must decide," said Gerry seriously, "What we are playing for."
"I got money," King said.
"We're not playing for your rubber check," Gerry said. "You probably used your payoff up by now. We won't play for money, but we got to play for something. Otherwise there's no game." (*LM* 261)

Lipsha suggests the car and, compelled by his fear of Gerry, King agrees. The game will thus decide the following question: should June's legacy be awarded to King, by right of the white man's law, or to Lipsha, by virtue of his compassion and good humor? The answer, of course, is Lipsha. Now holding all the cards, he deals King a pair, Gerry a straight, and himself a royal flush, a hand he describes as a "perfect family"(*LM* 264). As the king, queen, and jack of the royal flush suggest, Lipsha has imaginatively reconstructed his family through the game. This is literally true insofar as the Firebird, the symbol of June, serves as the vehicle by which Lipsha helps Gerry escape into Canada. Amid all the disunities and disruptions imposed upon the community by contact with white America, a simple card game becomes a symbol of agency, hope, and family tradition.

Erdrich's commentary on the role of traditional gambling stories and practices in the modern world continues in *Tracks* and *The Bingo Palace*. Set in the allotment era, *Tracks* follows the career of Fleur Pillager, a tribal gambler of great power. Demonstrating that the good gambler can be any gender, Fleur gambles to save the land from the grasp of the speculators. As we have seen in *Cogewea*, speculations on tribal land are related to speculations on tribal women. Suggesting this connection, Fleur's literal gambling opponents are four white men who run a butcher's shop. The men allow Fleur to join their game thinking she will be an easy opponent. To their great surprise, she proves herself to be an excellent card player. For several consecutive nights she wins a dollar on low hands such as pairs and straights. Increasingly frustrated with their inability to dominate the tribal woman, the men decide to raise the stakes of the game. This is the opportunity for which Fleur has been waiting. With more money on the table than ever before, she plays the winning cards. Her success brings out the worst in the men. Frustrated, angry, and lacking any semblance of good sportsmanship, they beat and rape Fleur, who later uses her winnings to pay the annual fees on Pillager allotments.[41] In this way she turns the tables on the vicious speculations that were produced by allotment. Justice is served to the men, who pay a heavy price for their misdeeds. During a tornado, apparently conjured by Fleur, they are trapped in a meat locker, where all but one freeze to death.

While the men have been killed, their spirits do not perish, but wait in the next world for an opportunity to continue the game. Their chance comes later in the novel. In labor in the midst of a winter famine, Fleur is brought to the brink of death by pregnancy complications. As narrated by Pauline, a mixed-blood Catholic convert, the shaman's spirit travels to Chippewa heaven, where the men are found waiting with their cards. In the game that follows, Fleur gambles for her own life, that of her newborn child, and that of her three-year-old daughter, Lulu. Of these she only loses the infant. While she again survives, Fleur's trouble are not over. In the end, she is beaten out by the speculators, who charge late fees on overdue allotment payments. Unable to pay the penalty, Fleur is forced to relinquish the land. In a last gesture of defiance, she wrecks the logging crews by causing the trees to fall on them. While Fleur must turn away, her gambler's talent will be passed on to future generations who will use it to make their own acts of resistance and survival.

In *The Bingo Palace*, Erdrich joins traditional gambling practices with high-stakes reservation gambling in Lipsha's sacred gamble for a grand prize van. Initially, the van is less important to him than the chance it offers to impress Shawnee Ray, a young woman with whom he has fallen in love. Not surprisingly, Lipsha wins the van. He had intended to bring it to Shawnee Ray, but finds that he enjoys the feeling that comes with driving a luxury automobile. His triumph turns to mockery when the van is totaled by some white men. Lipsha stoically accepts the loss and is optimistic about his future: "It makes no sense, but at this moment I feel rich ... it seems like everything worth having is within my grasp. All I have to do is reach my hand into the emptiness."[42] For Lipsha, mastery of the game, if only for brief intervals, is worth more than the things that can be won. He measures success in terms of his ability to play the game, not the possession of goods that results from winning.

The tribal gambling metaphors examined in the preceding pages hint at but do not directly engage the controversy over reservation gambling. For that we must turn to Vizenor's *Heirs of Columbus*, a 1991 novel, and "The Moccasin Game," a short story published in 1993. By foregrounding the effects on the tribes of reservation gambling, these texts join an exploration of tribal art and contemporary politics with a meditation on ritual games and for-profit gambling. The heirs referenced in the novel's title represent a modern cross-blood community that combines indigenous traditions and modern technologies. The tribal descendants of Christopher Columbus and a tribal healer, the heirs own and operate Santa Maria Casino, a floating casino caravel and replica of the explorer's flagship. High-stakes for-profit gambling thus serves as the symbolic fruit of the Columbian exchange. Through the success of the gambling operation, the entrepreneurial heirs fund genetic research to heal the world's children and isolate the gene for tribal survivance. Large public works projects include a giant statue of the Trickster of Liberty and a laser hologram show.

Along with running a modern casino, the heirs play a traditional tribal moccasin game. Described as the game that "saved the heirs from the water demons,"[43] it is accompanied by the story of the tribe's contest against Wiindigoo, a cannibal spirit associated with winter starving.[44] With his blond hair and perfect smile, Wiindigoo is deceptively attractive. His sly methods, combined with his European appearance, associate him with the white confidence man and speculator. At the same time, Wiindigoo is an ancient and familiar enemy of the people. In *Ojibway Heritage*, Basil Johnston describes him as an ordinary man driven mad by hunger. With the help of a magic hunting potion he is able to find game, but having lost his reason, he eats it all rather than sharing it with his family and village.[45] Wiindigoo is eventually killed, but his spirit lives on as an incorporeal being, the "spirit of excess" that captivates and enslaves anyone too preoccupied with sleep, work, play, drink, or other pursuit.[46] According to Johnston, children and the young were often warned, "Don't play too much, Wiindigoo will get you." Though

Wiindigoo was fearsome and visited punishment upon those committing excesses, he nevertheless conferred rewards upon the moderate. He was excess who encouraged moderation.[47]

In *Heirs of Columbus*, the people's sacred gamble against Wiindigoo is recalled in a ceremonial moccasin game played before a white anthropologist. According to the story that is told as the game is played, the children are staked on the outcome of the contest. All would seem to be lost when Wiindigoo reaches for the moccasin that hides the ceremonial coin. Before he can turn it, however, he is frozen solid by Mikwan, a winter spirit that comes to the tribe's aid. The frozen Wiindigoo and the accoutrements of the game are hidden in her cave. By this "breath of winter in the summer" (*HC* 21) the tribe is saved. The game, however, is not over; nor has Wiindigoo been defeated. Later in the novel, he returns to finish the game.

In the short story "The Moccasin Game," Vizenor elaborates on this story as it is presented in *Heirs of Columbus*. Evoking the pre-Columbian context and origins of tribal moccasin games, this story has no white characters or references to Europe or Euro-Americans. It begins near a fire circle on the shores of a moonlit lake, where "Native American Silent People" sign the moccasin game story; their hand movements are translated by Nawina, whose narration is the printed text.[48] With this framing device Vizenor reminds the reader that the story as read is several places removed from the lived experience of hearing a moccasin game story told in real time. Rejecting realist and modernist aesthetics, his work draws attention to the dialogic play of signification that constitutes a text in the oral tradition.

The first round of the game is played when Wiindigoo captures a copper ring engraved with "seventeen tribal figures carved on the wide rim" (*MG* 45). This circle, described as the "sacred tribal history," is staked against a newly fashioned canoe (*MG* 45). The tribal player guesses wrong and the canoe is lost. Wiindigoo offers the tribe another chance to win the ring, but only if it stakes the children; if the tribe wishes to reclaim the past, as represented by the ring, it musk risk its future, as represented by the children. Unwilling to relinquish history to the cannibal, the tribe agrees to his terms, knowing full well that the children are a prize it can ill afford to lose. It is only by Mikwan's intervention that the children are temporarily safe.

In the midst of the game, the tribal players participate in a Mediwewin, or Medicine Lodge Ceremony. With this episode, Vizenor joins gambling, medicine, and storytelling as parts of one curative ritual. Johnston describes the Mediwewin as a ceremonial that commemorates the knowledge of medicine and the healing of disease.[49] Moccasin games and tribal tricksters are associated with the ceremony. As Nora Barry reports, Manabozho, the good gambler of the stories, was sent with the gift of medicine to the Anishinabeg by the creator Kitche Manitou.[50] In Vizenor's story, the candidates are teased by Wiindigoo as they make their way into the Midewigaan, or Grand Medicine Lodge. Taunting them with "human temptations, mongrel names, and the treacherous powers of nature," he attempts to turn them from the path of goodness (*MG* 49). The word *Mediwewin* is probably a contraction of *mino*, meaning "good," and *daewaewin*, meaning "hearted."[51] As the etymology of the word indicates, knowledge of medicine is not enough to insure good health and well-being; one must also lead a moral life. Through the moccasin game, the people demonstrate their goodheartedness by balancing the destructive capability of Wiindigoo.

At the conclusion of *Heirs of Columbus*, the suspended moccasin game is resumed when federal agents thaw the cannibal. As Wiindigoo again reaches for the winning moccasin, Stone Columbus, the tribal player, warns him that the marked coin has been placed with a dangerous war herb (*HC* 181). The herb is said to be the "soldier weed" of "brute force and termination" revealed to Black Elk in his vision (*HC* 178). At first Wiindigoo suspects that Stone is bluffing, but hesitates long enough to be convinced that victory would result in his own demise. According to Stone,

> The war herb would terminate the world, a bioactivated evanescence, only you and the robots would survive, and you would be mocked by the robots forever....
> Who would you be without the heirs and the children to menace...?
> Your choice would be your last moccasin game, nothing would remain if you reveal the war herb, nothing more human than the robots, and our memories in the stone, but even a demon needs humans....
> The soldier weed would end your game forever. (*HC* 181–182)

Swayed by Stone's words, Wiindigoo raises his hand and "moves back into the shadows," cautioning the tribe that "the game will never end" (*HC* 182). In this context, the suspension of the game suggests that the long-term survival of the community depends upon the survival of its games and stories. By emphasizing the moccasin game as a sign of survivance, Vizenor dramatizes the importance of ritual play to the tribe's well-being. Like the word *performance*, the coined term uses the noun modifier "–ance" to emphasize the actions, processes, and functions by which the tribes continue.

In *Dead Voices: Natural Agonies in the New World* (1993), Vizenor offers more dialogues on the relationship between survival and gambling. In this text, gambling rituals and storytelling traditions find themselves at home on the urban streets of Oakland, California. The central character is Bagese, a tribal woman and storyteller. Her stories are introduced by Laundry, a university lecturer on tribal philosophies. While Laundry is positioned as an expert on tribal affairs and culture, Bagese perceives him as a "wordy" bound to printed books and the "dead voices" of classroom recitations.[52] She nicknames him Laundry because he has the generic smell of television soap: "The sweet smell of laundry," she informs him, "is a dead voice"(*DV* 16). With this comparison Vizenor distinguishes the language of a literate culture bound by printed words from the language of a culture that records and transmits its collective experiences aurally.

For Bagese, storytelling is related to a game of *wanaki* chance. Said to have been invented by a manidoo spirit in a time when the world was young, *wanaki* connects Bagese and Laundry to the sources of tribal experience, language, and power. Laundry describes it as Bagese's game of "natural meditation" of stories that "liberate shadows and the mind:"

Chance is an invitation to animal voices in a tribal world, and the word wanaki means to live somewhere in peace, a chance at peace.

She turned seven cards in the game, one each for the bear, beaver, squirrel, crow, flea, praying mantis, and the last was the trickster figure, a wild card that transformed the player into an otter, a rabbit, a crane, a spider, or even a human. The animals, birds, and insects were pictured in unusual poses on the cards. The bear, for instance, was a flamenco dancer, the crow was a medical doctor, and the praying mantis was the president. The cards and creatures were stories, and she insisted that nothing was ever personal in a game of wanaki chance.

Bagese told me that the poses of the creatures were the common poses of civilization, the stories and shadows of the animals and birds in the mirrors. She compared the wanaki peace cards to tarot cards that depict the vices and virtues of human adventures, but tarot was in the eye and wanaki was in the ear. The fortunes were never the same as the animal stories. (*DV* 16–17)

Every morning Bagese turns one of the seven cards and concentrates on the picture. As she becomes the creatures in the cards, she narrates her adventures in the first-person plural. Gathering bits of nature—leaves, stones, flower petals, and the like—and arranging them on the floor of her apartment, she creates a natural map of the surrounding urban terrain. Through this game Bagese reconstructs the features of an indigenous, pre-Columbian world in the midst of a "cold and chemical civilization" (*DV* 7). Describing a "new wilderness in the city," her stories reclaim the urban space as tribal (*DV* 10).

As a group, these texts demonstrate the fundamental relationship between gambling rituals, tribal storytelling traditions, and tribal literature. For Indian writers, gambling stories and the powerful metaphors they generate provide a means to comment upon a whole range of issues involving politics, philosophy, religion, and art. It is both ironic and telling that the fortunes of so many tribal corporations have been joined to high-stakes gambling. For Native peoples, dealing with hostile colonial forces has always been a high-stakes game of chance. Gambling stories, in both their spoken and written forms, instruct the players on how to play that game.

NOTES

1. William Wood, *New England's Prospect*, ed. Alden T. Vaughan (Amherst: University of Massachusetts Press, 1977), 103–104.

2. Ann Fabian, *Card Sharps, Dreams Books, and Bucket Shopts: Gambling in 19th-Century America* (Ithaca: Cornell University Press, 1990), 5; Reuven Brenner, *Gambling and Speculation: A Theory, a History, and a Future of Some Human Decisions* (Cambridge: Cambridge University Press, 1990), 12–13.

3. Robert Stewart Culin, *Games of the North American Indians* (New York: AMS Press, 1973), 809.

4. Neal Salisbury, *Manitou and Providence: Indians, Europeans, and the Making of New England, 1500–1643* (New York: Oxford University Press, 1982), 44–46.

5. Francis Parkman, *The Oregon Trail* (New York: The New American Library, 1964), 177.

6. Luther Standing Bear, *My People the Sioux* (Lincoln: University of Nebraska Press, 1975), 34–35.

7. Mourning Dove, *A Salishan Autobiography*, ed. Jay Miller (Lincoln: University of Nebraska Press, 1990), 102.

8. Ibid., 103.

9. Trudie Lamb, "Games of Chance and their Religious Significance Among Native Americans," *Artifacts* 8:3 (Spring 1980): 1, 10–11.

10. Ibid., 11.

11. Arthur C. Parker, *The Code of Handsome Lake*, in *Parker on the Iroquois*, ed. William N. Fenton (Syracuse: Syracuse University Press, 1975), 17.

12. Ibid., 18.

13. Joseph Henry Jackson, Introduction, *The Life and Adventures of Joaquin Murieta*, by John Rollins Ridge (Norman: University of Oklahoma Press, 1955), XIII.

14. John Rollins Ridge, *The Life and Adventures of Joaquin Murieta* (Norman: University of Oklahoma Press, 1955), 9. Subsequent citations will appear in the text as *JM*.

15. John Lowe, "'I Am Joaquin!': Space and Freedom in Yellow Bird's *The Life and Adventures of Joaquin Murieta, the Celebrated California Bandit*," in *Early Native American Writing: New Critical Essays*, ed. Helen Jaskoski (New York: Cambridge University Press, 1996), 116.

16. Mourning Dove, *Cogewea, the Half-Blood: A Depiction of the Great Montana Cattle Range* (Lincoln: University of Nebraska Press, 1991), 17. Subsequent citations will appear in the text as *CHB*.

17. D'Arcy McNickle, *Native American Tribalism: Indian Survivals and Renewals* (New York: Oxford University Press, 1973), 82–83.

18. Martha L. Viehmann, "'My People...My Kind': Mourning Dove's *Cogewea, the Half-Blood* as a Narrative of Mixed Descent," in Jaskoski, *Early Native American Writing*, 211.

19. Kathryn Gabriel, *Gambler Way: Indian Gaming in Mythology, History and Archaeology in North America* (Boulder: Johnson Books, 1996), 93.

20. Ibid., 91.

21. Ibid., 97.

22. Paula Gunn Allen, *The Sacred Hoop: Recovering the Feminine in American Indian Traditions* (Boston: Beacon Press, 1986), 17–18.

23. The summary of the Sun Man-Gambler story is taken from two sources, Franz Boas' translation in *Keresan Texts* (New York: The American Ethnological Society, 1928), 76–82; and Leslie Marmon Silko's translation appearing in *Ceremony* (New York: Penguin, 1986), 170–176. In *Storyteller*, Silko credits Elsie Clews Parsons with having collected the story that Boas later published: "In 1918 Franz Boas, ethnologist and linguist, passed through Laguna. His talented protégé Elsie Clews Parsons stayed behind to collect Laguna texts.... Boas, as it turns out, was tone-deaf and the Laguna language is tonal so it is fortunate he allowed Ms. Parsons to do the actual collecting of the stories." *Storyteller* (New York: Arcade, 1981), 254.

24. Susan J. Scarberry, "Grandmother Spider's Lifeline," *Studies in American Indian Literature*, ed. Paula Gunn Allen (New York: MLA, 1983), 100.

25. Boas, *Keresan Texts*, 82.

26. Gabriel, *Gambler Way*, 120.

27. Ibid., 136.

28. Allen, *Sacred Hoop*, 119.

29. Leslie Marmon Silko, *Ceremony* (New York: Penguin, 1986), 2. Subsequent citations will appear in the text as *C*.

30. Louis Owens, *Other Destinies: Understanding the American Indian Novel* (Norman: University of Oklahoma Press, 1992), 176.

31. Allen, *Sacred Hoop*, 19.

32. Ibid., 121.

33. Joseph Bruchac III, "Indian Storyteller Wins Pot of Gold," *The Greenfield Review*, ed. Joseph Bruchac III (Winter 1981/82): 104.

34. Gerald Vizenor, *anishinabe adisokan: Tales of the People* (Minneapolis: The Nodin Press, 1970), 140.

35. Ibid., 148.

36. Nora Barry, "Chance and Ritual: The Gambler in the Texts of Gerald Vizenor," *Studies in American Indian Literature* 5:3 (Fall 1993): 20.

37. Gerald Vizenor, *Bearheart: The Heirship Chronicles* (Minneapolis: University of Minnesota Press, 1978), 189–191. Subsequent citations will appear in the text as *BH*.

38. Barry, "Chance," 20.

39. Owens, *Other Destinies*, 234.

40. Louise Erdrich, *Love Medicine* (New York: Bantam, 1984), 254. Subsequent citations will appear in the text as *LM*.

41. Louise Erdrich, *Tracks* (New York: Harper and Row, 1988), 36.

42. Louise Erdrich, *The Bingo Palace* (New York: Harper Collins, 1994), 83.

43. Gerald Vizenor, *Heirs of Columbus* (Hanover: New England University Press, 1991), 20. Subsequent citations will appear in the text as *HC*.

44. Barry, "Chance," 19.

45. Basil Johnston, *Ojibway Heritage* (Lincoln: University of Nebraska Press, 1990), 166.

46. Ibid., 167.

47. Ibid.

48. Gerald Vizenor, "The Moccasin Game," in *Earth Song, Sky Spirit: Short Stories of the Contemporary Native American Experience*, ed. Clifford E. Trafzer (New York: Doubleday, 1993), 40. Subsequent citations will appear in the text as *MG*.

49. Johnston, *Ojibway Heritage*, 83.

50. Barry, "Chance," 18.

51. Johnston, *Ojibway Heritage*, 84.

52. Gerald Vizenor, *Dead Voices: Natural Agonies in the New World* (Norman: University of Oklahoma Press, 1992), 5–21. Subsequent citations will appear in the text as *DV*.

The Bingo Palace: Indian Gaming as a Literary Device

Karen L. Wallace

In his essay "On the 'Indianness' of Bingo," Paul Pasquaretta writes, "the 'casinoization' of Indian territories has tended to exploit the limited sovereignty tribal entities are granted under the law, and this has provoked controversy within Indian communities."[1] Always a point of contention between state and tribal governments, sovereignty appears to remain the primary subject of debate despite its current guise. Gaming has become the most controversial "Indian Problem" in the United States, overshadowing even hunting and fishing rights in most states.[2] Accusations of mismanagement and criminal tendencies abound and the more significant aspect of self-determination is obscured. As Don Cozzetto explains, "The passage of the 1988 Indian Gaming Regulatory Act (IGRA) is viewed by some as one vehicle whereby at least a small amount of self-determination can be realized. Others argue, however, that federal legislation permitting gaming on reservations amounts to yet another intrusion into tribal sovereignty."[3] In her novel *The Bingo Palace*, Louise Erdrich offers a fictional account of the rise of gaming on a reservation and the reasons that it emerges as a viable economic solution for tribal independence.

The novel emphasizes the politics of Indian gaming and how they impact the socialization of the Turtle Mountain tribe. According to Don Cozzetto and Brent LaRocque, the 1995 median income at Turtle Mountain was $12,020, slightly more than half that of the state population, while reservation unemployment was over seven times more prevalent than for non-Indians in the state of Minnesota.[4] Addressing the consequence of compulsive gambling at Turtle Mountain specifically, Cozzetto and LaRocque explain the social repercussions of high-stakes gambling for local Indians. They focus on the circumstances of communities that are far from urban centers: "Casino gambling … is the latest in a long history of attempts to empower tribal communities. The objective is that tribal governments utilize revenues from casino operations to invest in the tribal infrastructure, to create employment opportunities for tribal members, and to address social problems on the reservations."[5] While many of these goals have been achieved, they have resulted in new problems that are not easily remedied. Clearly, a new business enterprise is sorely needed, a condition Erdrich represents effectively in her characters' acceptance of the new casino and their devotion to Lyman Lamartine, the man who has brought solvency to the tribe.

In *Crossbloods: Bone Courts, Bingo and Other Reports*, Gerald Vizenor discusses the consequences of tribal gaming. He quotes William Houle, chairman at Fond du Lac: "'Gaming has always been part of our culture, and now it is an integral part of our economy as well.'" Vizenor agrees, but adds that "bingo as the new cash crop is based on losers, compulsive behavior, and most of the downtown gamblers are white."[6] Erdrich addresses the complexity of reservation gaming early on in her novel and, through Lyman, effectively shows the price tribal members must pay. "Lyman has run so many businesses that nobody can keep track—cafés, gas pumps, a factory that made tomahawks, a flower shop, an Indian Taco concession, a bar which he has added to and parlayed from a penny-card bingo hall and kitchen-table blackjack parlor into something bigger, something we don't know the name of yet, something with dollar signs that crowd the meaning from our brain."[7] Lipsha observes that,

> By day, the [bingo palace] looks shabby and raw—a rutted dirt parking lot bounds the rippled tin walls. Bare and glittering with broken glass, the wide expanse is pocked by deep holes.... But you can't see dents in the walls or rips or litter once darkness falls. Then, because the palace is decked with bands of Christmas lights and traveling neon disks that wink and flicker, it comes at you across the flat dim land like a Disney setup, like a circus show, a spaceship, a constellation that's collapsed. (*BP* 41)

In the chapter entitled "Lyman's Luck," Erdrich shows the inevitable loss that accompanies compulsive gambling, the flaw behind the facade.

As Paul Pasquaretta notes, "the high stakes game of chance is an important narrative device that assigns value and difference.... By negotiating chance in a traditional manner, characters attain individual and collective aspirations.... The Native American community's ongoing negotiation with colonial impositions might also be conceptualized as a high stakes game of chance with open and multiple outcomes."[8] The Gambler, an archetypal figure in Native American lore is, of course, a major figure in *The Bingo Palace*. The bingo palace and gambling recall to us the primacy of fate and the illusion of individual control. "Every gambler," writes Edmund Bergler, "gives the impression of a man who has signed a contract with Fate, stipulating that persistence must be rewarded. With that imaginary contract in his pocket, he is beyond the reach of all logical objection and argument."[9] We see this type of behavior in several of Erdrich's characters, especially Lyman and his brother Lipsha. Lyman in particular succumbs to the lure of easy money and the control it seems to allow him. Gambling is an activity familiar to tribal peoples, but as Cozzetto and LaRocque caution, "traditional Indian betting was certainly not organized, emphasized, or depended upon by tribal society to the extent characterized by the opening of casinos on Indian reservations.... Tribal life was also not complicated ... [by systems that] encourage competition for the accumulation of scarce resources."[10] Cozzetto and LaRocque found that, by virtue of their relative isolation, Turtle Mountain gamblers are most often Indian and the reservation has had to accommodate emerging addiction. In *The Bingo Palace*, Erdrich uses Lyman Lamartine to show the conflicts inherent in adapting to these pressures, especially when so few choices are available.

Sitting in the casino with Lipsha, Lyman agrees to forfeit the right to pursue a woman whom they both desire, Shawnee Ray, in exchange for their father Nector's sacred pipe: "'Here's the deal,'" Lipsha tells Lyman: "'I give you the pipe, and you lay low, step aside'" (*BP* 88). Though Lyman is initially offended by Lipsha's suggestion, he does agree, the legacy and power of the pipe outweighing Shawnee Ray's outrage. Next, Lyman attends the Indian Gaming Conference as Turtle Mountain's representative and takes the pipe with him. He flies to the Sands Regency in Reno, intending to participate in the conference, but he never leaves the casino: "He tried to contain it but a kick of adrenaline surged up when he walked into the lobby of the Sands and heard the high, manic warble of the slot machines, the controlled shouts of pit bosses, the whine and crash of someone's bad hand sinking, dark, out of view" (*BP* 89). In Reno, Lyman falls victim to the mystique of the casino. Knowing full well the outcome for most gamblers, Lyman watches his own "bad hand" sink out of view along with his sense of identity and self-possession.

Lyman's ordeal is long and heartbreaking and mirrors that of his community as a whole. He is a big winner at first and, despite his desire to quit, he plays too long: "His features were a mask. His outside expression was fixed, serene, but beneath that, on the real face that was hidden, he could feel his look of bewildered dread" (*BP* 92). Having spent all his own money, plus the money the tribe had allocated for the conference, Lyman does the unthinkable and sells the sacred pipe: "At six, he brought Nector's pipe to the all-night pawnshop and got a hundred dollars for it.... At seven in the morning he had nothing left" (*BP* 93). Lyman is defeated, and the narrative turns back to Lipsha and Fleur. In his discussion of *Love Medicine*, Paul Pasquaretta writes, "poker upholds traditional communal values like virtue, wisdom and self-sacrifice; in Erdrich's treatment, it becomes a medium through which the ancient tribal past is made manifest in the modern present. Amid all the disunities and disruptions imposed upon the family by contact with white America, an integrated and whole indigenous community is imagined and evoked through an appropriated material."[11] This moment is replicated in *The Bingo Palace*: the climax of the novel is, predictably enough, a game of cards, one in which Fleur gambles to recover the reservation. As the story follows a new thread, Erdrich illustrates the excitement inherent in games of chance as well as the implications for sovereign control.

Gerald Vizenor comments that "Federal Courts have ruled in favor of certain tribal rights based on treaties: for instance, state regulations over taxation … now bingo and other forms of gambling, have been issued based on the interpretation of treaties and advanced as tests of tribal sovereignties."[12] In *The Bingo Palace*, Erdrich describes the process by which land was lost, through treaties, through the Dawes Act, and by individual purchase. Erdrich's major trope, the Bingo Palace reflects the ongoing dilemma posed by Indian gaming.

For example, central to current legislation, California's Cabazon Band of Mission Indians, whose casino is named the Bingo Palace, took their case for tribal sovereignty to the Supreme Court, resulting in the *Cabazon* decision. In his history of gaming on the Cabazon Reservation, Ambrose Lane explains that, following its opening on 3 March 1983, the Cabazon Bingo Palace was continually threatened by Riverside County and maligned by the press:

> As a result, the Tribe would suffer terrible public credibility problems until February 25, 1987. On that day the US Supreme Court ruled that high-stakes Bingo and other gaming on Indian reservations could not be regulated by state and local governments, if state law allows such forms of gaming by anyone. That decision became known all over the nation as the 'Cabazon Decision.' The Tribe that had fought for seven years—and four for Bingo—had finally been vindicated.[13]

Erdrich's central metaphor reflects the Cabazon tribe's successful struggle for sovereign rights. Run by Lyman Lamartine, the Turtle Mountain tribe's answer to Donald Trump, the Bingo Palace seems like an effective means to tribal self-determination.

Lipsha observes that "[Fleur] takes the future of others and makes it her own, sucks it in through a hollow reed, through a straw, a bone" (*BP* 128). Reminiscent of a "sucking doctor," Fleur Pillager, the oldest and most traditional member of the community, "is out to reclaim the original reservation, no less" (*BP* 129). Lipsha, who, like the rest of the community, both fears and respects Fleur's power, describes her mystique, trying to explain the reactions she provokes: "She's older than any of them, so old no one remembers how old. She's a Pillager, the adopted daughter of Old Man Nanapush, this healing doctor witch. She must be a hundred. She's so old that people don't use her name anymore. She's just the Old Lady" (*BP* 126). In the Chippewa story of the Gambler, his nemesis is Trickster, or Nanabozho, who is sent to defeat the Gambler and restore the community. For Erdrich, Fleur occupies Trickster's position; by renaming Fleur simply the Old Lady, Erdrich reasserts the mythic structure upon which the novel is based, so that the outcome of Fleur's final gamble is predetermined.

The original reservation had been stolen through treaty agreements and it is the consistent loss of land that has impacted the tribe's sense of cohesion. Certainly sovereign status is reinforced by territory, so there is no doubt that recovering land is essential to self-determination. Erdrich writes, "After the Pillager land around the lake was stripped bare by the lumber company and of no more use ... it was put up for sale and bought by the former Indian agent, Jewett Parker Tatro, a man now wealthy in land but in little else" (*BP* 142). Seeking to recover Pillager land, Fleur returns one last time. The object of her business is Jewett Parker Tatro, the former agent who bought reservation land, "the land for which he had cheated so carefully and persistently" (*BP* 142). The community now watches Fleur, having lost interest in Lyman for a time: "Those of us who dared to notice saw that her braids had grown thick as tails and hung long down her back, bound together with a red strip of cloth. The oldest people frowned when they heard that detail, remembering how in the old days the warriors arranged their hair, tied back when they prepared to meet an enemy" (*BP* 139). Erdrich emphasizes the irony of Fleur's appearance through the car in which she arrives, satirizing the image of the warrior: "Fleur's car was also white and it was large, a Pierce-Arrow" (*BP* 139). Tatro sees the car, and covets it. He is so intent on his pursuit of the car that he misses Fleur's true goal.

Through the character of the Indian agent, Erdrich reveals the history of land mismanagement at Turtle Mountain. Tatro represents the legacy of government intervention and the attempts to undermine tribal sovereignty: "Jewett Parker Tatro had in his life managed with such thorough ease to acquire anything that pleased him—beaded moccasins, tobacco bags … property of course—that when he saw the car he made an immediate assumption. He could get it from Fleur, just like he had acquired her land.… He had not yet determined the method, but there was no question that this would happen" (*BP* 143). Yet even Tatro recognizes that there is something different about this game.

Fleur has brought a small, white boy. The scene recalls the Gambler of Chippewa lore. Gerald Vizenor describes the Great Gambler as "a curious being, a person who seemed almost round in shape, smooth and white."[14] The boy represents the power of the Gambler, now being used by Fleur. He sits with Fleur to play cards, attracting Tatro's attention. The spectators watch the game in awe, focussing on details of his appearance and difference:

> the smoothness of his face.… They saw the smallness of him, the child- ish candy fat, the tightness of his rich-boy suit. And then, unfurling from his cuffs and wrists, they saw his hands. His wrists appeared, his palms, and then the fingers—long and pale, strong, spidery, and rough. The boy shuffled with an organist's blur.… He dealt.… Once the Agent sat down, it didn't matter who stayed or who left. For to all, the out- come was obvious. (*BP* 144)

Fleur sits down with Tatro and proceeds to win back her tribe's source of power and basis for negotiation. In *The Bingo Palace*, the boy playing cards for Fleur against the agent assumes the Gambler's characteristics. Thus Fleur subverts and manipulates people's expectations to recover the tribe's land and restore its cohesion: "When the Agent got up from his chair she would have what he owned, or the boy would, the two one and the same" (*BP* 145).

Erdrich emphasizes Fleur's control. This is not an extraordinary moment of good luck, but rather the culmination of years of experiences and a result of tribal knowledge and skill: "Fleur had studied the situation and kept track of time, calculated possibilities.… Gamblers in the old days kept a powder of human bones—dried, crushed, pounded fine—to rub on their hands. So did she" (*BP* 143). Tatro is cautious while faced by Fleur, but then the boy begins to shuffle the cards and he loses his fear. Fleur's misdirection, relying so heavily on Tatro's greed, highlights the cultural difference that separates this card game from the others in the novel.

The narrator speculates on the boy's origin, suggesting that "[Fleur] should have been dead, but perhaps, knowing death was near, she had thrown a soul out into the world, a decoy, and lived on without harm" (*BP* 140). Fleur's super- natural qualities are paramount in this meeting with the Indian agent. Thus, the narrator concludes, "[the boy] must be a soul Fleur had tossed out in the face of death. An argument. Bait. He was a piece of her own fate used to divert atten- tion from her real business, which was something now thrown open for specu- lation" (*BP* 142). For the Turtle Mountain community, the introduction of a market economy coupled with loss of land has disrupted tribal cohesion. In this moment, Fleur has the capacity to restore both the land and the group's sense of identity as a whole. The boy begins to deal the cards, sitting between Fleur and Nanapush. As they watch the game, it is clear who the foreign element is: though they fear Fleur, it is Tatro who represents failure and dissolution.

The image of Tatro's loss at Fleur's hands is juxtaposed with Lyman's loss at Reno, complicating the notion of gaming and its benefits as we return to the world of the mundane. The chapter following Fleur's game with Tatro is called "Lyman's Dream." Dreaming of the slots in Reno, Lyman sees his reflection in the glass of the slot machines as he mechanically plays quarter after quarter. He imagines his own significance: "He was drive. He was necessity. If not him, there was no one who would plan his plans ... and bring the possibilities into existence" (*BP* 148). We see that Lyman's arrogance is his downfall, that when he loses sight of his community, he is lost. However, as Pasquaretta maintains in his discussion of traditional gaming, "Neal Salisbury has argued that northeastern woodland dice games like hubbub reinforced native systems of resource management and helped to maintain harmonious group relations. Within a classless society gambling losses and gains contributed to the fair and equal distribution of the group's communal resources."[15] Thus, Lyman sees Fleur in his dream, a counterpoint to his own image, and she corrects him, not condemning gambling, but exhorting him to maintain a certain focus. "*Land,*" she tells him, "*is the only thing that lasts life to life. Money burns like tinder, flows off like water, and as for the government's promises, the wind is steadier.... This time, don't sell out for a barrel of weevil-shot flour and a mossy pork*" (*BP* 148). Throughout her novel, Erdrich emphasizes self-determination and the danger of losing sight of future improvement in the face of immediate personal gain.

Through her fictional account of one tribe's struggle with gaming, Erdrich offers a complex picture of the dilemma it brings to reservation communities. Lyman Lamartine is juxtaposed with Fleur Pillager to show the conflicting sides to gambling and the various nuances it has for Native communities. Finally, however, in *The Bingo Palace*, Lyman comes to understand Fleur's message: "Use a patch of federal trust land somewhere, anywhere near his employee base. Add to it, diversify, recycle what money came in immediately into land-based operations" (*BP* 149).

For Turtle Mountain, as for the Cabazons or the Pequots, Indian gaming has the potential to enable tribal sovereignty. As Gerald Vizenor and many others point out, sovereignty is a concept fraught with conflict, for Indians as well as non-Indians. *The Bingo Palace* shows a picture of what gaming could mean and how it could be put to use. In that novel, the casino is a trope, useful for recalling the primacy of fate as well as tribal integrity. Erdrich's vision is a positive one. What will happen in Indian Country remains to be seen.

NOTES

1. Paul Pasquaretta, "On the 'Indianness' of Bingo: Gambling and the Native American Community," *Critical Inquiry* 20:4 (Summer 1994): 696.

2. For an excellent summarization of the history of Indian gaming, see Wayne J. Stein, "Gaming: The Apex of a Long Struggle," *Wicazo Sa Review* 13:1 (Spring 1998): 73–92.

3.   Don A. Cozzetto, "The Economic and Social Implications of Indian Gaming: The Case of Minnesota," *American Indian Culture and Research Journal* 19:1 (1995): 119.

4.   Ibid., 75–76: "The median income for all North Dakotans is $23,123. The median income on the Fort Totten Reservation is $15,394; on the Turtle Mountain Reservation it is $12,020. The unemployment rate for non-Indians in North Dakota is 4.5 percent. At Fort Totten and Turtle Mountain, the unemployment rates are 23.5 percent and 33 percent respectively."

5.   Don A. Cozzetto and Brent W. LaRocque, "Compulsive Gambling in the Indian Community: A North Dakota Case Study," *American Indian Culture and Research Journal* 20:1 (1996): 74.

6.   Gerald Vizenor, *Crossbloods: Bone Courts, Bingo, and Other Reports* (Minneapolis: University of Minnesota Press, 1990; 1976), xii.

7.   Louise Erdrich, *The Bingo Palace* (New York: HarperCollins, 1994), 15. Subsequent citations will appear in the text as *BP*.

8.   Paul Pasquaretta, "Sacred Chance: Gambling and the Contemporary Native American Indian Novel," *MELUS* 21:2 (Summer 1996): 32.

9.   Edmund Bergler, *The Psychology of the Gambler*, reprint, originally published: Hill and Wang, 1957 (International Universities Press, Inc., 1985), 3.

10.   Cozzetto and LaRocque, "Compulsive Gambling," 76.

11.   Pasquaretta, "Sacred Chance," 29.

12.   Vizenor, *Crossbloods*, 22.

13.   Ambrose I. Lane, Sr., *Return of the Buffalo: The Story Behind America's Indian Gaming Explosion* (Westport, CT: Bergin and Garvey, 1995), 127.

14.   Gerald Vizenor, *The People Named the Chippewa* (Minneapolis: University of Minnesota Press, 1984), 5.

15.   Pasquaretta, "On the 'Indianness' of Bingo," 700.

❤

◆

Tribal Perspectives

◆

Ron Andrade

Executive Director,
Los Angeles City/County Indian Commission

If you assume, as many researchers have, that an Indian dollar, or a dollar entering the reservation, turns over two or possibly three times, then you can see the economic impact that gaming facilities have on surrounding non-Native communities. Many tribes have gaming facilities bringing in $50 million a year in gross income. That means roughly a $100 million impact in the local community due to their involvement with the gaming facilities. Once the money leaves the reservation, the gaming facility's impact doubles.

This economic impact affects the gaming area's job market as well. For the 15,000 jobs created by Indian gaming in this state, there are actually 45,000 jobs dependent on Indian gaming since, as many researchers say, two or three jobs open up for every one job created in a new industry. In other words, several teenagers might land jobs at McDonald's because of the increased business near the gaming facility. If 90 percent of those jobs are given to non-Indians, there's a lot more than 15,000 people relying on these jobs.

When I hear comments by non-Natives discussing the possibility of Indian job loss due to outlawed gaming, I realize that it is not necessarily the Indians who are losing jobs. I do not believe that some of these people care if the Indians return to unemployment. They do care, however, if 45,000 non-Indians become unemployed. Therefore, I think we should focus on educating non-Indians about the impact of gaming on their livelihoods.

All economic development surrounding gaming, I think, turns on sovereignty. Self-determination is and should be the basis for our economic development enterprises. But one of the most ridiculous positions that tribes are in right now is that the Federal Deposit Insurance Corporation (FDIC) has determined that if a tribe has all of its money in a bank, the FDIC guarantees your accounts only to the level of $100,000. It has determined that the tribes hold their money in common and as a result it will only guarantee the tribe's account, one account, to $100,000. That means that if the tribe has $1 million in any one bank, it is only covered to $100,000.

The law allows the FDIC to cover the account of any public agencies above $100,000. The bank has to sign a special collateral agreement to collateralize the account. Housing authorities, the public housing authorities, the cities, the counties, the state, all have their money guaranteed above $100,000 with the bank, but FDIC refuses to do this for the Indian tribes.

I have checked with many of the gaming tribes. Many of them say, no, we're protected. One, our bank couldn't go under anyway because it's Bank of America or First Federal. And second, we're a public agency. But the FDIC has said that it will not at this point guarantee the tribe's account above $100,000. To change this policy, however, only requires a rule change.

I have a copy of a letter sent by a law firm that has been working on this issue with FDIC. I served at FDIC in Washington. While I was there, I approached them but we got into a screaming match in which they said that they did not see any reason to change the rule. So we need to help the tribes change that rule. Because I would really hate to see tribes come this far in economic development and have gained some money in their tribal accounts, and then watch it go under with the bank.

I worked for Resolution Trust Corporation (RTC), an organization created by Congress to help dispose of bank assets seized by the FDIC. I helped resell banks that had previously gone under. We resold 300 banks in the United States. These banks holding tribal funds, I can assure you, could go under at any time. It would not be hard for Bank of America or First Federal Union or any of these others to go under. I saw bigger banks than these go under and we simply assumed their accounts.

If the government is really going to talk about sovereignty and if this president is going to keep telling Indian tribes how much he believes in a government-to-government relationship, then he should be able to call the FDIC and order it to protect tribal accounts. That is sovereignty. What we are dealing with now is not even close to sovereignty.

And for those of you who follow Indian legislation, you might know that a few years ago the Congress in all of its wisdom passed a bill allowing Indian tribes to have 401(k) programs. For those of you who do not know, those are retirement plans. The reason Congress had to do this is that the federal treasury ruled all Indian 401(k) plans illegal. Bill Clinton signed the bill. The only reason the bill got through, as far as I'm concerned, is because the Pequot tribe got mad and told the White House that they would not donate any more money unless their 401(k) plan was certified as eligible. But the Treasury Department ruled four years ago that all Indian 401(k) plans are illegal. And we have the same situation now on the FDIC rule on the $100,000 deposit level. If you are going to begin to address economic development and investment strategies, you have to start with these problems.

One of the other things that I am interested in is the tribes' lack of regulatory authority over much of the goods and services sold within reservation boundaries. Most of the tribes allow corporations such as Pepsi, Coca-Cola, and Frito-Lay to come and sell in their gaming halls. However, they don't make them sign marketing or licensing agreements. Pepsi can come in and simply claim to offer the tribe a deal. There's no charge for signage or for any other kind of marketing. In other areas, however, these companies pay a lot of money, billions of dollars a year, for the kind of signage and marketing they do on the reservations.

When I was at the La Jolla Reservation, I made Pepsi pay me a marketing fee. A five-thousand-dollar marketing fee just to sell on the reservation. Then we made them cut their unit price by one-third, including all their cans and syrup. We basically told them what to do. I had them give me free cups for our water park and then I turned around and ordered Coke off the reservation. Coca-Cola was upset, but they left because I told them that I could seize their goods at the tribal store as abandoned goods. When they tried to not show up the next morning, I started unloading their stuff from our store. When they finally showed up, they took their products off the reservation.

Now I don't know if La Jolla's maintained this agreement, but the gaming halls and gaming enterprises should make all companies pay. R. J. Reynolds and all of the big cigarette companies would pay huge amounts to get signage up in those gaming halls because they can't get signs up anywhere else anymore. Five hundred thousand people a year come to some of these gaming halls. That's a lot of people seeing these cigarette signs. These companies should be acting through regulatory procedures. I suggest that tribespeople go to their own tribal store and ask the owners if they made Frito-Lay, for example, sign an agreement to sell and advertise on that reservation. Companies almost never sign anything. I guess we're just so happy to get Fritos near us, we don't care about the money. But we are losing all that money, and the companies will pay it. They do it for the non-Indian communities.

When I was at La Jolla, I just happened to live at the Rincon Reservation, so I stopped at a local store, a white store, and bought a two-liter bottle of Coke. It cost me about a dollar. When I went to La Jolla's store, however, the bottle was a buck and a half. The two stores are only seven miles apart. What's the difference? How did the price go up fifty cents? When I asked the Coke representative, he said that La Jolla is a little off the normal route. He hoped that if he sold Coke at a higher price, the shoppers would come down the hill to Pauma Valley to buy Coke. Tribes should stop this kind of unfair behavior.

We have also made suggestions to many tribes that they go into micro-lending. Indians are mostly accustomed to small lending. I know I used to be accustomed to a different type of micro-lending. To me, it meant that I would go down to the bank and ask for $5,000 but receive only $500. That was micro-lending to me. But seriously, tribes should get into micro-lending. This lending should not be limited to tribal members only. Every report I have seen suggests that tribes do micro-lending with their members, which is important. However, they should set up a micro-lending program for the non-Indian community— the people who disrupt us the most. For those of you who study small business, you know that getting a small business loan is a hard thing to do. Because these entrepreneurs generally want to start a small business with no income, assets, or prior experience, they cannot qualify for a loan. If the tribe offered micro-loans to small businesses starting on the reservation and in the surrounding communities, they could play a big part in these economic ventures.

In undertaking these lending programs, tribes do not necessarily need to be a straight lender. They can be equity investors. Saudi Arabia is doing this through its lending banks. While the Koran may not allow a Muslim to gain interest, it does not say that a person cannot make a profit. This is why they equity invest. Many Muslim banks are now using equity investment here in the

United States. There is no reason why the tribes couldn't do the same thing. These micro-lending programs would allow us to spread our influence.

Tribes should also make money the old-fashioned way—they should borrow it. White people don't spend their own money—they borrow it so that if it goes bad, they can declare bankruptcy and wipe out their debt. That's why we have all these banks in this country. So I don't know why tribes should use their own money. I see many tribes that want to put up 100 percent of their development financing. It makes no sense. It's more sensible for them to use regular leveraging of their money with other borrowed money to set up corporations that they can collapse if they have to. Then they can walk away, rather than acting as the 100 percent investor.

I also believe that tribes should stop donating their own money to private causes. Many people are now coming to the tribes and asking for donations. There are certain things that tribes should continue to do. I'm not saying they should stop 100 percent of their donating. However, the tribes should donate somebody else's money. For all the money that they're putting into these banks, the tribes should negotiate with these banks and say, you donate money to people and organizations we identify. If the bank refuses to donate money from their foundation, the tribes should just withdraw their money from the bank and take it to another one. Tribes should be telling the Pepsi-Cola people or the Coca-Cola people, "You're donating money from your corporate foundation, and we want to identify people for you. If you refuse, we will withdraw our account from you and find another soft drink seller who will donate." Many major corporations conduct their donation activities that way. They do it constantly. There's no reason why tribes should not be doing this, rather than try to meet every social need from the tribal money.

While I am saying this, I do applaud the tribes for their significant donations. Of course, the banks sit back and say, "Oh! Aren't you wonderful?" And they keep making interest on our money. One of the things we found out in San Diego, even though we have a quite extensive amount of money on deposit from our water authority, is that we cannot find a donation track record from the bank. It had never donated, as far as we could tell, but yet that tribe has more than $50 million on deposit. That seemed to me a big weakness. If the tribes are putting their money into the banks, the banks should donate.

This, of course, leads to corporate responsibility. Tribes should be buying stock. A lot of folks are doing this in the United States and there is no reason why the tribes can't do it, too. Tribes can buy stock in local companies in places such as San Diego and Green Bay—those businesses that think badly of us. Their stock is publicly traded. The tribes can make a good investment by buying stock in corporations that tend to dislike us. *The Washington Post* is publicly traded. *The Los Angeles Times,* I believe, is publicly traded. A whole lot of these folks who call us dirty names should have us at their board meetings so we can ask them as corporate investors why they call us dirty names when we own 25,000 shares of their company. That's what the Blacks and the Hispanics have done. And that's how the California Personnel Retirement Board (CALPERS) holds so much power in the United States—their money is invested in many corporations. There's no reason why tribes should not be doing this.

And finally, I think that tribes should look at utilizing Indian and other minority businesses in their economic enterprises. If Indian gaming goes tomorrow, all of our non-Indian friends are going to be gone. They all hang around while the times are good, but I want to know who is going to stay if gaming is outlawed tomorrow. But we know that come tomorrow morning, the Hispanics, the Blacks, and a lot of the other minority companies that have always worked with us will still be around. They were our friends when we were poor. They'll stick around. Yet, we haven't done much with them in our business investing and relationships. I think it only behooves us in the long term to remember who our friends were through the long haul and begin to use them. Because if it all goes away, we'll still need their political and economic support and friendship.

♦

Perspective of

Mary Ann Andreas

Morongo Tribal Chairperson

Traditionally, California Indian reservations are smaller than those in Arizona, New Mexico, the Dakotas, or Wisconsin. For example, while the Oneida tribe in Wisconsin has an estimated 15,000 tribal members, California reservations and rancherias tend to be smaller.

The Morongo Band of Mission Indians has one of the largest reservations in California, with about 1,100 members and 32,000 acres as our land base. Like many reservations, we have traditionally been very poor. There is a lot of welfare dependency in our past. The tribe had no ability to provide services for tribal members. We had HUD housing and minimal health care. We have had to fight in Congress for Indian Health Services, a service that other tribes already had. There wasn't much in the way of governmental income in the form of grants, special programs, or that type of thing. We had an 85 percent dropout rate among our students. Like many rurally located tribes, we were isolated economically. There was not a great deal of business activity or industry in our region.

As a result of tribal government gaming we have eliminated welfare. There is no welfare on the Morongo Indian Reservation. Unemployment is practically nonexistent. As a direct result of our gaming, anyone who wants a job can have a job.

Previously, our dependence on federal funds was something like $500,000 a year. That taxpayer burden has been eliminated by our gaming revenue. We have saved California taxpayers hundreds of thousands of dollars in annual welfare assistance that is no longer paid.

We employ about one thousand individuals in our casino operation and create another 450 jobs indirectly through the goods and services we purchase. We have established non-gaming jobs through our tribal government in providing water and waste disposal services, road maintenance, cable TV access, Head Start programs, public transportation systems, and emergency services.

We are updating and expanding our tribe's water system. The federal government and the Bureau of Indian Affairs put in miles and miles of cancer-causing concrete asbestos water lines. We have been able to eliminate those. We've installed two one-million gallon water tanks. Previously we always ran out of water in summertime or when there were dry seasons. So the two one-million-gallon water tanks were necessary. We've been able to sink wells. One of our wells has been able to surpass output of all of our previous wells combined.

The tribe has been able to provide fire flow to our tribal members' homes. Previously, if your house caught on fire, there was not adequate water to fight a fire—so we used dirt. Now we have been able to ensure a water supply and provide a fire station. In fact, we have a water system that surpasses many of the communities around us. We have a radio telemetry system that allows us to monitor and control our wells and the tanks in our canyons. From our tribal offices the system can determine what well is running properly and alert us when there is a problem. If there is a problem, the computer automatically calls a series of phone numbers to contact tribal leaders. The system will also switch tanks if there is a problem with the water supply and report on water usage. We've had many of the communities around us come and examine the system we have now.

We've invested $3 million installing silt basins to prevent flooding and erosion. The Morongo Reservation sits on a slant so we have lots of flooding during the rainy season. We've been able to acquire a school bus. Our students were bused sometimes two to three hours a day without being able to use the bathroom. So we bought a bus for $80,000 to provide our students with a direct trip to and from school.

The Morongo tribe is the second largest private employer in our area. Our gaming operation generates $12 million in payroll annually and $1.5 million in payroll taxes. More than two-thirds of our work force is composed of residents in the Banning and desert cities. We believe that gaming is a powerful economic engine for the cities, for the state, and for the tribe. An estimated $10 million alone goes into the economy surrounding us from our purchase of goods and services.

It is often said by opponents or enemies of Indian gaming that Indians don't pay taxes. That is not true. We pay taxes on goods and services and collect taxes on food and services sold in the casino. And tribal members annually pay federal and state income taxes.

As a result of our gaming success, our tribe has begun to share proceeds with the communities through donations in support of nonprofit organizations like the American Cancer Society and area high schools. In the spring of 1997, our tribe presented the Riverside County Sheriffs Association with $20,000 for two surviving families of officers who were shot in the line of duty. These officers used to visit our casino every day and have coffee. We knew these gentlemen. We felt it must be the ultimate nightmare for police officers to leave their families every day, get into their "black and whites" and know that, one day, they may not come home. It happened to these two gentlemen who were our friends. So we lent a hand to their families.

In 1996, our casino brought goods and services from more than five hundred regional vendors and did business with a total of 750 outside companies. About 25 percent of these businesses are minority owned and operated. Casino patrons took home another $200 million in winnings which are spent in the respective communities surrounding us.

A governor's task force in 1994 estimated that more than $6 billion currently leaves California and goes to Las Vegas in recreational spending. We see tribal gaming as a no-cost solution to California that both captures these tourism dollars and eliminates welfare dependency in our communities.

We believe that our future will be better because of gaming. We have two members currently enrolled at Cornell University. One is pre-med and one is studying engineering. We have others in the University of California system. And we are investing both in our people and our resources. In 1997, we constructed a $2 million gas station and retail store on our reservation. We also are in negotiation with several nationally recognized restaurant chains.

We have a master plan that incorporates retail shopping, golf course development, hotel projects, an RV park, and a truck stop. Because of tribal gaming, the Morongo Band is diversifying its economy and developing multiple income streams.

Most importantly, we think that gaming has meant a return to self-sufficiency. This has meant the return of economic independence, the restoration of tribal pride, and the ability to provide not only for our own, but also to claim a new role in the larger community. In the last two years we have really seen some dramatic success. We have been able to provide more for our tribal membership than the federal government has been able to provide in three hundred years. No one knows the needs of our community like we do, and we've really made some great strides.

To the Indian law students and to the law students at large, I cannot stress enough the importance of having knowledge of and commitment to tribal sovereignty. Don't ever compromise yourself on these issues. So many times I have seen our own people elected or appointed to positions and they forget who they are and where they come from. The past chairman of the National Indian Gaming Commission—Harold Monteau—did not forget where he came from. His heart was always Indian and he was a warrior for our people. We need to pass on that kind of mindset to our young as they become attorneys, professionals, business people, and elected leaders.

And while gaming has brought many good things, there is a potential downside we must be watchful to combat. We have to be ever watchful that we don't lose our culture, that we don't get caught up in all the glitz that gaming can bring. We must guard our cultural heritage and our spirituality ever more strongly. While it is inevitable that we will not be the same Indians going into the new millennium that we were coming into it, we still must preserve our spiritual legacy. Without it we just become brown white-people.

The battle ahead of us to protect our sovereignty, our culture, and our people's future will lie in utilizing both technology and human resources. From telephones, faxes, computers, and the Internet to lobbyists, lawyers, communications advisers, and other professionals, we must tap every advantage and prepare for this battle like never before. In all of this we must remember never to lose our culture.

♦

Perspective of
Priscilla Hunter

Chairwoman,
Coyote Band of Pomo Mission Indians

One question has been asked repetitively: is gaming advisable for tribes? I can only answer that question with another. What other form of economic development has been as successful on so many reservations as gaming?

Gaming is not necessarily for every tribe. One of the main reasons that tribes do not participate in gaming is because of compacting issues and other gaming issues in California, as well as the fear of trying to initiate economic development projects. Some tribes have decided that they simply do not want to do it, or they know that gaming would not be successful on their reservation. Others might just be waiting to see what is going to happen with other tribes.

There are numerous issues, problems, and regulations involved with gaming; it takes determination and a strong government or tribal council that tries to stick together to continue the business. Some tribal members get upset about problems on the reservations, but on the whole, I think that gaming works. We have to be strong and we have to be patient to continue working for the people and for the cause. It is unfortunate that people even wonder whether gaming is a positive step for tribes. What other state or country would have such interference in their governmental decisions? I think the most fundamental question to ask is why tribes are conducting gaming on their reservations. Tribes are governments, not unlike any other government with which you may be familiar. Tribes entered into federal treaties to preserve their land and resources for their people. The federal government entered into these treaties because they wanted the Indians' land in exchange for health, education, and welfare services for Indian people, which is kind of a laughing matter now that they do not want to live up to those agreements. These agreements are legally binding, and they are in effect forever.

What does the general public have to do with tribal governments? Why are they so infatuated with the judicial issues of tribal governments? There are several types of Americans interested in Indian people and their gaming. First, we have people who care and want to assist, and we are thankful for those people. Second, there are people with a general lack of knowledge and education regarding tribal governments and life on today's reservations. Third, there are those who fantasize that the Hollywood Indians, supposedly representing Native peoples of long ago, actually exist. Fourth, there are those who still hate Indian people. And finally, there are those who feel that tribal governments are in competition with the United States government. They either want to discourage or prevent tribes from being successful because their success might mean competition and loss of revenue. For example, the state of Nevada receives 30 percent of its revenue from Californians. Furthermore, the gamblers who come to Nevada to play their machines produce more than 60 percent of Nevada's gaming revenue. The tribes in California are nearing completion of tribal-state Class III gaming compacts, which might allow for machines. Wouldn't Nevada casinos try to prevent the California tribes from successfully completing this tribal-state compact?

Now, I want to talk about our tribe, the Pomo. Our tribe was illegally terminated and our lands were taken away from us for our water resources. When I was a child, we had 101 acres. I could see and hear mumbling among our elders. As a little child you wonder—you look up on the mountainside and see a construction site, and you wonder what is happening. Then, all of a sudden, I was taken away to five acres of land purchased near us. There we were, on another piece of land.

It was not until later that I knew what happened. My cousin was about to graduate and he wanted to go to college. When he filed for Bureau of Indian Affairs funding, he was denied because the bureau said that our tribe was terminated. We were shocked in the same way that we are shocked with the way that the gaming issue is handled here. Of course, I was also upset because he received no funding for college. Instead, he went to Vietnam and never returned. If he had been able to go to college, and if he had the necessary funds, he may be here today.

So we were really thankful for the California Indian Legal Services at that time. Lester Marston and California Legal Services helped us get to court. There, we were restored as a federally recognized tribe. After that, we started reform as a tribe and received a whopping $4,000 a year from the Bureau to run our government. Unfortunately, we still had no land. We underwent a big struggle. Some members were living in other places, even motels. Finally, we got a grant through the Housing and Urban Development (HUD) block grants; in 1979, we got some property, fifty-nine acres in Mendocino, as federal status land.

The land we received was bare. I was the administrator, and there was barely any money for anything. Now we have housing, thirty-four homes. We have a tribal office. We have a gym that we built with a HUD block grant. It is a large recreation center, and we are very proud of it. That is when we started to get involved in gaming.

Our tribe was not the only one that suffered. For years California Indians have been mistreated and killed for practicing our culture, our religion. Our lands have been taken, our people placed in boarding school, our tribes terminated. The tribes entered into treaties with the government, but the state of California persuaded the United States Congress not to ratify the treaties. Those treaties were purposely hidden away in the federal archives for decades.

We have had injustice, it's true. I'm not reminding anyone to make them feel bad or defensive, but to educate them to help us stop the injustices to tribes. Gaming is only one of the issues tribes are struggling to save. For more than two hundred years, tribes have struggled continuously to preserve their sovereignty against federal and state intrusions. To this day, we are fighting to protect our land, our water, our culture, our religion, and even our children.

During the last three years we have fought many pieces of anti-Indian legislation. We will face numerous issues in Congress and in our state legislatures again this year. However, the preservation of gaming is probably one of the most serious issues facing tribal government to date. If tribes lose gaming, tribal governments will lose the revenue that allows them to protect Indian people from drug and alcohol abuse and from illnesses such as diabetes that are uncontrollable in our community and threaten the lives of our people. We will also lose the revenue that enables us to have everyday necessities, including clean water, sanitation systems, electricity, telephones, health, law enforcement, cultural projects, and especially better education for our children and the tribal members.

To date we employ more than two hundred people because of gaming. We are host to numerous vendors. We also have been able to invest in and buy land for our tribe that was for sale next to us, and we want to invest in additional land. We need additional homes for our people. We need places where we can gather our foods, our native plants—places where we can hold ceremonies without intrusion. We had a bear dance ceremony in July, and our park is right across from the casino. It was really different because we put up a little fence, which was made out of willows and things. We were on one side of the fence doing the bear dance, and the casino was on the other side. We could just feel the spirits coming down. We should be able to have that space.

We have developed programs for our children—tutors and scholarships for our people. We are preparing our children to see the outside world, to enjoy life off the reservation. We have a law enforcement program that we recently started, and it has been very beneficial to our community as well.

We have a strong tribal government. When I was the administrator, I had to search for funds just to pay myself. I never knew if I would have a job or a staff in six months. It was a piecemeal process. Every time there was a job opening, twenty members would apply for the position. Only one tribal member could be employed for one year, and it was difficult to choose that person. The casinos have changed this, creating employment for our people and opportunities for our children.

I am shocked that we have to struggle to keep our enterprise going. However, this is nothing new. Indian people always have to struggle forward. Gaming has offered more to California Indian tribes in the past decade than the US government has offered in the past century. Indian people are strong. With all the obstacles placed in our path, we have survived. We will continue to survive, but we need assistance from non-Native people. We ask them to support the gaming compact regulations for tribes.

♦

Ernie L. Stevens, Jr.

Tribal Councilman,
Oneida Nation

In the late 1960s and early 1970s, my mother was a student at the University of California, Los Angeles. During that time she was a strong advocate for Indian rights. She was involved with the occupation of Alcatraz Island and participated in the Bureau of Indian Affairs (BIA) takeover. In fact, my mother, my older brother, and I all served at Wounded Knee II in 1973. She was active in almost every major uprising in Indian Country and was probably considered a militant activist.

When my mother went to the BIA on what is now called the Trail of Broken Treaties, my father was working there. It was weird to have my parents on different sides of the Indian civil rights debate. My father was a special breed. He worked at the Los Angeles Indian Center and the California Indian Council. Ernie, Sr. had a long track record of helping Indian people all over Indian Country. He did what he could to prevent bloodshed during the BIA takeover. To most, he was a hero; to others, he was considered too liberal and friendly with militant activists. He was eventually encouraged to leave his position at the bureau because of his understanding of and appreciation for activism.

Both my parents are special and strong motivators for me in helping me do what I can to help Indian people throughout the United States. We need to acknowledge that the days of taking up arms and taking over buildings are long gone—at least I hope they are. We must also remember the important impact of activism and the ways in which it changed the dominant society's views of Indian governments. Today, however, the lawyers, teachers, and tribal leaders are our best weapons. It is their dedication and knowledge that keep our dreams alive and our nations strong and progressive.

The National Congress of American Indians (NCAI) was founded in 1944 as a representative congress of tribal governments and individuals meeting to address priority issues at the national level. The NCAI stresses the need for unity and cooperation among Native governments and people for the security and protection of treaty and sovereign rights for the betterment in the quality of life for all Indian people.

I would like to discuss Indian gaming from a national perspective, and I have some specific points to make regarding Wisconsin and Oneida gaming. The debate over Indian gaming is actually over the rights of tribes to govern themselves and to engage in economic development activities. Indian tribes have the right to self-government. They were sovereign long before European settlers arrived in North America. Treaties signed by the tribes guaranteed the right to continue this type of self-government. Historically, many states have refused to treat Indian tribes as sovereign governments because they believe that it threatens their power.

Indian gaming is just one example of this conflict. The governors who issue compacts say they want a bigger piece of the pie. Meanwhile, we are breaking even in our gaming operations. Our budgets are going through a tough time right now. The governors throughout the states, however, say they want more of our money. This is unacceptable. If the states want more then they should give more. We are at the negotiating table and our sovereign nations are working hard to remain united. I encourage all tribes to stay united in all aspects of Indian government. We should share all our strategies, and we can bet that state governors are doing the same. Strength through unity is the key to our survival.

Under treaties signed with the federal government, the Constitution of the United States, and many federal court decisions, it is clear that the federal government has a special relationship with tribal governments. This relationship requires the federal government to protect tribes' lands, assets, and rights to self-government. It is important to protect tribes' right to engage in gaming because the loss of this right would set a precedent for other self-government rights to be taken away. This may include threats to our rights to speak our own language, direct the education of our children, or protect the environment on our tribal lands.

I want to briefly discuss some Indian gaming myths. First is this idea that Indian tribes are getting rich from their gaming. The fact is that on the average Indian reservations have a 31 percent poverty rate, the highest rate in the United States. Indian unemployment is six times the national average. Indian health, education, and income statistics are the worst in the country. The Oneida Nation has a good operation, but we are not satisfied with it because so many of our brothers and sisters run struggling operations. We are concerned about the benefits and the future of all of our brothers and sisters, and we cannot allow governors and legislators to choke what little we have. Second, many people falsely believe that Indian gaming is a huge industry. The fact is that Indian gaming accounts for only 8 percent of the gambling activity in the country, and it occurs on only one-third of the country's 558 reservations. Finally I want to address the misconception that tribes do not pay taxes, but use gaming money to buy sports cars and yachts. Well, I have two sports cars and I pay for them out of my check every week. I also have two teenagers who drive these cars. If the government did not take so much money out of my check, I might be able to buy myself a sports car. The federal law requires tribal governments to use gaming revenues to fund tribal services such as education, law enforcement, tribal courts, economic development, and infrastructure improvement. Why people do not understand this is beyond me. A lot of groups are getting rich because of gaming, but Indian tribes are not one of them.

Much like the revenues from state lotteries, tribal governments are also using gaming profits to fund social service programs, scholarships, health care clinics, new roads, new sewer and water systems, and adequate housing. In essence, gaming revenue serves as tax revenues for tribal governments. Like state and local governments, the revenues accruing to tribal governments are not taxed. State lotteries bring in $15.5 billion annually, more than five times as much as tribal gaming. Why is no one suggesting a federal tax on state lottery revenues? Governments should be treated equally.

Only a relatively small number of tribes have been fortunate enough to have very successful gaming operations. If one of these tribes is able to distribute some income to their individual tribal members, this income is taxed by federal government at a full federal rate. All Indian gaming revenue is taxed.

Indian gaming is planting the seed for economic recovery. It is without a doubt the most positive context in which gaming now occurs. The tribal government programs and infrastructure funded by gaming bring hope and opportunity to some of the most desolate places in America and to some of the country's most impoverished people. Where this economic development has occurred, Indian tribes have witnessed a drop in crime rates and in alcohol and drug abuse. In addition, individual initiative is improving.

The Oneida Nation has used its government's gaming revenues for health care, education, elder care, and many other improvements to the quality of life in our communities. In addition, Oneida gaming has created six thousand jobs for both Indians and non-Indians and pays more than $15 million annually in taxes. The unemployment rate for tribal members has been reduced from 47 percent to 5 percent. From a national perspective, it would be a horrible atrocity to reach the next century with a federal policy that discourages Indian gaming and moves tribes back into the poverty out of which we are now rising.

There has been a lot of discussion surrounding the proliferation of Indian gaming, and as we all know, the pros and cons can and have been debated to death. The question before us today is, Indian gaming: who wins? In Wisconsin we have answered this very question. The eleven Wisconsin tribes have mounted a statewide public relations advertising campaign to educate the public and encourage a positive attitude toward Indian gaming and what tribes are doing for gaming revenues. We have placed ads in major newspapers throughout Wisconsin. These ads convey a very important message to Wisconsin citizens—with Indian gaming, Wisconsin wins. The positive effects Indian gaming has had in tribal communities has been lauded by all of us over and over again. It is amazing to me that we end up under attack when we are not only helping our people, but also the people around us. There are over 15,000 jobs in the state of Wisconsin. AFDC (Aid to Families with Dependent Children) payments to the counties where casinos are located have decreased since 1990 as much as 28 percent. Furthermore, we pay excellent wages and provide excellent benefits. The Oneida minimum wage is much higher than the federal minimum wage.

We still have social problems that have plagued our reservations for years, such as problems with compulsive behavior disorders relative to alcohol, drugs, domestic violence, and other harmful behaviors. However, we now have gaming-generated revenues that allow us to address those problems through education, prevention, and treatment. This year we gave $30,000 to the Wisconsin Council on Problem Gambling. We are the only tribe and the only agency to fund this organization. It survives on our $30,000. It receives no federal or state support. We gave $120,000 to the Amerindian Center Urban Support Group that handles various issues for Natives living in an urban setting. We pay service agreements to the cities and municipalities for providing services to the tribe and we are not required to do this—it is voluntary.

As for education, I have two sons that are getting ready for college. These benefits will be a great asset to their education. Today I have a twelve-year-old daughter who is on a national science fair trip to Albuquerque. Without gaming support, these young boys and girls from our tribal Turtle School would not be able to enjoy these experiences. These same students attend a brand new school with state-of-the-art equipment and facilities. The school is built in the shape of a turtle, reflecting our culture. This facility and quality of education would not be possible without the support of gaming dollars. This is particularly encouraging considering that the highest grade I completed in school was fourth grade. I never completed another grade or year in school. Without my GED and my ability to attend class everyday, I never would have made it through college.

Things are a lot better for our people now, and it is a direct result of us taking care of our people through gaming. We have a long way to go to reach our vision of success, but as Native people we now have some cash to buy a ticket so we can at least get on the right track. With Indian gaming, everybody wins.

In closing, I would like to impress upon readers that Indian gaming is more than just a goose that lays a golden egg. It is the practice of the sovereign rights secured to Native Americans in our treaties. We have a right to exercise our sovereignty and operate and regulate our affairs on the reservation as independent nations. Too often we are scrutinized about our regulation, but I assure you that our industry is heavily regulated and run completely by Oneida. While it may not be perfect—we do have our bumps and bruises throughout Indian Country—we are rebounding from our pitfalls and are rebuilding our communities. We are particularly proud of the scrutiny that is built into our operations through security, audit departments, independent investigators, state-of-the-art surveillance equipment, and well-trained gaming commissioners. For the most part, Indian gaming is very productive.

Tribes are not traditional businesses that distribute earnings to shareholders, but are governments that deliver their members essential services not provided by municipalities, state, or federal governments. Nobody is getting rich. Native people are taking care of one another and having a great impact on the non-Native community as well. Viable gaming establishments operated by tribal governments are the economic foundation of a revitalized Native American economy. I will commit myself always to work on behalf of all nations. Oneida Nation and the National Congress of American Indians are committed to standing by Native people and supporting and lobbying for our future success. I stand here today to make this commitment to all of you.

♦

Perspective of

Erma J. Vizenor

Secretary/Treasurer,
White Earth Reservation

White Earth Reservation is located about one hundred miles south of the Canadian border and seventy miles east of the North Dakota-Minnesota line. I am from the largest reservation in Minnesota, and it is one of the six reservations that comprise the Minnesota Chippewa tribes. My constituency is made up of 25,000 members, most of whom live off the reservation. Only approximately 5,000 members live on the reservation. We know the history of what happened—why 20,000 of my people are living off the reservation and in urban settings such as Los Angeles, Denver, San Francisco, Albuquerque, and Phoenix. Assimilationist policies of the 1950s and 1960s gave our people one-way tickets off the reservation. Other members left the reservation because we were starving. People left looking for work.

Now we are looking for ways to unite our people, to bring our people together—to be of one mind, one spirit, and one heart. This is very difficult to do. We face tremendous challenges today because we are so scattered. I am not saying it is impossible—we just have to work very hard at it. I'm an idealist. I really believe that in order for us to exercise our sovereignty—and I believe sovereignty is synonymous with self-sufficiency—we cannot depend on the federal government for our daily bread. In order for us to be sovereign, we need economic self-sufficiency. We need to unite around this theme and principle.

In 1989, gaming started in Minnesota. We have twenty-two compacts with the state of Minnesota. A compact is a negotiated agreement which usually gives the state restrictions on our gaming enterprises. In Minnesota, we are fortunate thus far because our gaming compacts are in perpetuity. However, every day becomes a threat as guards and arms go up around Indian gaming.

We have gaming on our eleven reservations in Minnesota, six within the Minnesota Chippewa tribe, the Red Lake Nation, as well as the Lakota/Dakota reservations in the southern part of the state. Gaming is the seventh largest employer in Minnesota, generating $1.5 billion in revenues alone, and that is without any kind of state taxes imposed or without any public investment from the state of Minnesota. Indian gaming contributes $1.5 billion to the state.

We have a number of gaming industries throughout Minnesota. They range from the six-hundred-strong Dakota Sioux's gaming center, which is the most lucrative successful gaming industry in this country, to the 25,000-member White Earth Reservation, where the Shooting Star casino is located in one of the poorest counties and most isolated parts of Minnesota. The Sioux's Mystic Lake Casino makes more in one day than we make in one year.

On 11 March 1997, I was elected to the tribal council. I filled the secretary/treasurer position on a council in which three of our five tribal council members are now in federal prison in Minnesota. When I discuss the White Earth story, please pay attention. It holds the pain that can hurt all our people. When something happens to the Ojibwa, the people of White Earth, as far as government is concerned, it happens to every tribe across this country. It has an impact.

We had horrendous corruption within our tribal system. There was fraud and embezzlement, symptoms of a holocaust happening to our people. This holocaust was not instigated by the federal government, but by our own people. I think of this and it scares me.

My involvement with tribal affairs started when I came home from college with a degree in 1973. I went into the classroom to teach on the reservation and found that I was making very little impact as an educator. Our people needed education and knowledge outside of the classroom. I began to see that tribal services really did not benefit most of our people, only a select few. I became active in the community, and became an organizer. I was disliked by the tribal government. I was falsely charged many times for questioning the government. In 1988 I left home to attend Harvard. When I came back two and a half years later, the tribe's elders came to me and asked me to lead a reform movement, which I did.

Political clashes happen in many tribes. Indian politics are vicious. Our worst enemies are ourselves. As we worked for reform at White Earth, we had to be extremely careful to ensure that we would not regret our actions ten or twenty years down the road. Sometimes it is easy to align yourself with anti-Indian forces; and sometimes it is simple to side with the federal government, the Bureau of Indian Affairs, and all of the different government agencies and departments. But I am telling you, students and scholars, we as tribal people need to come to our own tribal solutions to take care of the problems within our tribes. When I was working for reform, I did not have anywhere to turn. We had no tribal fora to attend. No one listened to us.

We have a casino located in Mahnomen, Minnesota. We employ 950 people there, but prior to August of 1996, because of our corrupt tribal council, we had a management firm from the East Coast that was reaping the profits. This company took 40 percent of the profits, a direct violation of the Indian Gaming Regulatory Act. The management firm was receiving all the benefits, yet all the papers from the regulating agency said the tribe was in full compliance. The papers showed full compliance, but who was really benefiting from Indian gaming? The outsiders.

Last summer, on the eve of the conviction of our corrupt council, we came in as a reform tribal council and took over. We led a coup. It was a risky thing to do. We had just had an election with a chairman and a district councilman, and I started to help clean up the government. We had an election for my position on the tribal council, which I won. When we looked into our government, we found that our tribe was $6 million in debt; our gaming industry was $22 million in debt; and the HUD program was $5 million in debt.

What are the issues that have evolved from such a legacy? For one, we must ensure that our tribal leadership is accountable to our tribe. Who do our tribal leaders really serve? Do we have checks and balances within our government? We need to look at accountability within our tribes because it is this dividing line that can hurt us the most.

We need to develop some kind of mechanism at a national level to resolve tribal disputes. In 1992, I was working on reform and going through many arrests. I went to the National Lawyers Guild and described our conflict, but they did not have a clue as to what I was talking about. So it behooves us as tribal people to develop dispute-resolution mechanisms among ourselves.

Gaming is here to stay—it's just what kind of shape or form it will take in the future that is uncertain. We now have a national commission to study the effects of gaming. We have never had such a concerted, concentrated effort to study the effects of diabetes on our reservations. On my reservation we have a diabetes clinic one day a week. The federal government never studies the high dropout rates among our people, but now we have a commission to study gaming and its effects. This study is targeted at Indian people. For forty years, we have not had any kind of study on Indian gaming when gaming was thriving throughout Nevada and New Jersey.

We have a conflict between the state and the tribe. We know that the states want a greater chunk of gaming revenues. We face this issue in Minnesota. Our casino is located on fee land with taxes of $1 million per year. These are property taxes in the poorest county in Minnesota. Of that one million $340,000 goes to the local school district where 50 percent of our students—Indian students—attend school. Both the county and school district benefit from the property taxes. When the casino is placed in trust status, the tribe will need to work cooperatively on a new agreement with the county and school district. It is the politically prudent action to take and it is the right thing to do.

Gaming in Indian Country is young. It is only twelve years old. We have not even gotten our feet wet; however, there are assaults on all corners.

◆

About the Contributors

Ron Andrade (La Jolla) is the executive director of the Los Angeles City/County Indian Commission and former director of the National Congress of American Indians. Andrade served on the National Advisory Council on Indian education as a presidential appointee and was a member of the board of directors for the National Education Association, the National American Indian Council, and the Literacy Volunteers of America.

Twice elected tribal chairperson, **Mary Ann Andreas** (Morongo) has a reputation as a strong champion of Indian issues. She is one of the country's leading Native American women advocates on subjects ranging from child welfare and education to the protection of Indian sovereignty and tribal gaming rights. She led her tribe's expansion into gaming and now oversees one of the most successful tribal government gaming operations in California. A frequent congressional visitor, Andreas has spoken often on behalf of those issues affecting the Morongo community, including education, youth programs, health care, water resources, and tribal gaming rights. She has spent more than ten years working on Indian housing and is a determined and hard-working advocate for California's Native Americans. Andreas recently studied at Harvard University's Kennedy School and received the state of California's Woman of the Year award.

James V. Fenelon (Lakota/Dakota) teaches sociology at California State University, San Bernardino, and taught at John Carroll University after receiving a Ph.D. from Northwestern University. Fenelon also holds graduate degrees from the School for International Training and Harvard University. He teaches race and ethnic relations, urban issues, and specializes in research on the cultural domination over Native nations.

Thomas Gede is a special assistant attorney general and US Supreme Court counsel, as well as a policy advisor to the California attorney general. He acted as counsel for thirty-one states supporting Florida in *Seminole Tribe* v. *Florida* in the United States Supreme Court. After graduating from Stanford University in 1970, Gede served in the United States Navy in Vietnam, Japan, and Washington, D.C. He earned his law degree in 1981 from Hastings College of Law. He subsequently served as a clerk for California Court of Appeals Justice Edwin Regan and became a deputy attorney general in the criminal division in 1987.

Carole E. Goldberg joined the law school faculty at the University of California, Los Angeles in 1972, and directs the law school's joint degree program in law and American Indian Studies. She has served as associate dean for the School of Law twice as interim director of UCLA's American Indian Studies Center, and is chair of the Academic Senate. She is co-principal investigator with Professor Duane Champagne of Project Peacemaker, which develops and implements curricula in tribal legal studies at tribal colleges.

Chad M. Gordon (Muscogee Creek) received his bachelor's degree from the University of California, Santa Barbara, his master's in American Indian studies from the University of California, Los Angeles, and his Juris Doctor from the UCLA School of Law. Gordon worked on Proposition 5 in the fall of 1998 and remains active in defending the rights of sovereign Indian nations.

Sioux Harvey holds a Ph.D. in American history from the University of Southern California. Her dissertation, entitled "Igniting Tribal Fires: Indian Sovereignty, Gaming, and Incorporation into the World System, 1946–1996," focuses on the ways in which recent tribal gaming initiatives have provided tribes with greater self-sufficiency and self-determination.

Priscilla Hunter (Pomo) is the chairwoman of the Coyote Band of the Pomo Indians. Her tribe operates the Coyote Valley Shodaki Casino, which employs over two hundred people. She is also the chair of the Inter-Tribal Sinkyone Wilderness Council. Hunter was appointed by the governor of California to serve as a commissioner on the Native American Heritage Commission and by the secretary of the Interior to serve on the advisory council on California Indian policy. Hunter also advocates at the international level for human rights of indigenous people.

The **Indian Law Professors** are primarily instructors of federal Indian law. Rennard Strickland, dean at the University of Oregon School of Law; David Getches, professor at the University of Colorado School of Law; Richard B. Collins, professor at the University of Colorado School of Law; Monroe Price, professor at Cardozo Law School, Yeshiva University; Reid Chambers, part-time faculty member at Yale Law School; Robert N. Clinton, professor at the University of Iowa College of Law; and Charles Wilkinson, professor at the University of Colorado School of Law are all co-editors and co-authors of the 1982 edition of *Felix Cohen's Handbook of Federal Indian Law*. Nell Newton, dean at the University of Denver School of Law, is editor of the handbook's forthcoming edition. In addition, Getches, Wilkinson, Clinton, and Price have authored casebooks in the field of Indian law studies. The others, including Jo Carrillo, professor at Hastings College of Law; Arturo Gandara, professor at the University of California, Davis School of Law; Gerald Gardner, part-time faculty member at the University of California, Berkeley, Boalt Hall; and Raleigh Levine, part-time faculty member at Loyola, Los Angeles School of Law are professors of federal Indian law at California law schools.

Joseph G. Jorgensen is professor of anthropology and social science at the University of California, Irvine. He has worked for and among America's Indians and Eskimos for thirty-eight years.

Joseph G. Nelson (Tlingit/Eyak) is a second-year law student at Loyola Law School in Los Angeles. He received a master's degree in American Indian studies in 1998 and his bachelor's degree in political science in 1996, both from the University of California, Los Angeles.

Paul Pasquaretta is an assistant professor of English and cultural studies at State University of New York's Empire State College. He is the author of "On the Indianness of Bingo" (*Critical Inquiry* 1994), "Sacred Chance" (*Melus* 1996), and "Gambling Against the House" (*Mosaic* 2000). He is currently working on *Tricksters at Large: Native American Survivance and the Politics of Chance* (forthcoming).

Alexander Tallchief Skibine (Osage) is a professor of law at the University of Utah. Skibine was born in France and served as deputy counsel for Indian affairs on the Interior Committee of the United States House of Representatives between 1981 and 1989. He received his law degree from Northwestern University.

Katherine A. Spilde is the director of research for the National Indian Gaming Association in Washington, D.C. Prior to this position she was a policy analyst and writer for the National Gambling Impact Study Commission. She holds a Ph.D. in cultural anthropology from the University of California, Santa Cruz.

Ernie L. Stevens, Jr. (Oneida) is presently a tribal councilman, elected to his second term. In 1995 he was elected to serve as the first vice president of the National Congress of American Indians, the oldest and largest organization in the United States devoted to promoting and protecting the rights of American Indians and Alaskan Natives. Stevens received his bachelor's degree in criminal justice and sociology from Mount Senerlo College in Wisconsin. In his capacity as a tribal councilman, he serves as the liaison to the city of Green Bay, the Green Bay AmerIndian Center, the Oneida Nation governmental services and gaming divisions, and the Oneida Gaming Commission. Stevens is also a member of negotiating teams currently working with surrounding municipalities on service agreements and with the state of Wisconsin on a gaming-compact renewal.

Erma J. Vizenor (Chippewa) is secretary/treasurer of the White Earth Reservation Tribal Council in Minnesota. She is a graduate of Harvard University and received her Ph.D. in administration, planning, and social policy.

Karen L. Wallace received her master's in American Indian studies and her Ph.D. in English from the University of California, Los Angeles. She is currently an assistant professor of English at the University of Wisconsin, Oshkosh.

About the Editors

Angela Mullis is currently a doctoral student in English at the University of Arizona. She completed her master's in American Indian studies at the University of California, Los Angeles and received her bachelor's degree in English from Florida State University.

David Kamper is a doctoral student in anthropology at the University of California, Los Angeles. He holds a master's degree in American Indian studies from the University of California, Los Angeles.

Index